AF600387

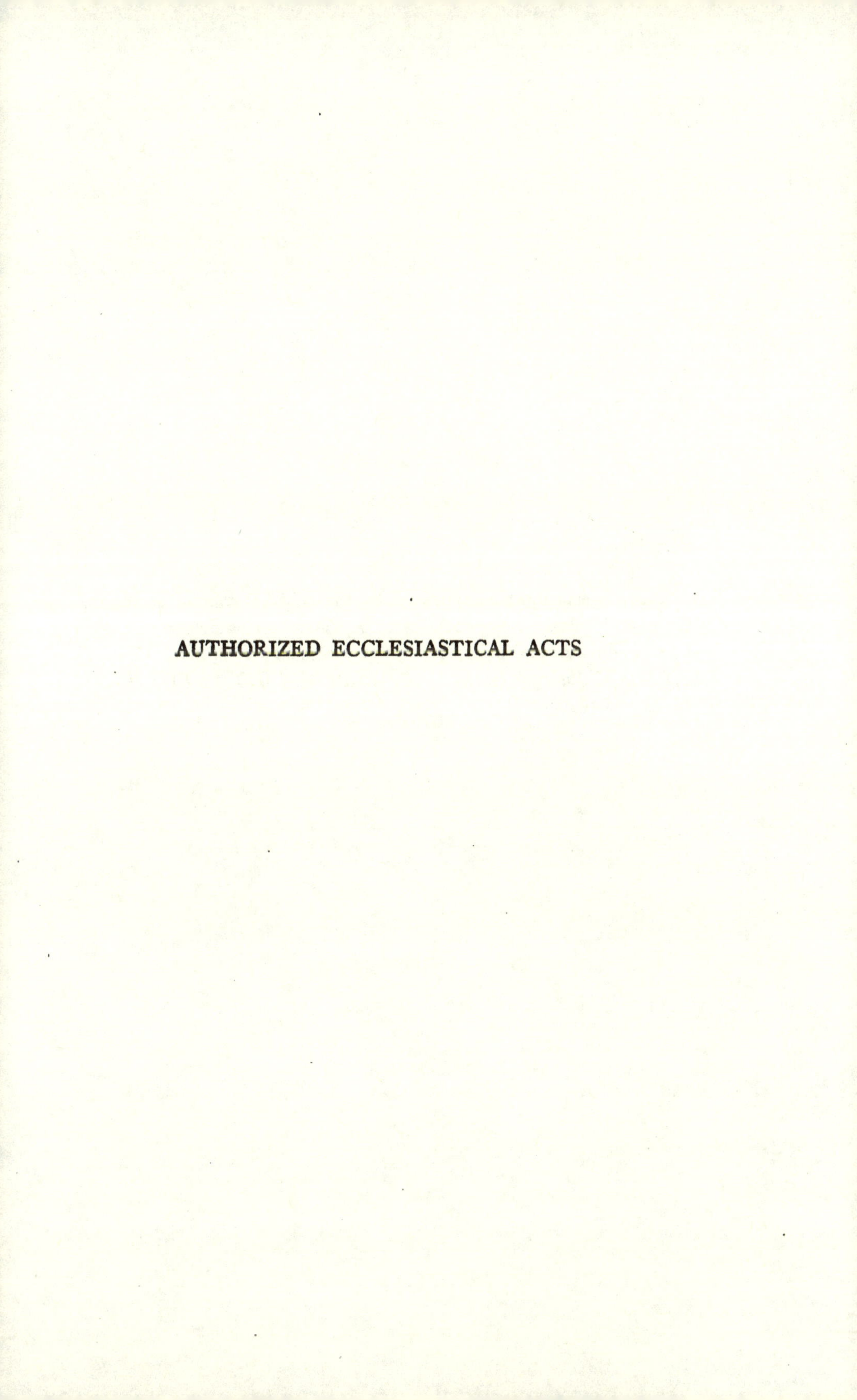

AUTHORIZED ECCLESIASTICAL ACTS

This dissertation was approved by the Right Reverend Monsignor Clement V. Bastnagel, S.T.L., J.U.D., Associate Professor of Canon Law, as director and by the Reverend Meletius M. Wojnar, O.S.B.M., S.T.L., J.C.D. and Stephan G. Kuttner, J.U.D., S.J.D., J.C.D., LL.D., as readers.

THE CATHOLIC UNIVERSITY OF AMERICA
CANON LAW STUDIES
No. 414

Authorized Ecclesiastical Acts

A DISSERTATION

SUBMITTED TO THE FACULTY OF THE SCHOOL OF CANON LAW OF THE CATHOLIC UNIVERSITY OF AMERICA IN PARTIAL FULFILLMENT OF THE REQUIREMENTS FOR THE DEGREE OF DOCTOR OF CANON LAW

BY

WILLIAM J. TIERNEY, A.B., J.C.L.
PRIEST OF THE DIOCESE OF ROCKVILLE CENTRE

THE CATHOLIC UNIVERSITY OF AMERICA PRESS
WASHINGTON, D. C.
1961

NIHIL OBSTAT:

CLEMENT V. BASTNAGEL, S.T.L., J.U.D.

Censor Deputatus

Washingtonii, die 2 maii, 1961.

IMPRIMATUR:

✠ WALTER P. KELLENBERG, D.D.

Episcopus Petropolitanus In Insula Longa

Petropoli, die 4 maii, 1961.

TO MY MOTHER AND THE MEMORY OF MY FATHER

FOREWORD

The Church has ever been solicitous that those who fill positions of responsibility in the carrying out of its end and purpose be persons of upright life in matters both of faith and morals. This fact is ably attested to by its present legislation as found in the Code of Canon Law. To realize that this has always been the case, one need only investigate its previous discipline.

In canon 2256, n. 2, the Code of Canon Law lists 17 distinct functions which aid in the carrying out of the purpose for which the Church exists. These are known as authorized ecclesiastical acts. In order to insure the correct carrying out of these actions, the Church excludes certain classes of people from their performance. It is the purpose of this dissertation to explore the origin and development of this legislation and to analyze it in its present form.

The exclusion from or the inability for the performance of authorized ecclesiastical acts is governed by those canons which forbid them to those who are excommunicated, to the infamous at law, to the infamous in fact, and to those who fall under this prohibition in consequence of a vindictive penalty. Thus, it is with these matters that the present study will be concerned.

The writer welcomes this occasion to express his sincere gratitude to the Most Reverend Walter P. Kellenberg, D.D., Bishop of Rockville Centre, for the opportunity of pursuing advanced studies in canon law. He also wishes to thank the Canon Law Faculty of the Catholic University of America for their kind and patient assistance during the past three years. In particular he is grateful for the assistance of the Right Reverend Clement V. Bastnagel, S.T.L., J.U.D., the director of this dissertation. Finally, the writer wishes to thank his classmates for their assistance and encouragement in the completion of this work.

TABLE OF CONTENTS

CHAPTER I

Introductory Notions

Article I. purpose and scope of this dissertation

In canon 2256, n. 2, the Code of Canon Law introduces the concept of *"actus legitimi ecclesiastici,"* and states that in the following canons this term has a definite content and meaning. The law lists 17 distinct acts or capacities as comprised within this concept.[1]

It is clear that there are several avenues of approach in one's dealing with this institute. One could, for example, analyze historically each of the individual actions in an effort to determine their exact origin and development. It was felt, however, that, since much of this work has already been accomplished in several fine works,[2]

[1] The office of administrator of ecclesiastical goods: functioning in the capacity of judge, auditor, referee, defender of the bond, promoter of justice, promoter of the faith, notary, chancellor, messenger, apparitor, advocate and procurator in ecclesiastical causes; the office of sponsor in baptism and confirmation; voting in ecclesiastical elections, and exercising the right of patronage.

[2] Bottoms, *The Discretionary Authority of the Ecclesiastical Judge in Matrimonial Trials of the First Instance,* The Catholic University of America Canon Law Studies, n. 349 (Washington, D. C.: The Catholic University of America Press, 1955); Metz, *The Recording Judge in the Ecclesiastical Collegiate Tribunal,* The Catholic University of America Canon Law Studies, n. 287 (Washington, D. C.: The Catholic University of America Press, 1949); Dolan, *The Defensor Vinculi,* The Catholic University of America Canon Law Studies, n. 85 (Washington, D. C.: The Catholic University of America, 1934); Glynn, *The Promoter of Justice,* The Catholic University of America Canon Law Studies, n. 101 (Washington, D. C.: The Catholic University of America, 1936); Duerr, *The Judicial Notary,* The Catholic University of America Canon Law Studies, n. 312 (Washington, D. C.: The Catholic University of America Press, 1951); Prince, *The Diocesan Chancellor,* The Catholic University of America Canon Law Studies n. 167 (Washington, D. C.: The Catholic University of America Press, 1942); Hogan, *Judicial Advocates and Procurators,* The Catholic University of America Canon Law Studies, n. 133 (Washington, D. C.: The Catholic University of America Press, 1941); Kearney, *Sponsors at Baptism According to the Code of Canon Law,* The Catholic University of America Canon Law Studies, n. 30 (Washington, D. C.: The Catholic University of America, 1925); Godfrey, *The Right of Patronage According to the Code of*

another plan should be followed, with reference namely to the institute as a whole. It is, then, the purpose and scope of this dissertation to deal with these *actus legitimi ecclesiastici* in the setting and context in which they are found in the Code of Canon Law itself. A brief study of the text and context of the canons dealing with this institute reveals the following general outline:

Canon 2256, n. 2, introduces the concept and describes just what is included under it. Canon 2263 states that the excommunicated are excluded from the performance of these acts within the limits set in the respective norms of law. Canon 2291, n. 8, mentions the exclusion from the exercise of these acts as one of the Church's principal vindictive penalties. Canon 2294, § 1, teaches that those who have incurred infamy of law are incapable of performing these acts, while the second paragraph of this canon points out that those who have incurred infamy of fact must likewise be excluded from the performance of these acts.

It is clear, then, that if one desires to follow the Code of Canon Law in the study of this institute, one shall, under the several headings employed, deal with the exclusion from or the inability for the performance of the acts which the Church accounts as authorized ecclesiastical acts.

Accordingly, the writer proposes to present a historical analysis and canonical interpretation of this institute under the various prohibiting and invalidating elements affecting it. But, before he can attempt to do so, he must explore certain basic preliminary notions in relation to it. This is the purpose of the following article.

Canon Law, The Catholic University of America Canon Law Studies, n. 21 (Washington, D. C.: The Catholic University of America, 1924); Parsons, *Canonical Elections,* The Catholic University of America Canon Law Studies, n. 118 (Washington, D. C.: The Catholic University of America Press, 1939); Mock, *Disqualifications of Electors in Ecclesiastical Elections,* The Catholic University of America Canon Law Studies, n. 218 (Washington, D. C.: The Catholic University of America Press, 1958); Comyns, *Papal and Episcopal Administration of Church Property,* The Catholic University of America Canon Law Studies, n. 147 (Washington, D. C.: The Catholic University of America Press, 1942); Blaher, *The Ordinary Processes in Causes of Beatification and Canonization,* The Catholic University of America Canon Law Studies, n. 268 (Washington, D. C.: The Catholic University of America Press, 1949).

ARTICLE II. ORIGIN OF THE INSTITUTE

Section 1. Selection of the Term "Authorized"

The choice of a designation for the acts enumerated in canon 2256, n. 2, centers in the expression *authorized* ecclesiastical acts. A variety of English words could be employed in a translation of the Latin *"legitimi."* To the writer the word *authorized* seems the one best suited for conveying the true meaning involved.

Most authors seem content to render the term into English as "legitimate ecclesiastical acts." [3] It sounds rather strange, however, to deal with those who are excluded or incapable of performing actions which are legitimate in themselves. Perhaps, then, one should seek to use a more precise term. Thus the writer has chosen "authorized." Surely it is a precision in terminology, and brings out more distinctly the nature of these actions, if one consider them as "authorized." Thus the law means that certain classes of people, determined in law, are not permitted to perform actions which are authorized for those who are in good standing.

Section 2. Difference in Terminology Between the Former and the Present Law

Part of the purpose of this dissertation is the historical analysis of the institute of authorized ecclesiastical acts in so far as their performance is simply prohibited, or affected also with invalidity. This task is impossible in the *strict* sense, for the institute as such derives its immediate origin from the Code of Canon Law itself.

[3] Abbo and Hannan, *The Sacred Canons* (2 vols., Vol. II, Revised Edition, St. Louis and London: B. Herder, 1957), II, 835; Hyland, *Excommunication,* The Catholic University of America Canon Law Studies, n. 85 (Washington, D. C.: The Catholic University of America, 1928), p. 123; Ayrinhac and Lydon, *Penal Legislation* (New York: Benziger Brothers, 1936), p. 92; Bouscaren and Ellis, *Canon Law* (2. ed., Milwaukee: Bruce, 1953), p. 897; Jone and Adelman, *Moral Theology* (rev. English trans. of 13th German ed., Westminister: Newman Press, 1953), n. 480, p. 332; Mahoney, *Priests' Problems* (ed. by L. McReavy, New York, Chicago, Cincinnati, Boston, San Francisco: Benziger Bros., 1958), p. 63; Davis, *Moral and Pastoral Theology, A Summary* (New York and London: Sheed and Ward, 1952), p. 208.

The institute of authorized ecclesiastical acts as it is known today, that is, as it is described in canon 2256, n. 2, begins with the Code; it has no exact counterpart in the former law. The phrase now employed in the Code does not seem to be found in the law of past times; one must look to the Code for the very coining of the phrase.

It must be pointed out, however, that there is a great similarity between the institute spoken of in canon 2256, n. 2, and the *"legitimi actus"* in the older law. The similarity is indeed so much a fact that one could at first glance be led to conclude that the two are in reality the same.

The writer's position may briefly be stated in this manner: The authorized or legitimate acts of the older law do not evince a scope and meaning that coincide exactly with the authorized ecclesiastical acts mentioned in canon 2256, n. 2. Though it is true that many or even most of the acts involved may be the same, the 17 acts comprised in the Code under the term "authorized ecclesiastical acts" are not strictly synonomous with the acts which in the former law were included under the expression "legitimate acts."

The truth of this position is obvious first of all from the recent institution of some of the offices which the Code recognizes as authorized ecclesiastical acts. Thus, for example, it seems that the office of the chancellor, as precisely outlined in the present law, is a creation of the Code itself.[4] The office of the *Defensor Vinculi* was canonically established by means of the constitution *Dei miseratione* on November 3, 1741, by Pope Benedict XIV,[5] and that of the Promoter of Faith by Pope Clement XI in 1708.

It must be remarked, however, that the argument stated above may not be as apodictic as it appears. It is always to be remembered that the institutes of law are not created or brought into existence from nothing at any particular moment. They are, for the most part, the fruit and culmination of centuries of development. Their basis and foundation is to be found in the legislation of the past. And so it may well be that, although an institute is specifically proclaimed or inaugurated at a precise moment in time, it has

[4] Prince, *op. cit.*, p. 118.

[5] *Fontes*, n. 318.

existed in practice for many years. Thus it is that the writer must seek a more fundamental basis, one founded in the law itself, for his opinion. And thus it is that he goes back to the former law itself to establish that what the pre-Code law meant by *"legitimi actus"* was not what the Code of Canon Law refers to as *"actus legitimi ecclesiastici."*

The expression "authorized" or "legitimate acts" is found in the law prior to the Code. It is not of frequent occurrence, but indeed both the text of the law itself and the glosses of the commentators contain it. The position stated above is supported not only from an analysis of these texts themselves, but also by the general impressions that remain from a study of the pertinent passages of the former law.

The former law and the commentary upon it (glossa) mention authorized or legitimate acts at least 8 times.[6] None of these citations supports the position that the *actus legitimi* were identical with the authorized ecclesiastical acts which receive mention in the Code. A careful analysis of the texts reveals two basic arguments in support of this negative opinion. In the first place, the former legislation and commentary point to certain legitimate or authorized acts of which no mention occurs among the authorized ecclesiastical acts listed in canon 2256, n. 2. This argument of itself opens a twofold hypothesis. Either it serves as proof for the contention stated above, or it presupposes that the enumeration in canon 2256, n. 2, is not a complete one, so that the basic question regarding the identity of the *actus legitimi* of the older law with the "authorized ecclesiastical acts" of the Code remains open and therefore unsolved. An investigation of the texts compels one to accept the first conclusion,

[6] C. 47, X, *de testibus et attestationibus,* II, 20; c. 5, *de poenis,* V, 9, in VI°; c. 14, *de sententia excommunicationibus,* V, 11, in VI°; c. un., *de poenis,* tit. XII, in Extravag. Ioan. XXII; Council of Milan (1287), c. 18—Mansi, *Sacrorum Conciliorum Nova et Amplissima Collectio* (53 vols. in 60, Parisiis, Arnheim, Leipzig, 1901-1927), XXIV, 878 (hereafter cited Mansi); Paulus IV, const. *Cum secundum,* 16 dec. 1558, n. 2, 3, 5—*Bullarum Diplomatum et Privilegiorum Sanctorum Romanorum Pontificum Taurinensis Editio* (24 vols. et Appendix, Augustae Taurinorum, 1858-1872), VI, 545 (hereafter cited *Bull. Rom. Taur.*); *glossa ordinaria* ad c. un., *de poenis,* tit. XII, in Extravag. Ioan. XXII, s.v. *perpetuo sit infamis.*

for the simple reason that the acts in question are among the ones most frequently cited in the former law, and if the content of the "authorized acts" of the former law was to be transposed, even if only in a substantial if not in an identical fashion, these acts would certainly have been included. The prime example in this regard concerns the capacity to act as a witness in a judicial process. Thus the law stated that those who did violence to ecclesiastical authorities or cooperated in such actions were branded as perpetually infamous, so that they were not to be allowed to testify, or also to perform *other* authorized acts.[7] This certainly lets one conclude that under the former law the capacity of acting as a witness pointed to the performance of an authorized act. It is not such under the Code, and thus one must conclude that the two sets of acts are not mutually to be identified.

The glossator on the Decretals of Gregory IX strengthened this impression through his inclusion of the *intestabiles* among those who were excluded from the exercise of authorized acts.[8] The *intestabiles* were those who through punishment by law became disabled from witnessing the drawing up of a will and, at a later date, even of making one themselves. This notion was closely linked with that of the incapacity of being a witness. This identification of one's acting as a witness with one's performing of an authorized act was pointed out again in the decretals in connection with the giving of testimony in matrimonial causes.[9]

The texts of the former law also support the position proposed above in that in several places one finds mention of acts which are now recognized by the Code as authorized ecclesiastical acts but in the former law were listed separately from, though on a par with, the authorized acts as expressed in the law. It thus follows that these acts were not regarded as authorized acts by the older law, at least not in the strict sense. Yet these acts are now listed in the Code's authorized ecclesiastical acts. Therefore, the two are not identical. This is illustrated in the Constitution of Pope

[7] "Perpetuo sit infamis: ut nec ad testimonium vel alios actus legitimos admittatur: . . ."—c. un., *de poenis,* tit. XII, in Extravag. Ioan. XXII.

[8] *Glossa ordinaria* ad c. 13, X, *de haereticis.,* V, 7, s.v. *sit etiam intestabilis.*

[9] C. 47, X, *de testibus et attestationibus,* II, 20.

Paul IV (1555-1559), in which he punished those who meddled in papal elections by depriving them of the right of patronage, the right of suffrage and, among other penalties also, the performance of authorized acts.[10]

As will be pointed out at greater length in a following chapter, the former law listed many punishments which resulted from the incurring of infamy of law. In one such text the capacity to function in two positions, which capacity the Code now counts among the authorized ecclesiastical acts, is indeed listed on a par with, but nevertheless distinct from, the *actus legitimi.* Thus the *Extravagantes* of John XXII point out that the infamy resulting from acts of violence committed against ecclesiastical authorities brings with it the deprivation of the office of procurator and notary in addition to the forfeited exercise of the *actus legitimi.*[11]

In all fairness it must be admitted that perhaps these arguments, even though they are taken from the former law itself, may not be conclusive. It must be pointed out that there are also passages which give the appearance of distinguishing at least in some general manner between the *actus legitimi* and other closely related acts, which even today are not listed by the Code as authorized ecclesiastical acts.[12] In view of this fact, coupled with the general impression of equivocation and indefiniteness that the former law sometimes presents in regard to the content of its authorized acts, perhaps one should conclude that the former law had no set and definite number of acts which fell within the category of *actus legitimi.* Hyland seems to tend toward this conclusion when he remarks in reference to a particular text of the decretals: "True it is in the Decretals of Boniface VIII, there is a reference to the

[10] Paulus IV, const. *Cum secundum,* 16 dec. 1558, n. 2, 3, 5: ". . . necnon iurium patronatus et iurisdictionem quarumcumque; careantque voce activa et passiva . . . et incapaces omnium dignitatum, honorum, bonorum, iurium et legitimorum actuum, . . ."—*Bull. Rom. Taur.,* VI, 545.

[11] "Perpetuo sit infamis: ut nec ad testimonium vel alios actus legitimos admittatur: . . .: nec ipse ad patrocinandum aliis admittatur: instrumenta confecta pereum, si forte officium tabellionatus exerceat, nullam habeant firmitatem: . . ."—c. un., *de poenis,* tit. XII, in Extravag. Ioan. XXII, . . .

[12] Cf. *glossa ordinaria* ad c. un., *de poenis,* tit. XII, in Extravag. Ioan. XXII, s.v. *perpetuo sit infamis.*

removal of public excommunicates from legitimate acts. It is very difficult however to ascertain just what were included within the scope of legitimate acts, for in the very same sentence the canon speaks of avoiding public excommunicates not only in judicial but extrajudicial affairs." [13]

Thus, because of the general imprecision of the former law the arguments presented here may not be apodictic. The answer may lie in a general state of confusion and indefiniteness regarding the exact extension of the concept of *actus legitimi* in the former law. In either case, that is, whether one accepts the arguments as sufficiently conclusive, or whether one sees only vagueness in the former law regarding the meaning and import of its authorized acts, the submitted thesis appears sustained. The legitimate or the authorized acts of the older law are not to be identified exactly with the scope and meaning now attaching to authorized ecclesiastical acts as listed in canon 2256, n. 2.

Section 3. Differences in Terminology in the Present Code

Though one believe it to be firmly established that the *actus legitimi* of the former discipline are not synonymous with the authorized ecclesiastical acts as now enumerated in the Code, one must at the same time admit that the terminology of the Code itself presents some difficulties. The problem briefly is this: Although in the great majority of passages in the Code the expression *actus legitimi ecclesiastici* is used when reference is intended for the acts enumerated in canon 2256, n. 2, there are also several passages wherein simply the term *actus legitimi* is found. Such a slight variance in the wording has been duly stressed in the comparison made between the wording of the Code and that which obtained in the former law. Is one to make the same distinction within the Code itself, or do these various phrases have exactly the same meaning within the context of the present law?

There can be no doubt that these two variations in wording

[13] Hyland, *op. cit.*, p. 123; c. 14, *de sententia excommunicationis*, V, 11, in VI°.

nevertheless reflect the same meaning in the present law of the Code.

These phrases are found in 17 canons of the Code. There are 14 direct references, that is, passages where the full and complete expressions are used,[14] and three indirect allusions to these expressions.[15] In 11 passages there is a direct mention of *actus legitimi ecclesiastici,* while canon 2358 indirectly refers to this term. *Actus legitimi* are mentioned directly three times, and referred to indirectly twice, in those canons that deal with the requirements for valid and licit sponsorship at confirmation. These canons—795, n. 2 and 796, n. 3—refer back to conditions previously established in regard to baptism.[16]

There is little difficulty in determining the meaning of *actus legitimi* in those canons which state the requirements for valid and licit sponsorship at baptism and confirmation.[17] The law there simply restates what is clear from canon 2256, n. 2. Since the functioning as a sponsor at the conferral of either of these sacraments is an authorized ecclesiastical act, it is obvious that one cannot be a valid or a licit sponsor should one be excluded from the valid or the licit performance of these acts.

This point seems to present no difficulty to either moralists or canonists, for they are unanimous in agreeing that the *actus legitimi* as mentioned in these canons are synonymous with the *actus legitimi ecclesiastici* listed in canon 2256, n. 2. Thus Kearney, when commenting on the *actus legitimi* mentioned in canon 765, lists them in exactly the same manner as they are found listed in canon 2256, n. 2, and refers the reader to the latter.[18] Vermeersch (1858-1936) offered an interesting description of the acts in question, and identified them with the authorized ecclesiastical acts as they receive men-

[14] Canons 2256; 2263; 2291, n. 8; 2294, § 1, § 2; 2315; 2350, § 2; 2353; 2354; § 1; 2357, § 2; 2375; 2385; 765, n. 2; 766, n. 2.

[15] Canons 2358; 795, n. 2; 796, n. 3.

[16] Canons 765, n. 2, and 766, n. 3.

[17] Canons 765, n. 2; 766, n. 2; 795, n. 2; 796, n. 3.

[18] Kearney, *op. cit.,* p. 91.

tion in canon 2256, n. 2.[19] Others may also be cited in defense of the same doctrine.[20]

There remains in the Code only a single passage which presents a difficulty in terminology. Canon 2256, n. 2, points out that in the canons which follow it the expression "authorized ecclesiastical acts" signifies the 17 acts which are there enumerated. The proper terminology is used in all the canons which follow and deal with the subject in hand, save one. Canon 2315 provides that only exception. Whereas the other canons use the phrase *"actus legitimi ecclesiastici"* this canon employs the expression *"actus legitimi."* There is no reason for any change of terminology at this point; there seems no alternative but to conclude that this canon likewise refers to the authorized ecclesiastical acts as listed in canon 2256, n. 2. This is the opinion of Conte a Coronata who, when commenting on the phrase in question, equates it with the content of canons 2256, n. 2, and 2291, n. 8.[21] Woywod (1880-1941) and others reflected the same doctrine.[22] No authors seem to propose any doctrine to the contrary.

[19] *Theologiae Moralis* (4 vols., Vol. III, 4 ed. by Creusen, Roma: Pontificia Universita Gregoriana, 1948), III, 146.

[20] Regatillo-Zalba, *Theologia Moralis Summa* (3 vols., Vol. III, *De Sacramentis De Delictis et Poenis,* Madrid: Biblioteca de Autores Cristianos, 1954), III, p. 364; Jone-Adelman, *op. cit.,* p. 332; Jorio, *Theologia Moralis* (3 vols., Vol. III, *De Sacramentis in genere et de Sacramentalibus,* Neapoli: M. D'Auria, [S. Sedis Apostolicae Typographus], 1954), III, 42; Davis, *Moral and Pastoral Theology* (4 vols., Vol. III, *Sacraments,* 7. rev. ed., London and New York: Sheed and Ward, 1958), III, 63; Merkelbach, *Summa Theologiae Moralis* (3 vols., Vol. III, *De Sacramentis,* 10. ed., Brugis: Desclée de Brouwer, 1956), III, p. 139; Jone, *Commentarium in Codicem Iuris Canonici* (3 vols., Vol. I, 1950, Vol. II, 1953, Vol. III, 1954, Paderborn: Ferdinand Schöningh), II, 36.

[21] "Quid sint actus legitimi cfr. in 2256, 2° una cum 2291, 8°.—*Institutiones Iuris Canonici* (5 vols., Vol. I, *Normae Generales, De Clericis, De Religiosis, De Laicis,* 4. ed., Taurini et Romae: Marietti, 1950; Vol. II, *De Rebus,* 4. ed., Taurini et Romae: Marietti, 1951; Vol. III, *De Processibus,* 4. ed., Taurini et Romae: Marietti, 1956; Vol. IV, *De Delictis et Poenis,* 4. ed., Taurini et Romae: Marietti, 1955; Vol. V, *Index Rerum et Appendices,* 3. ed., Taurini et Romae: Marietti, 1951), IV, p. 319, footnote 4. (Hereafter cited Conte a Coronata.)

[22] *A Practical Commentary on the Code of Canon Law* (2 vols., 3. printing, New York: Wagner, 1929), II, n. 2159, p. 467; Jone, *op. cit.,* III, p. 499; Augustine, *A Commentary on Canon Law* (8 vols., Vol. VIII, St. Louis and London: B. Herder, 1922), VIII, 286.

Article III. description of each authorized ecclesiastical act

Section 1. The Administrator of Ecclesiastical Property

The Church is a perfect, i. e., a juridically self-contained society, and as such is endowed with those means which are necessary for the accomplishment of its end and purpose.[23] Although this purpose is primarily a spiritual and eternal one, it is carried out among men and temporal affairs. Thus, one of the means necessary for its realization is the acquiring, owning, and administration of temporal property.[24] Thus the Catholic Church and the Apostolic See have an inherent right to acquire, own, and administer temporal property in the carrying out of the purposes for whch they were established. This right is independent of any civil power or interference.[25] This right also belongs to individual churches and other moral persons which have been established as juridic persons by ecclesiastical authority.[26] It is with the third of these rights that this study is here concerned in that the performance of the office of administering ecclesiastical property is an authorized ecclesiastical act.

Ecclesiastical property consists of that temporal property, both movable and immovable, corporeal and incorporeal, which belongs either to the universal Church and the Apostolic See or to some other moral person in the Church.[27] This property is called sacred, when it is destined by consecration or blessing for use in divine worship.

23 Ottaviani, *Institutiones Iuris Publici Ecclesiastici* (2 vols. in 1, 3. ed., Typis Polyglottis Vaticanis, 1947), I, 80-128; Cappello, *Summa Iuris Publici Ecclesiastici* (6. ed., Romae: Apud Aedes Universitatis Gregorianae, 1954), pp. 88-102, n. 105-125; Vermeersch-Creusen, *Epitome Iuris Canonici* (Vol. I, 7. ed., 1949, Vol. II, 7. ed., 1954, Vol. III, 7. ed., 1956, Mechliniae-Romae: H. Dessain), II, p. 570, n. 817; Woywod, *op. cit.*, II, p. 166, n. 1478.

24 Abbo-Hannan, *op. cit.*, II, p. 705; Vermeersch-Creusen, *op. cit.*, III, n. 817, p. 570; Comyns, *op. cit.*, p. XIII; cf. the condemnation of the opposed doctrine by Pope Pius XI: Denziger, *Enchiridion Symbolorum* (29. ed. by Rahner, Friburgi Brisg.: Herder, 1953), p. 486, n. 1726; p. 242, n. 590; p. 243, n. 612; p. 243, n. 616.

25 Canon 1495, § 1.

26 Canon 1495, § 2.

27 Canon 1497, § 1.

It is called precious when it is of notable value by reason of its artistic quality, historical significance, or the material of which it is made.[28]

Administration concerns those actions which pertain to the conservation and improvement of ecclesiastical property itself as well as to the reception, conservation, improvement, and application of the fruits or income of such property.[29]

In the early days of the Church the administration of ecclesiastical property was entrusted to the deacons.[30] Thus it was in later times that the bishops entrusted this duty to the care of their archdeacon.[31] As the Church grew and prospered the administration of its property came to be an undertaking of more magnitude, and thus it was that special provision was made for the appointing of *oeconomes* to handle this matter. The Council of Chalcedon (a. 451) threatened to punish any bishop who did not appoint one of these officers.[32]

It was customary in various parts of the Church to administer church property by dividing it into different portions. Thus, for example, in Italy there was a fourfold division. One part each for the bishop, the clergy, the poor, and the church. In other sections the division was somewhat different.[33]

The administrative activity of the popes increased decidedly from the 5th century to the time of the Decretals of Gregory IX (1234). The power of the bishops decreased during this period in consequence of the growing recognition of the rights of local churches over their income by conciliar legislation.[34]

[28] Canon 1497, § 2.

[29] Wernz-Vidal, *Ius Canonicum* (7 vols. in 8, Vol. IV, Para. II, *De Rebus*, Romae: Apud Aedes Universitatis Gregorianae, 1935), IV, n. 746, pp. 211-212; Conte a Coronata, II, n. 1058, p. 482; Vermeersch-Creusen, *op. cit.*, II, n. 838, p. 591; Berutti, *Institutiones Iuris Canonici* (6 vols., Vol. VI, *De Delictis et Poenis*, Taurini-Romae: Marietti, 1938), VI, n. 60, p. 165; Comyns, *op. cit.*, p. 1.

[30] Acts of the Apostles, 6:1-5.

[31] Comyns, *op. cit.*, p. 22.

[32] C. 26—Mansi, *Sacrorum Consiliorum Nova et Amplissima Collectio* (53 vols. in 60, Parisiis, 1901-1927), VI, col. 1230.

[33] Wernz-Vidal, *op. cit.*, Vol. IV, Pars II, n. 736, pp.187-188.

[34] Comyns, *op. cit.*, p. 27.

From the 12th to the 16th century the exercise of the administration of temporal property was continued on a larger scale than before. The popes of this period asserted their supremacy over all the Church's possessions. The rights of bishops in this regard were continually reduced in favor of those of the pastors of the individual parishes.[35]

The rights of the papacy which had been so clearly defined in these past centuries remained intact in the legislation from the Council of Trent to the Code. The rights of the bishops which had been reduced to the administration of the cathedral and of the common diocesan property, and simply to the supervision of parochial administration, were likewise maintained.[36]

The present law states that the Roman Pontiff is the supreme administrator and dispenser of all ecclesiastical property.[37] Local ordinaries are to carefully supervise and regulate the administration of ecclesiastical property in their territory.[38] In order that they may carry out this duty properly they are to establish a diocesan council of administration. The ordinary is to be the president of this council and is to be assisted by at least two qualified men. These men should be proficient in civil law and are selected by the ordinary upon consultation with the Board of Consultors, unless another system of law or custom is approved for this establishment.[39] In addition to this board, the ordinary is to appoint men who are prudent, qualified, and of good reputation to administer the property of a church or pious place which does not have its own administrator.[40] When the administration of ecclesiastical property is carried on by laymen, it is nevertheless to be executed in the name of the Church and without prejudice to the right of the ordinary to inspect the property, to demand an accounting, and to prescribe the mode of administration.[42]

[35] Comyns, *op. cit.*, pp. 37 and 41.
[36] Comyns, *op. cit.*, pp. 46 and 48.
[37] Canon 1518.
[38] Cf. canon 1519.
[39] Canon 1520, § 1.
[40] Cf. canon 1521, § 1.
[42] Cf. canon 1521, § 2.

The administrators of ecclesiastical property are required to fulfill their office with that diligence with which a good father of a family would. They must therefore be vigilant lest the property entrusted to their care be destroyed or damaged; observe the prescripts of both canon and civil law as well as those laid down by the founder or donor or imposed by legitimate authority; collect promptly and accurately the income and profits, and safeguard and distribute them in accordance with the intention of the founder or with established laws or norms; invest, for the benefit of the church itself, with the consent of the ordinary; that money which is left over after the payment of expenses; keep the records of receipts and expenditures in good order; arrange and keep the documents and instruments, upon which the property rights of the church are based, in the archives or in a suitable safe; and authentic copies of these documents should be kept in the archives or safe of the diocesan curia when this can be done conveniently.[43] In addition to these general duties, the administrators appointed for a particular church or pious place, before they assume this position must: take an oath before the local ordinary or dean that they will faithfully and efficiently carry out their work; make an accurate and specific inventory, to be signed by all the administrators, of immovable and precious movable goods as well as of all other property, with a description and appraisal of each; if they use an inventory previously drawn up, the things acquired or lost in the interim are to be noted; one copy of this inventory is to be deposited in the archives of the place of administration, and another in the archives of the curia; any change which the goods undergo is to be noted in each copy.[44]

In addition to these responsibilities, the administrators of ecclesiastical property are bound to render an account of their administration each year to the local ordinary. This is a strict obligation and is to be fulfilled even though particular law requires the rendering of such an account to others as well.[45] They are also bound to

[43] Canon 1523.

[44] Canon 1522.

[45] Cf. canon 1525.

provide a living wage and to be moderate in their demands upon their employees.[46] They have no right to engage in lawsuits without permission.[47] Acts of extraordinary administration performed without the required permission are invalid.[48] And, finally, the administrators are bound to restore any loss suffered by the church as the result of having abandoned their administration on their own authority.[49]

Section 2. The Judge

Canon 1572, § 1, states the concept of the bishop as the principal member of the diocesan tribunal. In every diocese and for all causes not expressly excepted by law, the local ordinary is the judge of the first instance. This judiciary power the local ordinary can exercise either in person or through others according to the canons.[50]

The judicial power of the tribunal lies in the bishop. He is the visible representative of the court, and as such it is to him that matters of delegation and rogatory commissions are addressed. He may always preside over the tribunal in person with the exception of causes in which he is an interested party.[51] He may act as the sole judge or as the presiding judge when a collegiate tribunal is necessary. On the other hand, the law demands that he appoint an *officialis,* i. e., a presiding officer for the diocesan court.[52] It also urges that he arrange to have the hearing of causes, especially the criminal and the important civil causes, undertaken by

[46] Cf. canon 1524.

[47] Cf. canon 1526.

[48] Canon 1527, § 1.

[49] Cf. canon 1528.

[50] Canon 335 points out that it is the right and duty of the bishop to govern his diocese in both spiritual and temporal matters with legislative, judicial, and coactive power, which is to be exercised according to the norms of the sacred canons.

[51] Canon 1572, § 2.

[52] Canon 1578; cf. Roberti, De Processibus (2 vols., Vol. I, 4. ed., Romae: Apud Custodiam Librariam Pontificii Instituti Utriusque Iuris, 1956), I, nn. 89-91, pp. 207-211.

the ordinary tribunal under the presidency of the *officialis* or the *vice-officialis*.[53]

The judicial power of the bishop is further demonstrated in that he may reserve any cause, whether criminal or civil, to himself, apart of course from such as have been expressly excepted by the law.[54] The law further points to certain situations in which the bishop and he alone must act.[55] There are many other examples of this.

In general, a judge is a public person who enjoys ecclesiastical jurisdiction in order that he may deal with and settle controversies according to law.[56] It is not his office to make law; rather he is to apply it to particular causes under litigation. The *officialis* is the ordinary judge of the diocesan tribunal. He is the priest whom the bishop has deputed, and to whom belongs the ordinary power of dealing with all causes which the bishop has not reserved to himself.[57]

In Roman Law a twofold procedure was observed in judicial matters. The controversy was presented to the magistrate, whose function it was to determine whether the cause fell within the scope of the law. If it did, it was then presented to the judge or *iudex* with the instructions of the magistrate. The cause was then investigated and settled.

Roman jurisprudence developed under the *praetors,* who were civil magistrates charged with the administration of justice in regard both to Roman citizens and strangers.

Both the legislative and the judicial powers were clearly exercised

[53] Canon 1578; cf. Roberti, *op. cit.*, I, n. 109, p. 244.

[54] Canon 1572, § 1; Roberti, *op. cit.*, I, n. 109, p. 244.

[55] Canons 1614, § 1; 1625, § 1; 1576, § 3; 1586; S.C. de Sacramentis, *Instructio servanda a tribunalibus diocesanis* in pertractandis causis de nullitate matrimoniarum, 15 aug. 1936, Art. 16, § 1—*Acta Apostolicae Sedis, Commentarium Officiale,* (Romae, 1909-) XXVIII (1936), 313-361 (hereafter cited *AAS*); Bouscaren, *The Canon Law Digest* (4 vols. and supplement, Milwaukee: Bruce, 1934-1959, II, 471-573. (This document will hereafter be cited as *Provida* along with an indication of the article and paragraph number.)

[56] Cappello, *Summa Iuris Canonici* (Vol I, 5. ed., 1951, Vol. II, 5. ed., 1951, Vol. III, 4. ed., 1955, Romae: Apud Aedes Pontificae Universitatis Gregorianae), III, n. 71, p. 75.

[57] Cappello, *op. cit.*, III, n. 73, p. 78.

in the early Church. Christ, the Divine Founder, gave both of these powers to the Apostles and their successors, and there is abundant testimony that they were employed.[58]

The title *officialis* is found as early as the fourth century. At that time, however, the one so designated was chiefly concerned with aiding the bishop in his dealings with matters that were strictly spiritual in nature. Rarely was he involved in the administration of justice.[59]

There are various theories regarding the exact origin of the office. It seems to have appeared, in its proper sense, for the first time in Rheims in the middle of the 12th century. The person referred to was not always designated as the *officialis,* but the office existed and soon spread to other regions and nations. Thus one finds it established in Germany and Poland by the beginning of the 13th century, and in Spain fifty years later. Thc *officialis* soon appeared in Italy also, but there as in other places his title and duties were often intermingled with those of the vicar general.[60]

The reasons for the institution of the office of the *officialis* are somewhat clouded. As the judiciary system of the Church developed, the archdeacon became second in importance only to the bishop himself. According to Thomassinus (1619-1695)[61] the *officialis* was created for the purpose of putting a check on these powers. This opinion however no longer enjoys favor, for it can be demonstrated that the office already existed during the time the archdeacon was at the height of his influence. Further, the archdeacon's office did not cease with the introduction of the *officialis,* for in fact the same man sometimes held both positions. The true explanation seems to lie in the fact of the tremendous increase of

[58] St. John, 21:15; St. Matthew, 16:17-18; Acts of the Apostles, 15:8; I Cor., 11:2, 33, 34; I Tim., 5:19; St. Matthew, 18:14-18; cf. Dugan, *The Judiciary Department of the Diocesan Curia,* The Catholic University of America Canon Law Studies, n. 26 (Washington, D. C., The Catholic University of America, 1925), pp. 32-35.

[59] Roberti, *op. cit.,* I, n. 110, p. 250.

[60] Roberti, *op. cit.,* I, n. 110, p. 251.

[61] *Vetus et Nova Ecclesiae Disciplina circa Beneficia et Beneficiarios* (Lucae, 1728), Pars I, Lib. 1-2, cap. 17; as cited by Roberti, *op. cit.,* I, n. 110, p. 251, and Bottoms, *op. cit.,* p. 13.

causes referred to the diocesan tribunals and the deepened interest in the study of church law and its problems. This explanation does not deny however that the development of the office of the *officialis* provided an opportunity for the curtailing of the authority of the archdeacon.[62]

By the general law of the Latin Church every bishop is bound to appoint an *officialis*.[63]

Before any priest can be appointed to this office he must meet the requirements stated by law. He must be a priest of irreproachable reputation, must possess the degree of Doctor or Licentiate of Canon Law or at least have a thorough knowledge of it, and be at least thirty years of age.[64]

The *officialis* may be removed from office at the will of the bishop.[65] The bishop must have a reason in order to act licitly. Should the episcopal see be vacant, the *officialis* remains in office and cannot be removed by the *vicar capitular*. Upon the arrival of the new bishop his appointment must be confirmed.[66]

The *officialis* constitutes one tribunal with the bishop.[67] He judges with ordinary power.[68]

> "The tribunal or court of the official is to be considered as one and the same with that of the bishop, that is, of the same grade. This does not imply that the *officialis* is equal in person to the bishop. The *officialis* derives his jurisdiction from the bishop. The bishop has the power to limit the jurisdiction of the official by reservation of certain cases. But since the tribunal of the *officialis* is a court of the first instance, and since his jurisdiction extends to all persons and things within the diocese, it is said to be '*unum tribunal cum Episcopo loci.*' "[69]

62 Cf. Roberti, *op. cit.*, I, n. 110, pp. 251-252.
63 Canon 1573, § 1.
64 Canon 1573, § 4.
65 Canon 1573, § 5.
66 Canon 1573, § 5.
67 Canon 1573, § 2.
68 Canon 1573, § 1.
69 Dugan, *op. cit.*, p. 38.

The *officialis* constitutes one tribunal with the bishop. Thus there can be no appeal to the bishop from a decision of the *officialis,* for the latter constitutes as it were a projection of the judicial person of the bishop. Since this unity is present, there cannot be several *officiales* in the diocese. The need for assistance is provided for by the law in that assistants may be assigned to the *officialis.* Each is termed a *vice-officialis.*[70] These officials have the same ordinary power as the *officialis,* and whatever is done by any one of them is considered as done by the *officialis.* They must possess the same qualifications as the *officialis* and their office is terminated in the same way.[71] They are to exercise their office in subordination to the *officialis.*[72]

The *officialis* exercises not only judicial power but also administrative power when this is necessary for carrying out his judicial functions. This is true when he acts as the sole judge or as the *praeses* of a collegiate tribunal.[73]

The *officialis* performs matters of administration mixed with judicial power especially when causes are assigned to the synodal judges in rotation.[74]

In addition to the *officialis* other judges are to be appointed either in the synod or apart from it. These priests serve with the *officialis* in deciding certain types of causes.

Canon 1574 points out that in every diocese priests of good reputation and of outstanding knowledge are to be appointed as synodal judges, or as pro-synodal if appointed outside of the synod. These judges may be appointed from the clergy of another diocese, but are not to be more than twelve in number. They are to take part in the handling of causes with power which is delegated to them by the bishop. Their appointment, substitution, forfeiture of

[70] Canon 1573, § 3.

[71] Canon 1573, § 4, § 5; Cf. Conte a Coronata, III, n. 1116, pp. 31-34; Roberti, *op. cit.,* I, n. 111, pp. 252-254; Cappello, *op. cit.,* III, nn. 73 and 74, pp. 78-80.

[72] Roberti, *op. cit.,* I, n. 112, p. 256.

[73] Cf. canons 1909, § 1; 1715, § 1; 1727; Roberti, *op. cit.,* I, n. 111, p. 253.

[74] Cf. canon 1916, § 1; *Provida,* Art. 65, § 1; *Provida,* Art. 58; *Provida,* Art. 226.

office and removal from office is governed by the rules of canons 385-388. The law considers pro-synodal judges on a par with synodal judges.

The origin of these offices seems to lie in the middle ages. In the course of handling certain causes it was found necessary for certain ecclesiastical persons to be commissioned by the Holy See to execute a mandate or a rescript. In order to prevent unworthy parties from carrying out this function with consequent harm to both the Church and the parties involved, Pope Boniface VIII (1294-1303) laid down certain qualifications in this regard. The ones appointed were to be capable and worthy of such trust. If the cause involved judicial procedure it was to be handled in a place of some importance, where the service of men skilled in the law was available. The Council of Trent adopted this same policy; in its XXV session it called for the appointment of synodal judges. This legislation is substantially contained in the Code today.[75]

The synodal and pro-synodal judges are considered as auxiliary judges. They are selected and given power by the bishop in order that they may assist in the settlement of disputes in the ecclesiastical courts. In the consideration of their exact functions one must recall that a cause brought before a court of the Church may be adjudicated by one or several judges. If it is a cause in which several judges are necessary in order to render a decision, it is said to be handled by a collegiate tribunal. Such a tribunal may be composed of three, five, or even more judges. The vote of the majority of these judges will determine the decision to be rendered.[76]

The present law of the Church demands that certain causes be tried before a collegiate tribunal, while others are left to the prudent discretion of the bishop as to whether the collegiate body shall be employed.[77]

Another function of the synodal and pro-synodal judges is pointed to by canon 1575, which provides that in every trial conducted by a single judge two *assessores* or counsellors may be employed.

[75] Cf. Dugan, *op. cit.*, pp. 40-42; Roberti, *op. cit.*, I, n. 116, p. 260.

[76] Cf. Cappello, *op. cit.*, III, nn. 77-79, pp. 81-84; Conte a Coronata, III, n. 1118, pp. 34-38.

[77] Cf. canons 1576, § 1, n. 1; 1576, § 1, n. 2; 1576, § 2.

These are to be chosen from the body of synodal and pro-synodal judges.

Section 3. The Auditor

"An *auditor* is a cleric, who, by reason of jurisdiction delegated to him, is empowered to cite witnesses before an ecclesiastical court, hear their testimony and perform other judicial acts in keeping and within the limits of the commission through which he acts." [78] Others, considering the office in a more limited way, describe the *auditor* as one who in past times was commissioned by the Holy See to gather information in a particular cause. The data were then presented to the judge, who himself rendered the sentence.[79]

The office of the *auditor* has its origin in the middle ages. When the number of causes presented to the Pope transcended his ability to deal with them, he appointed others to hear some of these causes. It was the making of such appointments that gave rise to the *Roman Rota.* This group of *auditores* not only heard various causes alloted to them by the Holy See, but also contributed a great deal of legal advice and counsel.

This institute has passed down into the diocesan as well as the papal curia.[80]

The appointment of the *auditor* is left to the discretion of the bishop, who may appoint either one or several. This appointment may be permanent or for a special cause.[81] Should the ordinary fail to appoint an *auditor,* the judge may do so for the particular cause which he is adjudicating.[82]

The *auditores* of the diocesan tribunal are to be selected, in so far as it is possible, from the body of the synodal or the pro-synodal judges.[83] This requirement is one of lighter import, how-

[78] Dugan, *op. cit.,* pp. 50-51.

[79] Cf. Dugan, *op. cit.,* p. 51.

[80] Dugan, *op. cit.,* p. 51; Cappello, *op. cit.,* III, n. 87, pp. 91-92; *Roberti, op. cit.,* I, n. 124, pp. 273-274; Conte a Coronata, III, n. 1121, pp. 39-40.

[81] Canon 1580, § 1.

[82] Canon 1580, § 2.

[83] Canon 1581; Cf. Roberti, *op. cit.,* I, n. 126, p. 279; Dugan, *op. cit.,* p. 52; Cappello, *op. cit.,* III, n. 87, p. 92; Conte a Coronata, III, n. 1121, p. 40.

ever. For any proportionate reason will excuse from its fulfillment.[84]

The function of the *auditor* is to summon the witnesses of the cause and examine them as well as to draw up the judicial acts of the cause according to the tenor of their mandate.[85] The Code refers to the bearers of this office as both "*auditores*" and "*actorum instructores*." [86] The former label is given them because they hear the witnesses who have been cited, the latter, because they set in order and drew up the judicial acts relating to the procedure.[87]

The extent of the functions of the *auditor* is not fully treated by the Code. Some hold that the *auditor* is an aid to the judge, an auxiliary who carries out the will of the judge. His power thus depends on the judge. Is the *auditor* himself a judge? There can be no doubt that he does exercise some jurisdiction in the carrying out of his office. The Code considers him rather as a subsidiary judge in regard to the principal judge. His power is therefore completely derived from the principal judge. Should this judge lack jurisdiction, the *auditor* would be in a similar condition. In this view the jurisdiction employed by the *auditor* is ordinary or delegated depending on whether the ordinary or the judge has stably constituted him as *auditor* in the tribunal or selected him for an individual cause under litigation.[88]

Others contend that the power of the *auditor* is ordinary, since the office is stably constituted as such by the Code. Thus, regarding the actions expressly committed to him by the Code, he exercises ordinary power. He exercises delegated power in regard to other acts carried out in virtue of a special mandate. This is especially true if he is selected by the ordinary or the judge for the hearing of a particular cause. The question whether the *auditor* loses his jurisdiction or office if the principal judge should lose it must seek its answer on the basis of these principles.[89]

[84] Cappello, *op. cit.*, III, n. 87, p. 92.

[85] Canon 1582.

[86] Canon 1580, § 1.

[87] Cappello, *op. cit.*, III, n. 87, p. 93.

[88] Roberti, *op. cit.*, I, n. 125, p. 276.

[89] Cappello, *op. cit.*, III, n. 87, p. 93.

The mandate of the *auditor* is very important in the matter of determining his functions in a particular cause. Generally he will perform these duties: (1) He will summon the witnesses who are to appear before the tribunal; (2) he will examine the witnesses and hear their testimony, (3) and he will set in order and draw up the judicial acts relating to the procedure. The Instruction *Provida* furnishes many examples of the acts that may be performed by the *auditor*.[90]

The *auditor* may, depending on his mandate, be required to perform other functions in particular causes. Thus he may be commissioned to handle the many duties in the process from the joinder of issues to the publication of the process. In civil causes it may be his task to make the necessary preparations for the formal opening of the cause. These would include the acceptance or rejection of the bill of complaint (*libellus*), the citation of the parties, and the sealing of the joinder of issue (*contestatio litis*).

It is to be noted that the duties of the *auditor* concern the preliminary acts relating to the cause. They do not pertain to those acts in the process by means of which the cause becomes a settled issue.

This is true of both contentious and criminal causes, and thus he is excluded from employing the *"iusiurandum decisorium"* mentioned in canon 1834. This concerns the settlement of the cause by means of a statement under oath by one of the parties before the judge. The *auditor* likewise cannot resort to a court settlement by way of a compromise action as related in canon 1925. This also must be handled by the judge. There are many other examples of this kind.

The fact that the *auditor* is prohibited from adjudicating these questions flows from the very nature of his office in line with which he cannot pronounce the final sentence in the cause.[91] Thus, not only the rendering of the final decision cannot be undertaken

[90] *Provida,* Arts. 71, § 2; 77, § 2; 96; 97; 101; 110; 152; 167, § 3; 115; 104, § 2; 113; 123; 124; 126; 129; 134; 108; 130, § 1; 140, § 2; 147, § 1 and § 4; 131; 163, § 2; 166; 168; 174; 175, § 1; 178, § 3; 188, § 1; 206; 152; 168.—AAS, XXVIII (1936), 329-354.

[91] Canon 1582.

by the *auditor,* but also all those actions which concern the direction of the process and the determination of the question involved cannot be executed by him.[92]

It is not absolutely necessary that an auditor be appointed. If there is no such appointment, the duties outlined above fall to the judge. If an *auditor* is appointed, he must be a priest and is expected to fulfill his office faithfully [93] and keep the secrets he may come to know.[94] Further, he is forbidden, as are the other officials, to receive any presents on the occasion of a trial.[95] He may be removed from office at any stage of the trial by the one who appointed him. His removal should follow only upon a just reason and without prejudice to the parties.[96]

Section 4. The Referee

When one considers the judiciary procedure as carried out by the collegiate tribunal one must carefully distinguish among the functions assigned either to the tribunal as a whole, or to the presiding official (*praeses*), or to the referee (*ponens* or *relator*). The complete cause is referred to the *collegium integrum,* especially those things which directly and immediately pertain to the definitive judgment. Certain other acts are reserved to the *praeses* and the *relator,* as well as to the *auditor,* as pointed out above.[97]

"The *relator,* according to the Code, is one of the judges of a collegiate tribunal who is selected by the presiding judge as the one who is to render a written statement of the proceedings within the judicial assembly." [98]

The office of the *relator* is found in the ancient tribunals of the

[92] Cf. Roberti, *op. cit.*, I, n. 125, p. 276; Dugan, *op. cit.*, pp. 53-54.

[93] Canon 136, § 1.

[94] Canon 1623, § 1, § 2.

[95] Canon 1624.

[96] Canon 1583.

[97] Cappello, *op. cit.*, III, n. 82, pp. 86-87; Roberti, *op. cit.*, I, n. 119, pp. 264-265.

[98] Dugan, *op. cit.*, p. 56; cf. Cappello, *op. cit.*, III, n. 83, p. 86; Roberti, *op. cit.*, I, n. 121, p. 269; Conte a Coronata, III, n. 1122, p. 41.

Roman Rota.[99] According to Metz,[100] however, the institute of the *relator* as it is now known in the diocesan collegiate tribunal is new with the Code of Canon Law. The office as it is carried out today is completely different from the function as carried out in the *Rota* of old.

The *relator* is to be appointed by the *praeses* or presiding judge, who is to select him from judges of the collegiate tribunal.[101] There is some discussion whether such an appointment is necessary. Conte a Coronata holds that it is.[102]

The primary function of the *relator* is to report on the case in the meetings of the judges and to commit the sentence to writing.[103] This sentence should be written in Latin.[104] The *relator* must make a profound study of the cause which the court presents to him. He then sets down his opinion as to the law and the facts which govern the particular cause. He presents his opinions to the tribunal on the day determined by the *praeses*. Each of the judges is to have his opinion prepared for this meeting. The *relator* then reads his opinion, and is followed in this by the other judges. A discussion of the cause is then directed by the *praeses,* and the sentence determined by majority vote. The *relator* then must write this decision in the correct legal form and indicate the motives that determined the decision. If the judges so desire, they may determine, by a majority vote, that the specific motives upon which their decision was based be set down in this sentence. If such a vote is not taken, it is left to the discretion of the *relator* to include the proper mention of the motives in the sentence.[105]

99 Dugan, *op. cit.*, p. 55.

100 *Op. cit.*, p. 108.

101 Canon 1584.

102 *Op. cit.*, III, n. 1122, p. 42.

103 Canon 1584.

104 Doheny, *Canonical Procedure in Matrimonial Cases* (2 vols., Vol. I, 2. ed., *Formal Judicial Procedure,* Milwaukee: Bruce, 1948), I, 81; *Provida,* Art. 22, § 1; Metz, *op. cit.*, p. 108.

105 Canon 1871, §§ 1-4; canon 1577, § 2; canon 1873, § 2; canon 1584; Doheny, *op. cit.*, I, 82; Dugan, *op. cit.*, pp. 55-56; Cappello, *op. cit.*, III, n. 83, p. 88; Roberti, *op. cit.*, I, n. 121, pp. 269-270; Metz, *op. cit.*, p. 108.

Section 5. The Defender of the Bond

A defender of the bond is to be appointed in every diocese. He is to take part in causes in which there is question of the validity of the bond of marriage or of sacred orders.[106] The defender is an attorney for the Church. His function is similar to that of the prosecuting attorney in criminal causes of the civil law. He defends the bond of the marriage or of orders that is being impugned. He is a public person or minister of the tribunal to whom two things are committed, namely, the protection of the bond of sacred orders as also of the bond of matrimony. Thus he is entitled the defender of the bond.[107] His office is a species of that of the promoter of justice for the particular type of cause mentioned.[108] It was introduced as a safeguard against the danger of collusion by parties who might attempt to obtain a dissolution of the bond in contravention of the divine law.[109] The defender of the bond is for the causes that relate to matrimony and to holy orders what the promoter of justice is for all other causes.

The origin of the office of the defender of the bond is found in the constitution *Dei miseratione,* Nov. 3, 1741, of Pope Benedict XIV.[110] The same pontiff mentioned and confirmed it in his encyclical letter *Nimiam licentiam* of May 18, 1743.[111] Many later instructions of the Sacred Congregations mentioned and retained the office. The present law of the Code once again confirms it in canon 1586.[112]

The defender of the bond is appointed in the same way and should be cited and appear in court in the same manner as the promoter of justice. All that is said in the following section on the promoter of justice in this regard may be applied here.[113]

[106] Canon 1586.

[107] Cappello, *op. cit.,* III, n. 98, p. 105.

[108] Conte a Coronata, III, n. 1124, p. 45; Dolan, *op. cit.,* p. 9.

[109] Conte a Coronata, III, n. 1124, p. 45.

[110] *Fontes,* n. 318.

[111] *Fontes,* n. 337.

[112] Cf. Dugan, *op. cit.,* p. 68; Roberti, *op. cit.,* I, n. 133, pp. 294-295; Cappello, *op. cit.,* n. 98, pp. 105-106.

[113] Cf. canons 1586; 1587, § 1; *Provida,* Art. 15.

The defender of the bond of matrimony is to stand for and legally defend the bond until such time as its invalidity is definitely established. The carrying out of this office places a check on the powers of the judge, and thus prevents a hasty trial and decision which might declare the contract null. The parties involved are also checked by the defender, lest through their fraudulent cooperation one of them should refuse to answer the summons to court, give false testimony, or use other deception in order to obtain a favorable decision.[114]

The defender of the bond of sacred orders exercises a similar role when questions of the validity of orders are involved. His office was instituted by means of an Instruction of the Sacred Congregation of the Council in 1836.[115] The provisions of this Instruction form the basis for the present legislation.[116]

When causes arise concerning the bond of marriage or of holy orders the presence of the defender is required.[117] Should the judge fail to cite him, the acts are null unless he is present, even though not cited. If he was legitimately summoned though not present during some sessions, the acts are valid, but must be submitted to him afterwards so that he may offer his objections either orally or in writing and propose whatever he believes necessary or useful in the cause.[118]

The offices of the promoter of justice and the defender of the bond may be combined in one appointee unless the great number of causes on the docket forbids it. It is left to the discretion of the bishop whether the defender is to be appointed in a general way for all causes or simply for individual causes.[119]

The defender is to appear in matrimonial causes whether they be carried out in formal or summary procedure. This is true whether the bond is impugned by the Catholic spouse, the non-Catholic spouse, or the promoter of justice; whether both parties are alive

[114] Dugan, *op. cit.*, pp. 68-69.
[115] Cf. Dugan, *op. cit.*, p. 69.
[116] Dugan, *op. cit.*, p. 69.
[117] Canon 1586.
[118] Canon 1587.
[119] Canon 1588; cf. Dugan, *op. cit.*, p. 71.

or after the death of either. The law makes no distinction among these causes, and the public good demands that the bond be properly defended even after the death of one of the parties. From this rule the law likewise does not except unions contracted between a baptized person and an infidel. The public interest demands that even a non-sacramental marriage bond be sustained. It is required that in all causes in which the defender is called to act there be present at least the semblance of marriage ("*species matrimonii*") to which canon 1014 adverts.

The law does not require the defender to take part in causes concerning the separation of the spouses, in questions arising from engagement, or in matters relating to the free status of parties, unless these questions derive from a preceding doubtful marriage.

It is the position of the defender of the bond to be opposed to those who seek to have a marriage declared null or to prove that it was not consummated, as well as to those who seek a declaration of nullity of sacred orders or of the burdens attached to them. The defender always must uphold this position, and thus in questions of procedure he must urge those reasons which prove favorable to the existence of the bond. His position is not merely a defensive one, however. He is to use positive means to prevent crimes against matrimony and sacred orders.

The defender is never the plaintiff in the process. When the bond is impugned, he comes to its defense. He can and must, however, use positive and aggressive means in order to defend the bond. He enjoys in the process all the rights which belong to a litigating party.[120]

The defender has certain special rights and duties set down by law in line with his function. Thus he must be present at the examination of the parties and of the witnesses and experts. He must present the questions to the judge in a sealed envelope, which the judge may open only during the course of the questioning. He must suggest to the judge new questions which arise in the course of the examination. He is to study the points proposed by the

[120] Canons 1968, n. 3; 1969, n. 2; 1996.

parties and, if need be, to contradict them. He must also examine the documents presented. He must make a written defense against the claim for nullity and seek to uphold the validity or vindicate consummation for the marriage.[121]

In addition to these obligations, the defender has the right to inspect the acts of the cause at any stage of the trial, even though they have not as yet been published. It is also his right to seek more time from the judge in order to complete his written defense. He has a right to be informed of all the proofs and allegations in such a way that he may have an opportunity to prepare his objections. He may also request that other witnesses be summoned or that those already questioned be recalled for re-examination. This is true even though the taking of evidence has been completed and the evidence published. He may also submit new evidence and objections.[122]

It is the right of the defender to be heard last in the oral defense. The court is not to render a decision until the defender has been asked and has stated that he has nothing further to propose or investigate. This is presumed if he has not proposed anything before the final day fixed for that purpose by the judge.[123] It is his duty to appeal to the superior court within the fixed time from a first sentence of nullity of a marriage. If he neglects this, he is to be forced to do so by the judge.[124]

If in causes proposed by way of a summary procedure the bishop has declared the nullity of a marriage and the defender has good reason to maintain that there is no certainty about the impediments, or that there probably was a dispensation, he is obliged to appeal to the judge of the court of second instance to whom the acts of the cause must be forwarded, and who is to be reminded by way of a written notice that the cause is one that in first instance involved the summary procedure.[125]

[121] Canon 1968.

[122] Canon 1969.

[123] Canon 1984.

[124] Canon 1986.

[125] Canon 1991.

The defender of the bond of orders enjoys the same rights and has the same duties as the defender of the matrimonial bond.[126]

Section 6. The Promoter of Justice

The promoter of justice is a public person who in trials safeguards the law and carries out the duty of public prosecution. This office is found in all modern civil law codes. What the Canon Law calls the promoter of justice is often referrred to by the civil law as a public prosecutor or minister.[127]

There is much conflicting opinion among the authors on the history of the office of the promoter of justice. There seems to be general agreement that it did not have its origin in Roman Law.[128] There is, however, much debate regarding its exact origin. Many hold that its origin is found in canon law itself, while others contend that civil processes gave birth to the office. It is true that it was only with the advent of the Code that this office was regularly established. A survey of the history of the office reveals that prior to the Code its very existence depended on local custom and legislation. The duties carried out by the incumbent varied according to the discretion of the ordinary.[129]

A promoter of justice is to be appointed in every diocese.[130] He is to be appointed permanently or for individual causes.[131] The appointment should be made in writing in accord with canon 364, § 1. The promoter is to be duly cited by the presiding judge for the fulfilling of his office in accordance with the ruling of canon 1587. He is to be a priest of good reputation, a doctor in Canon Law or at least well versed in it, and of tried prudence and zeal

[126] Canon 1996; Roberti, *op. cit.*, I, n. 137, pp. 311-316; Cappello, *op. cit.*, III, nn. 99-102, pp. 107-112.

[127] Conte a Coronata, III, n. 1124, pp. 44-45; Cappello, *op. cit.*, III, n. 94, p. 100.

[128] Glynn, *The Promoter of Justice*, p. 3.

[129] Glynn, *op. cit.*, p. IX; Dugan, *op. cit.*, pp. 66-68; Roberti, *op. cit.*, I, n. 133, pp. 292-294.

[130] Canon 1586.

[131] Canon 1588, § 2; *Provida*, Art. 16, § 2.

for justice.[132] The office is not lost upon the vacancy of the see when the promoter was appointed for all causes in general. Nor can he be removed by the diocesan administrator. He must be confirmed in office by the new bishop. The bishop may remove him from office for a just cause.[133]

The promoter of justice is bound to fulfill his office faithfully,[134] to observe the secrets it entails,[135] and to refuse any gifts in the handling of a cause.[136] Should he be negligent or remiss in the fulfilling of his office he is to be punished.[137]

The promoter of justice is to appear in contentious trials in which the ordinary believes that the public welfare is at stake. He is also to appear in criminal causes.[138] The Church has the duty and obligation to correct and punish those who transgress its laws. In these matters the Church is represented by the bishop, who seeks correction and satisfaction in its name. Since the bishop is to sit in judgment on the accused, the law transfers his right of prosecution to the promoter of justice. Thus he is a public official whose job it is to assist the bishop in preserving and defending the good order of the diocese.[139]

Each diocese in the Church is a moral person and as such possesses certain rights. It is the office of the promoter of justice to guard and protect these rights by acting as the plaintiff or defendant for this moral person. His chief duties lie in the prosecuting of criminal offenses before the diocesan courts and in acting as the representative of the diocese, and therefore as plaintiff or defendant in judicial proceedings which involve the rights, perogatives, and property of the diocese.

The office and duty of the promoter were outlined in the Instruc-

132 Canon 1589, § 1.

133 Canon 1590.

134 Canon 1621, § 1.

135 Canon 1623, § 1.

136 Canon 1624.

137 Canon 1625.

138 Canon 1586; *Provida*, Art. 16, § 2.

139 Cf. Noval, *Commentarium Codicis Iuris Canonici, Liber IV De Processibus*, Pars I, *De Iudiciis*, (Romae, 1920) n. 140 (hereafter cited *De Iudiciis*).

tion of 1880,[140] which prescribed that this official be appointed to every diocesan tribunal. The Code has made minor changes and given more security and distinctness to the position and its functions than are found in the Instruction. The Code has canonized the office described in tre Instruction as the ***Promotor Fiscalis*** and has renamed it the ***Promotor Iustitiae***.

In practice, in our diocesan tribunals the chief function of the promoter concerns the impugning of the validity of marriages and the safeguarding of the procedural law. His intervention is determined by the bishop or the collegiate tribunal either *ex officio* or on the insistence of the parties, the defender of the bond, or the promoter himself.[141]

The promoter of justice does not enjoy judicial power in the strict sense. He does have a certain authority, however, which is clear from the canons that determine his rights and obligations.[142]

If the promoter was legitimately summoned but was not present during some sessions, the acts are valid, but they must be submitted to him afterwards in order that he may offer his objections and propose whatever he believes to be useful or necessary for the cause.[143]

Section 7. The Promoter of the Faith

The office of the promoter of the faith was officially instituted in 1708 by Pope Clement XI (1700-1721). Its purpose was to provide for the prevention and detection of fraud in the beatification and canonization processes. The office involved nothing else than a specialized type of the *promotor fiscalis*. The functions of the promoter of faith in the canonization process run parallel to those of the defender of the bond in marriage causes.[144] Thus it is that the promoter of faith is sometimes referred to as the devil's advocate.[145]

140 S.C. Ep. and Reg., 11 iun. 1880, art XXIII—*Acta Sanctae Sedis* (41 vols., Romae, 1865-1908), XIII (1880), 328 (hereafter cited *ASS*).

141 Cf. Doheny, *op. cit.*, I, 72-73; *Provida*, Art. 16, § 2.

142 Cappello, *op. cit.*, III, n. 95, p. 107.

143 Canon 1587, § 2.

144 Dolan, *The Defensor Vinculi*, p. 13.

145 Cf. Jone, *op. cit.*, III, 308.

The first mention of this office in causes of canonization is found in the cause of Saint Laurence Justinian (1381-1455) during the pontificate of Pope Leo X (1513-1521). It was his duty to oppose the canonization. There are other examples of his participation in processes of this period. Nevertheless, the full development of the office came about in the time of Pope Urban VIII (1623-1644).[146]

The promoter of faith in the Sacred Congregation of Rites, which alone has competence in canonization causes,[147] has the title of general promoter of the faith. The *assessor* of this Sacred Congregation who assists him is known as the general sub-promoter of the faith.[148] These officers are appointed by the Supreme Pontiff. The general promoter nominates the promoters of the faith in diocesan courts if they are to act in the apostolic process. They have the title of sub-promoters. Those promoters who act in the proceedings initiated by the local ordinary are to be appointed by the ordinary before he issues the decree calling for the writings of the servant of God whose cause is being investigated.[149] The appointment of the promoter is to be mentioned in the decree of the ordinary establishing the tribunal.[150]

The one selected to be the promoter of faith should at least possess the qualifications required of the promoter of justice or of the defender of the bond. He must be a priest of good reputation, a doctor of Canon Law or otherwise proficient in this subject, and a man of prudence and zeal. He should be thoroughly familiar with procedural law and have sufficient time at his disposal for the carrying out of this office.[151]

The promoter of faith must take part in every process in causes of beatification and canonization.[152] He is to be cited according to the norms laid down for the citation of the promoter of justice and

146 Blaher, *The Ordinary Processes in Causes of Beatification and Canonization*, p. 29.

147 Cf. canons 253, § 3; 1999, § 2.

148 Canon 2010.

149 Canon 2011.

150 Canon 2040, § 2.

151 Blaher, *op. cit.*, p. 140; Canon 1589, § 1.

152 Canon 2010, § 1.

the defender of the bond. Thus, the acts are null if the promoter of the faith was not cited, unless he was present despite the lack of citation. If he was cited but absent, the acts are valid, but must be submitted to him afterward.[153]

The principal duty of the promoter of faith is to safeguard the interests of the Church and the faithful in the causes of beatification and canonization. More specifically, it is his duty to prepare the interrogatories for the questioning of the witnesses; to insist that the witnesses be summoned *ex officio;* to propose objections to the testimony of the witnesses.[154] It is also within his province to provide the Sacred Congregation with information concerning the credibility of the witnesses and the legitimate execution of the procedural acts. This is to be done at the completion of the ordinary informative process.[155] The Code also outlines other duties for the promoter of faith.[156]

Section 8. The Notary

The notary is a public person appointed by one in authority. His records carry an authenticity which surpasses that of a private person acting without authorization.[157]

There must be present at every trial a notary who acts as a secretary or actuary. The acts of the causes are invalid unless they are drawn up or at least signed by the notary.[158]

A notary may be judicial or extra-judicial in the sense that he records judicial acts such as the acts of ecclesiastical trials or authenticates other acts and documents such as wills and contracts of various kinds.[159] If constituted for judicial acts, this officer is frequently referred to as an actuary. If constituted for extrajudicial acts he is simply called a notary.[160]

[153] Canon 2010, § 1; canon 1587.

[154] Canon 2012.

[155] Canon 2063, § 2.

[156] Cf. canons 2051; 2052; 2053; 2024; 2025, § 2; 1773, § 2.

[157] Dugan, *op. cit.*, pp. 72-73.

[158] Canon 1585, § 1.

[159] Dugan, *op. cit.*, p. 73; Conte a Coronata, III, n. 1123, p. 42; Cappello, *op. cit.*, III, n. 89, p. 98; Roberti, *op. cit.*, I, n. 130, p. 284.

[160] Conte a Coronata, III, n. 1123, p. 42.

The historical development of this office is not clear. This lack of clarity derives in large measure from the various terms which have been used in description of the incumbent of this office. Despite this confusion of title, a notary has been employed throughout the history of ecclesiastical trials. This official was a public person. The office can be traced in its origin to the Roman Law system and was in use in ecclesiastical courts before the 13th century. It was permanently established by the IV General Council of the Lateran (1215). The office has been for the most part occupied by clerics. There is some evidence that at one time the notariate was considered as a minor order.[161]

The judge is to designate a judicial notary before beginning the trial. This notary is to be selected from the legitimately appointed notaries, unless the ordinary has already designated one for the cause.[162] In addition to the chancellor spoken of in canon 372, the bishop may appoint other notaries for the purpose of authenticating acts and documents. It is this group who are referred to as the legitimately appointed notaries.

The removal of the notaries is in the hands of the one by whom they were appointed as well as his superior and successor. The diocesan administrator, however, needs the consent of the consultors in order to dismiss a notary.[163]

The law states that the functions of the notary are: to draw up acts or documents attesting to enactments, orders, commitments, judicial summonses and notifications, decrees, sentences and similar matters in which their intervention is required. They are also to draw up records of what transpires in meetings to which they are assigned. They are to sign this record upon attaching the name of the place, day, month, and year. It is also their function to give access to records to those who have a right to them. They are to furnish authenticated copies of the originals in due observance of the norms of law.[164] Further, there must be a notary present at

[161] Duerr, *op. cit.*, p. 89; Roberti, *op. cit.*, I, n. 129, p. 281; Dugan, *op. cit.*, p. 73; Conte a Coronata, III, n. 1123, pp. 42-43.

[162] Canon 1585, § 2.

[163] Canon 373.

[164] Canon 374, § 1.

every trial, and the acts of the trial are invalid unless they have been drawn up, or at least signed, by him.[165] It is his duty to record everything carefully and faithfully; to draw up and preserve the record; to certify all parts of the record and sign them along with the presiding judge; to keep a register of causes; to draw up the interrogatories; to be present whenever an oath is legally administered; to subscribe the summons and record the return made; to be present at the trial; to certify copies of documents; to see that rescripts, decrees, and decisions are delivered for execution; to communicate to the parties the dispositive part of the judgment; to sign the original copies of the judgment and to certify copies of it.[166]

All documents drawn up by the notary have the value of public documents, since he is regarded as a qualified witness.[167] Since he actually is never more than a qualified witness he does not exercise jurisdiction in the strict sense.[168] His ability to draw up these official documents is restricted to the diocese of his appointment and concerning the matters for which he was appointed.[169] Should he exceed his mandate or the scope of his powers, then the documents drawn up by him would not have their official value.[170]

Should the amount of work necessitate additional notaries, they may be appointed by the bishop in virtue of canon 373 and Article 19 of the *Provida.*

The office of the notary is an essential one for the formation of the tribunal.[171]

165 Canon 1585, § 1.

166 *Provida,* Art. 73; cf. Cappello, *op. cit.,* III, n. 89, p. 98; Dugan, *op. cit.,* p. 75; Roberti, *op. cit.,* I, n. 130, pp. 284-286; Conte a Coronata, III, n. 1123, p. 44.

167 Canons 1581, § 1; 1813, § 1, n. 2, 3; *Provida,* Art. 156, § 1, n. 2; Doheny, *op. cit.,* I, 74; Duerr, *op. cit.,* p. 53.

168 Doheny, *op. cit.,* I, 74; Abbo and Hannan, *The Sacred Canons,* I, 392.

169 Canon 374, § 2.

170 Doheny, *op. cit.,* I, 75; Duerr, *op. cit.,* p. 54; Conte a Coronata, III, n. 1123, p. 43.

171 Roberti, *op. cit.,* I, n. 130, p. 284; Conte a Coronata, III, n. 1123, p. 44.

Section 9. The Chancellor

In every curia there shall be a chancellor appointed by the bishop. He shall be a priest and his principal functions are the preservation of the curial acts in the archives, their arrangement in a chronological order, and the drawing up of an index of them.[172] The chancellor is a notary by reason of his office.[173]

In Roman Law the chancellor was a civil official who assisted the magistrate in admitting petitioners to court and in carrying out various secretarial duties. In later times, after the decline of the Roman Empire, the barbarian kings adopted this office and made it one of great importance. The chancellor then performed many duties of importance, among which was the keeping of the seal of the king.[174]

There is no evidence of the existence, as it is known today, of the office of the chancellor in the early history of the Church. In 1205 Charlemagne granted every bishop the power to constitute his own notary public. This legislation reflected the incipient development of the office of the chancellor. There is little evidence to show that this office was anything more than a mere civil function at that time.[175]

There are various indications that the 9th century saw the inclusion of the notarizing of and the caring for documents within the concept of the office of the chancellor.[176]

It is not surprising that such little evidence concerning the functions of an ecclesiastical chancellor is to be found when one considers that it was not until the 12th century that the diocesan curia actually became organized under the direction of the bishop.[177] Once this organization began to take shape, however, the office of the chancellor began to become more clearly defined. Its scope was enlarged by the expansion of educational activities and the need for

172 Canon 372, § 1.
173 Canon 372, § 3.
174 Prince, The Diocesan Chancellor, pp. 1-5.
175 Prince, *op. cit.*, p. 12.
176 *Ibid.*, p. 14.
177 *Loc. cit.*

judicial notaries in the judicial procedure of the 13th century.[178] Thus the ground work was laid for the office of chancellor as it is known today.

The first legislation concerning the chancellor was given in the 16th century. The III Provincial Council of Milan (1753) set down a clear concept of the office of the diocesan chancellor, as it is known today. The documents of the curia were to be preserved in the episcopal archives by the chancellor, who was to have the key to them. The chancellor's position as a notary was also made clear. The chancellor was a notary distinct from the other judicial notaries or actuaries.[179] This particular legislation was confirmed and amplified in particular synods, in papal documents, and in the replies of the Sacred Congregation of the Council. These pointed out that the practice of employing the chancellor as the guardian of the archives and as the public notary of the curia was well established by the end of the 18th century.[180]

It was not until promulgation of the present Code of Canon Law that there was any general legislation treating directly of the diocesan chancellor as his office is known today. It seems that what was already the established practice became the foundation for the law of the Code.[181]

The chancellor, as a rule, is to be appointed and removed by the bishop.[182] He holds an office in the strict sense.[183] He must be a priest of good reputation and a person above all suspicion.[184] The chief duties of the chancellor concern the preservation of the acts of the curia in the archives, their arrangement in chronological

[178] Prince, *op. cit.*, pp. 20-21.

[179] *Ibid.*, pp. 25-27; *"De iis quae ad Episcopale forum pertinent,"* III Conc. Prov. Mediolen. a. 1573—Ratti (Pope Pius XI), *Acta Ecclesiae Mediolanensis* (3 vols., Mediolani, 1890-1892), II, 275.

[180] Prince, *op. cit.*, pp. 29-32.

[181] *Ibid.*, pp. 35-36.

[182] Canons 372, § 1; 373, § 5.

[183] Abbo and Hannan, *The Sacred Canon*, I, 372.

[184] Canons 372, § 1; 373, § 4.

order, and the drawing up of an index of them.[185] The chancellor is of course a notary.[186]

The chancellor has many other specific duties. He is charged with the custody of the public episcopal archives, which the bishop is required to establish by canon 375. He is the sole custodian of the key to these archives.[187] He is also to keep an account of the receipts that must be signed by anyone authorized to remove a document from these archives.[188]

The chancellor is also to aid in the safeguarding of the secret episcopal archives and to compile their contents.[189]

Section 10. The Messenger and the Apparitor

Couriers or messengers are to be constituted for all trials generally, or simply for individual causes. They are to give notice of the judicial acts, unless the approved custom of a tribunal dispenses with these officials. Apparitors or constables should be appointed for the purpose of executing the sentences and decrees of the judge at his command. The same person may hold both offices.[190]

These functions are offices in the wide sense of the term.[191] Those who exercise them do not possess jurisdiction, but they participate in the exercise of jurisdiction held by others. These offices are not an essential part of the diocesan tribunal, as is clear from the words of the Code.[192] The work of the messenger can be handled by the notary or by any other safe means.[193] The mere threatening of ecclesiastical penalties may well achieve the function of the apparitor in many instances.

The offices of the messenger and the apparitor take their origin from Roman Law whereby their occupants performed various menial

[185] Canon 372, § 1.
[186] Canon 372, § 3.
[187] Canon 377, § 1, § 2.
[188] Canon 378.
[189] Canon 379.
[190] Canon 1591.
[191] Canon 145, § 1.
[192] Canon 1591, § 1.
[193] Canon 1719.

tasks such as carrying messages and reports for the magistrates and legislators. They were also commissioned to execute certain sentences. The Gallic law regarded the courier merely as a messenger for the judge. After the French Revolution, however, the office assumed greater stature, and its incumbent could execute a sentence of the court independently of a judicial order or mandate from the judge.[194]

These officers are regularly to be laymen of upright life and character. If prudence should dictate the use of clerics in a special cause, then preferably the latter are to be employed.[195] They are bound to fulfill the office faithfully,[196] to observe the secrecy involved,[197] and to receive no gifts in connection with the conduct of the trial.[198] These obligations are to be sworn to by oath. The officers may be punished if they do not fulfill their charge.[199]

These officers are to be appointed for all causes in general or simply for particular causes. Their nomination, suspension, and removal is governed by the same rules that are given for notaries in canon 373.[200]

The functions of the messenger and the apparitor are theoretically distinct. The messenger is appointed to give notice of the judicial acts. Apparitors have the task of executing the sentences and decrees of the judge. The acts which they write in the execution of their office are public documents and are legal proof of the assertions they make.[201]

The written summons is to be handed to the defendant personally by the messenger. The messenger may enter another diocese to do this if the judge thinks it advisable and so orders him. The Code is very specific as to the procedure to be followed by the messenger when, unable to locate the defendant, he leaves the

[194] Dugan, *The Judiciary Department of the Diocesan Curia*, p. 76.

[195] Canon 1592.

[196] Canon 1621, § 1.

[197] Canon 1623, § 1.

[198] Canon 1624.

[199] Canon 1625, § 3; cf. Roberti, *op. cit.*, I, n. 139, p. 318; Cappello, *op. cit.*, III, nn. 92-93, pp. 99-100; Conte a Coronata, III, n. 1125. p. 48.

[200] Cf. canons 1591 and 1592.

[201] Canons 1591 and 1593; Doheny, *op. cit.*, I, 76.

summons or citation with a member of the family or a servant.[202] When the messenger leaves the citation with the proper party he is to sign it upon noting the proper date and hour at which he delivered it to the defendant.[203] When the messenger leaves the written citation in the hands of a member of the family or of a servant of the defendant he shall add this person's name to the other information. If the summons is made by way of public notice, that is, by its being posted on the door of the curia in the manner of a public notice,[204] the messenger shall note the day and the hour at which the summons was posted, and eventually also the length of time it remained there. If the defendant should refuse to accept the summons, the messenger shall note the day and the hour, sign the summons, and then return it to the judge.[205] Regarding his work in the delivery of the summons the messenger is to make a written report. This report is to be signed by him, given to the judge, and then included in the acts.[206]

The function of the apparitor is that of executing the sentences and decrees of the judge. His duties may include his demand that certain documents be shown, his procuring of guarantees and judicial fees, the sequestering of articles, the restoring of articles in the event of spoliation and the collection of fines. His principal duty consists in his execution of the definitive sentence. It is evident, however, that this function is greatly restricted in our day.[207]

The same person may hold both the office of messenger and the office of apparitor.[208] It is the common practice not to use these officers in the diocesan tribunals of this country. Thus the phrase "*nisi alia sit probata tribunalis consuetudo*" of canon 1591 is applied. It is the custom in this country to employ registered mail in place of the messenger.[209] This and other means are found to

[202] Canon 1717.

[203] Canon 1720.

[204] Canon 1720.

[205] Canon 1727.

[206] Canon 1722; cf. Doheny, *op. cit.*, I, 76-77; Cappello, *op. cit.*, III, n. 92, pp. 99-100; Conte a Coronata, III, nn. 1125 and 1127, pp. 48-49.

[207] Cf. Roberti, *op. cit.*, I, n. 139, p. 318; Cappello, *op. cit.*, n. 93, p. 100.

[208] Canon 1591, 2.

[209] Canon 1719.

be adequate for the ordinary needs. For their employment in extraordinary circumstances these officers can be appointed temporarily.[210]

Section 11. The Advocate

"As it is commonly used in everyday life, the term advocate denotes a person who has been called upon to render assistance: *ad auxilium vocatus*. In particular, the ecclesiastical judicial advocate is one, approved by competent ecclesiastical authority, who conducts a case for a client before a Church tribunal." [211]

The origin of the office of advocate in Roman Law derives from the institute of patronage. Despite the collapse of this institution, the position of the advocate grew in scope and significance until during the imperial era the Roman advocate was considered as a member of a definite order of society. This order had certain rights and privileges as well as rigid standards of entrance and conduct.[212]

As is noticed in the treatment of the procurator, it was only after the time of the persecutions that the Church began to develop a judicial system and process. Thus it is that no legislation is found concerning the judicial advocate in the first two centuries. The Church found it expedient in the period following the persecution to borrow from the Roman legal system and to adopt the offices that existed in this system.[213]

It is clear that the office of the advocate was in use throughout the Church from the early fifth century. In many places these officers are referred to as defenders of the Church, and they were accustomed to act not only in ecclesiastical but secular courts as well. Their duties included protecting the poor, safeguarding Church property, and acting as agents of the pope in regard to Church discipline.[214]

There is little legislation reflecting a development in this office until the time of the Decretals. The old Roman Law concerning the

[210] Doheny, *op. cit.*, I, 77; Dugan, *op. cit.*, p. 77.

[211] Hogan, *Judicial Advocates and Procurators*, p. 3; Roberti, *op. cit.*, I, n. 236, p. 562.

[212] Hogan, *op. cit.*, pp. 7-12; Roberti, *op. cit.*, I, n. 235, p. 560.

[213] Hogan, *op. cit.*, pp. 18-20.

[214] Cf. *ibid.*, pp. 21-25; Roberti, *op. cit.*, I, n. 235, p. 561.

needed qualifications for the office was still followed in a modified form. Further restrictions and qualifications were, however, added during this period.[215]

Subsequent papal constitutions tended to define the office, its relation to that of the procurator, and the qualifications necessary for its undertaking. They also sought to eliminate abuses connected with the office. Responses of the Sacred Congregations and regulations of the Roman Tribunals as well as legislation of particular councils sought to apply the law of the Decretals in a more concrete manner.[216]

The advocate must be a Catholic, at least 21 years of age, and of good reputation. Non-Catholics are not admitted except by way of exception and in a case of necessity. The advocate must further be a doctor of Canon Law, or at least an expert in this field.[217] In order that an advocate be admitted to court there is needed his approval by the ordinary. This may be a general approval for all causes, or a particular approval for an individual cause.[218] If the cause is carried on before a judge delegated by the Holy See, it is the right of this delegate to approve and admit the advocate.[219] The advocate must have from the party or the judge a commission similar to the mandate of the procurator, which commission must be incorporated in the acts of the cause.[220]

In criminal trials the defendant must always have an advocate chosen by himself or appointed by the judge. In civil causes, when minors are involved or when the cause concerns the public welfare, the judge is *ex officio* to assign an advocate to a party who is unrepresented. If the cause at trial demands it, he may assign an additional advocate as well. Apart from these specifications the party is free to choose or to abstain from choosing an advocate, unless the judge deems the services of an advocate necessary.[221]

215 Hogan, *op. cit.*, pp. 38-40.
216 Hogan, *op. cit.*, p. 180.
217 Canon 1657, § 1, § 2.
218 Canon 1658, § 2.
219 Canon 1658, § 3.
220 Canon 1661.
221 Cf. canon 1655, §§ 1-3.

There may be, therefore, more than one advocate for a party in the same cause at trial.[222]

The advocate may be rejected by way of a decree of the judge given either *ex officio* or at the petition of one of the parties when there is a just ground for this rejection.[223] He may also be removed by the one who appointed him. In this event, however, he has a right to his fee. Further, as in the case of the procurator, the removal is not effective until it has been made known to him. If the joinder of issue (*contestatio litis*) has taken place, the removal does not become effective until after the judge and adverse party have also been notified.[224] The same restrictions that are mentioned in the case of procurators apply also to the advocate.[225] He is expected to fulfill his trust diligently and in good faith,[226] and to observe secrecy when necessary.[227]

Section 12. The Procurator

A procurator is an agent for another. "He is a person commissioned by a principal to act in the latter's name, to transact his business, and to manage his affairs when he, the principal, is unable or unwilling to attend to them personally. More particularly, the judicial procurator *ad lites*, is a person legitimately appointed, and admitted by the ecclesiastical court, for the purpose of representing one of the principals, or parties, before that tribunal."[228]

The accepted principle, *"Nemo alieno nomine agere potest,"*[229] of early Roman Law left little room for agency of any kind, and thus the office of the judicial procurator was unknown.[230] There were some few exceptions to the general principle which formed

222 Canon 1656, § 3.

223 Canon 1663.

224 Canon 1664, § 1.

225 Cf. canons 1665 and 1666.

226 Normae S. Romane Rotae Tribunalis, 29 iun. 1934, Art. 56, § 1—*AAS.*, XXVI (1934), 465.

227 Cf. canon 1623, § 3.

228 Hogan, *op. cit.*, p. 4; cf. Roberti, *op. cit.*, I, n. 236, p. 549.

229 G. (4, 82).

230 Cf. Roberti, *op. cit.*, I, n. 230, p. 547.

the foundation for the emergence of this office during the formulary period of Roman procedure. By the time of Justinian (527-565) the principle of representation was firmly established, and the procurator *ad lites* was an important person in Roman Law.[231]

It is easily understood that no mention is made of the procurator in the legislation of the first two centuries of the Church. It is only with the closing of the period of persecution that a judicial process was formed. It was natural that the Church should tend to borrow from the Roman legal system and adopt the offices that existed in this system.[232]

There is little legislation concerning the procurator up to the time of the Decretals. The existing requirements were adopted and considered sufficient for the purposes of ecclesiastical law. The decretals concerned themselves with adapting the principles of Roman Law to the needs and requirements of the Church.[233]

Subsequent papal constitutions, responses of the Sacred Congregations and regulations of the Roman Tribunals sought to eliminate abuses and promote the application of the Decretal Law to this office.[234]

The procurator is to be a Catholic, at least 21 years old, and of good reputation.[235] Every person so qualified can be appointed by a party as procurator, and it is not necessary that the ordinary approve this choice beforehand.[236] The procurator shall not be admitted to plead, however, until he has deposited a special written mandate from the party to represent him in the action at court.[237] The procurator may be rejected by the judge *ex officio* or at the petition of one of the parties if there is a just reason for such action.[238] The procurator can also be removed by the party who appointed him. The removal, however, does not take effect until he learns

231 Hogan, *op. cit.*, p. 14.
232 Hogan, *op. cit.*, pp. 18-20.
233 Hogan, *op. cit.*, p. 40.
234 Hogan, *op. cit.*, p. 180.
235 Canon 1657, § 1.
236 Canon 1658, § 1.
237 Canon 1659, § 1.
238 Canon 1663.

of it, and, if the joinder of issue (*contestatio litis*) has taken place, it takes effect only when the judge and the adverse party have also been notified.[239]

It is not absolutely necessary that a procurator be appointed.[240] It is advisable, however, and the judge may appoint one himself if he feels that it is necessary in the particular cause at court.[241] As a rule a party may appoint only one procurator, unless a proportionate reason suggest the appointment of more than one.[242] The procurator's name is to be included in the written sentence.[243]

The procurator is expected to fulfill his trust diligently and with good faith.[244] He cannot choose a substitute for himself unless this power has been explicitly granted to him.[245] He is bound to secrecy as often as the judge feels that this is necessary for the reasons stated in law.[246] He is forbidden by purchase to make the lawsuit his own or to make an arrangement for immoderate profits or for part of the thing in litigation. Such an agreement would be invalid, and the procurator could be punished with a fine.[247] Procurators who have violated the duties of their office shall be deprived of it, and are bound to make restitution. They shall also be punished with fines and other appropriate penalties.[248]

Section 13. Sponsor At Baptism

In common parlance a sponsor is one who undertakes the obligation of promising the satisfaction of a debt or the fulfillment of some duty.[249]

239 Canon 1664, § 1.

240 Canon 1655, § 1.

241 Canon 1655, § 3.

242 Canon 1656, § 1, § 2.

243 Canon 1874, § 2.

244 Normae S. Romane Rotae Tribunalis, 29 iun. 1934, Art. 56, § 1—*AAS.*, XXVI (1934), 465.

245 Canon 1656, § 1.

246 Cf. canon 1623, § 3.

247 Canon 1665.

248 Canon 1666.

249 Kearney, *Sponsors at Baptism*, p. 33.

The sponsor at baptism is as it were a spiritual parent who receives to his care the baptized person who has been reborn to the life of grace.[250]

The office of the sponsor at baptism is a very ancient one in the Church. The precise origin of the function is very difficult to determine. There is solid indication, however, that it was in general use during the second century.[251]

The source of this custom is a disputed point; [252] its practice, however, is widely attested in the early centuries of the Church and up to the present.[253]

The sponsor at baptism is to be designated by the one who receives baptism, or by his parents or guardians, or, in default of these, by the minister.[254] The Church, in consideration of the grave nature of this office, has set forth certain qualifications which must be met in order that one may be admitted to the valid and lawful performance of this function. Thus in order that one may validly be sponsor he must himself be baptized, possess the use of reason, and have the requisite intention. He cannot belong to a heretical or a schismatic sect, be excommunicated, infamous at law or excluded from authorized ecclesiastical acts in consequence of a condemnatory or declaratory sentence, or be a deposed or a degraded cleric. Further, he cannot be the parent or spouse of the one who is to receive baptism. He must be designated in the manner indicated above and must in person or by proxy hold or touch the baptized person in the act of baptism, or immediately lift or receive him from the sacred font or from the minister.[255]

In order that one be admitted to the lawful performance of this office it is further required that he have reached the 14th year of

[250] Cf. St. John, 3:5; Cappello, *De Sacramentis* (5 vols., Vol. I, *De sacramentis in genere, de Baptismo, Confirmatione et Eucharistia,* Taurini et Romae: Marietti, 1954), I, n. 179, p. 157; Vermeersch-Creusen, *Epitome,* I, n. 46, p. 27.

[251] Cf. Kearney, *op. cit.,* pp. 22-30; Woywod, *A Practical Commentary,* I, n. 655, p. 345.

[252] Kearney, *op. cit.,* pp. 22-27.

[253] Kearney, *op. cit.,* p. 32.

[254] Canon 765, n. 4.

[255] Canon 765, nn. 1-5.

his life, unless the minister permits otherwise for a sufficient reason. Further, he must not be excommunicated, excluded from authorized ecclesiastical acts or under legal infamy in consequence of a notorious delict, even though there has been no pronouncement of sentence. Further, he is not to be under an interdict or publicly known as a criminal or affected with factual infamy. He must also know the rudiments of the faith. A novice or a professed member of a religious institute likewise acts unlawfully except in a case of necessity when, in addition, the express permission of at least the local superior is had. The express permission of one's proper ordinary is necessary for one who is in sacred orders.[256]

The duty of the sponsor is a most solemn and serious one. He is to consider the baptized person as his spiritual child perpetually entrusted to him, and to provide for the spiritual training of this child, so that he may live up to the Christian ideal throughout his whole life.[257]

A sponsor is to be employed at the administration of baptism whenever this is possible.[258] Only one sponsor, even though he or she differ in sex from the one to be baptized, or at the most two, a man and a woman, are to be used.[259] The sponsor contracts a spiritual relationship with the person baptized as a result of his office.[260] This relationship constitutes a diriment impediment to marriage.[261]

Section 14. Sponsor At Confirmation

As baptism is the sacrament of supernatural birth, so confirmation is the sacrament of supernatural maturity. The baptized are mere infants in the life of grace, the confirmed are adults. Confirmation thus perfects the life which baptism has bestowed, and for this reason is called the perfection of baptism. In the early stages of

[256] Canon 766, nn. 1-5.
[257] Canon 769.
[258] Canons 762 and 763.
[259] Canon 764.
[260] Canon 768.
[261] Canon 1079.

the Church confirmation was administered immediately after baptism.[262]

The basic notion of sponsorship as outlined in the treatment of the sponsor at baptism applies likewise to this office. The function of the sponsor at confirmation is also a very ancient one, and its historical aspects run parallel to those noted above for the sponsor at baptism.[263]

It is evident that many of the terms which have been used in designation of this office have been borrowed from Roman legal parlance. No matter what terminology has been used, however, the basic notion of the office has remained the same.[264]

The sponsor at confirmation is to be designated by the person who is to receive confirmation, by this person's parents or guardians, or, if they are not available or refuse to take action, by the minister or by the pastor.[265] In view of the gravity of this office the Church has established qualifications which are required for its valid and licit performance. The requirements for a valid performance are virtually the same as those which are called for in the sponsor at baptism, with the additional note that the sponsor at confirmation must be not only baptized but also confirmed.[266]

The requirements for the lawful carrying out of the role of sponsor at baptism as noted above are also required of the sponsor at confirmation, with the following additions: the person is not to be the one who was sponsor at baptism, unless the minister judges otherwise for a justifying reason, or when the sacrament is lawfully conferred immediately after baptism. The sponsor is to be of the same sex as the person confirmed, unless in a particular cause a contrary application seems to the minister to be justified.[267]

There is a spiritual relationship between the one confirmed and the sponsor in virtue of which the sponsor is obliged to regard the

262 Cf. *The Teaching of the Catholic Church* (2 vols., Vol. II, ed. by Canon George D. Smith, New York: Macmillan Co., 1953), II, 803.

263 Kearney, *op. cit.*, p. 33.

264 Kearney, *op. cit.*, pp. 33-36.

265 Canon 795, n. 4.

266 Cf. canon 795, nn. 1-5.

267 Canon 796, nn. 1-3.

confirmed person as perpetually commended to his charge. The sponsor is to care for the Christian upbringing of the one confirmed.[268]

If possible, a sponsor is to be employed in the administration of confirmation.[269] A sponsor should act for only one or two persons to be confirmed, unless another arrangement seems to be warranted to the minister. There should be no more than one sponsor for each person to be confirmed.[270]

Section 15. Voting In An Ecclesiastical Election

Election is a term which is used in various senses. In its widest sense it denotes any selection. In a more restricted sense, and the one in which it is used here, it designates the method by which the votes of lawful electors confer the right to an ecclesiastical office.[271] It is the right to cast such a vote in such an election that constitutes an authorized ecclesiastical act.

The Church has employed different methods throughout history in selecting those who are to fill positions of authority within its ranks. One of these means is election.

In the earliest days of the Church those in authority for the most part simply appointed their successors and assistants.[272] After the period of persecution, however, election came into common use, especially regarding the selection of bishops.[273] Royal interference reduced the election to a mere formality until the Church won back its right under Pope Gregory VII (1073-1085).[274] After the 13th century, however, its use was curtailed. This was due to the fact that bishops were then generally appointed directly by the Holy See. In addition the religious institutes that were founded in the

[268] Canon 797.

[269] Canon 793.

[270] Canon 794.

[271] Abbo-Hannan, *The Sacred Canons,* I, 222; Parsons, *Canonical Elections,* The Catholic University of America Canon Law Studies, n. 118 (Washington, D. C.: The Catholic University of America Press, 1939), p. 2.

[272] Conte a Coronata, I, n. 224, p. 258; Acts of the Apostles, 6:3-6; Parsons, *op. cit.,* pp. 11-12.

[273] Conte a Coronata, *loc. cit.;* Parsons, *op. cit.,* pp. 13-40; Mock, *Disqualifications of Electors in Ecclesiastical Elections,* p. VI.

[274] Parsons, *op. cit.,* p. 82.

16th century were often modeled along military lines and made less use of election than the older orders had.[275]

Election is, however, still in use in the Church. It is used primarily by religious institutes,[276] but also as a means of selecting abbots and prelates *nullius* in some places,[277] and the *vicar capitular*.[278] The election of the Roman Pontiff is governed by Pope Pius XII's Constitution *Vacantis Apostolicae Sedis* of December 8, 1945.[279]

There are three species of election. It can be by ballot, that is, when the voters cast individual ballots; by commitment to deputies, that is, when the voters set up a committee to select someone; by quasi-inspiration, that is, when the voters unanimously agree upon the appointee without any previous discussion.[280]

Not only the general law, but also particular law, custom, and privilege must be taken into account when there is question of determining the ones who are qualified to cast a vote in an ecclesiastical election. Once the convocation has been lawfully carried out, the right of electing by ballot belong to those who are present.[281]

The law of the Code deals extensively with election and the right to vote. The right to vote is modified by the disqualification of the unworthy[282] and by other restrictions.[283] The vote itself is ruled on by canon 169. The law concerning religious specifies some additional rules for their elections.[284]

The primary function of the one who casts his ballot in an ecclesiastical election is to choose, before God, a candidate whom he considers worthy of election to office, that is, one who is in all respects qualified to share in the ruling power of the Church.

[275] Mock, *op. cit.*, p. VI.

[276] Cf. canon 506, §§ 1-4.

[277] Cf. canons 231; 329, § 3.

[278] Canon 432, § 1.

[279] *AAS.*, XXXVIII (1946), 65-99.

[280] Cf. canon 173; Vermeersch-Creusen, *Epitome*, I, n. 278, p. 251; Abbo-Hannan, *op. cit.*, I, 222.

[281] Canon 163.

[282] Canon 167.

[283] Cf. canons 101; 162; 163; 164; 165; 166; 170; 171; 174.

[284] Canons 506 and 507.

Section 16. Exercise of the Right of Patronage

The right of patronage is a body of privileges, together with certain obligations, which through the concession of the Church belongs to Catholic founders of a church, a chapel or a benefice, or to those whose title derives from the founders.[285] This right is either real or personal, inasmuch as it adheres to some object or is vested directly in some person. It is ecclesiastical, lay, or mixed, insofar as the title upon which it is founded is ecclesiastical, lay or mixed. It is hereditary, family, tribal, or mixed, according as it passes to the heirs, the family, the members of the clan or to those who are at the same time heirs or members of the clan or family of the founder.[286]

The privileges connected with this right are those of presenting a cleric for appointment to a vacant church or benefice, of receiving equitable support under certain conditions specified in law, and of having a coat of arms as well as precedence over other laymen and a seat of honor in the church.[287] Of these, the principal privilege is that of presentation, that is, the presenting of a cleric for appointment to a vacant church or benefice.[288]

The obligations are concerned primarily with the repair and the income of the church involved.[289]

The person who possesses this right of patronage, to whom these privileges and rights pertain, is the patron. The individual or specific exercise of this right of patronage is an authorized ecclesiastical act.

The terms "patron" and "right of patronage," as they are understood today, did not appear in Canon Law until the latter half of the 8th century, although the canonical right which forms their basis arose at least three centuries earlier. It was not until the 13th and 14th centuries that these terms were in common use, and even at

[285] Canon 1448; cf. Abbo-Hannan, *op. cit.*, II, 674; Godfrey, *The Right of Patronage*, p. 18.

[286] Canon 1449, nn. 1-3.

[287] Cf. canon 1455.

[288] Godfrey, *op. cit.*, p. 12; canon 1455, n. 1.

[289] Cf. canon 1469, §§ 1-3.

that time they were not clearly distinguished from other canonical rights.[290]

The terms designating the patron and the right of patronage (*patronus* and *ius patronatus*) were used equivocally even in the canon law itself from the 14th to the 18th centuries. In time, however, this equivocation disappeared, and when patronage was spoken of by the later canonists it referred to the founders of churches. In later times there was some disagreement among canonists as to just what the precise notion of patronage was. Perhaps this confusion was brought about by the adoption of parts of the Roman Law system. At any rate, the concept of the right of patronage has been defined and settled by the Code.[291]

The right of patronage is not to be granted in the future. Certain privileges are still permitted however.[292] The Code contains many regulations concerning the conveyance of the right,[293] the proof of its existence,[294] and its exercise by married women and by children.[295] There are also laws which govern the act of presentation, which is the outstanding privilege of this right.[296] It is to be recalled that a real distinction exists between the right of patronage and the right of presentation.[297]

Canon 1470 describes the various ways in which the right of patronage becomes extinct.

Article IV. THE EXHAUSTIVE NATURE OF THE ENUMERATION OF THE AUTHORIZED ECCLESIASTICAL ACTS

The list of authorized ecclesiastical acts as provided in canon 2256, n. 2, is an all-inclusive and exhaustive one. The Code exclusively recognizes these actions when there is question of authorized ecclesiastical acts.

290 Cf. Godfrey, *op. cit.*, pp. 11-13.
291 Cf. Godfrey, *op. cit.*, pp. 14-18.
292 Cf. canon 1450.
293 Canon 1453.
294 Canon 1454.
295 Canon 1456.
296 Cf. canons 1457-1468.
297 Cf. canon 1471; Godfrey, *op. cit.*, pp. 135-140.

That this is true is clear first of all from the text. "In canonibus qui sequuntur: 2° Nomine autem actuum legitimorum ecclesiasticorum significantur: . . .[298] This construction leaves no room for the supposition that the list is given only by way of example, that is, that the functions listed are examples of authorized ecclesiastical acts, but that there are others as well. These and these alone are recognized by the law as authorized ecclesiastical acts.

The fact that canon 2256 is concerned with penal matters likewise tends to support this opinion. Since in these matters the mind of the Church is primarily one of mercy and charity,[299] the more benign interpretation is to be followed; there is no room for any analogical application,[300] and a strict interpretation alone may be employed; [301] in a word, the Church is careful to define all terms as clearly and precisely as possible. Surely the interpretation and application of later canons in Book V of the Code would be all but impossible were not the list presented as an all-inclusive one.[302]

There is no doubt among the authors about the all-embracing nature of the list provided in canon 2256, n. 2. Although the majority of them do not mention specifically that it is an exhaustive list, their treatment indicates that they take this for granted.[303] Others, however, are clearer on this point when they specifically declare that the list is complete and all-inclusive.[304] None of the authors consulted even suggested that this might not be the case.

298 Canon 2256.

299 Canon 2214, § 2.

300 Canon 2219, § 1, § 3.

301 Canon 19.

302 Cf. canons 2263 and 2294, § 1, § 2.

303 Cocchi, *Commentarium in Codicem Iuris Canonici* (8 vols., Vol. VIII, *De Delictis et Poenis,* 4. ed., Torino: Marietti, 1938), n. 84, p. 142; *Chelodi, Ius Poenale et Ordo Procedendi Juxta Codicem Iuris Canonici* (Tridenti, 1925), n. 37, p. 46; Vermeersch-Creusen, *Epitome,* III, n. 458, p. 281; Jone, *Commentarium,* III, 464; Regatillo-Zalba, *Theologia Moralis,* III, n. 1055, p. 921; Bouscaren, *Canon Law,* p. 897; Ayrinhac-Lydon, *Penal Legislation,* p. 84.

304 Berutti, *Institutiones,* VI, n. 60, p. 165; "Enumeratio est taxativa . . ."; Hyland, *Excommunication,* p. 124; Conte a Coronata, IV, n. 167, p. 201; Beste, *Introductio in Codicem* (4. ed., Neapoli: M. D'Auria, 1956), p. 1005; Blat, *Commentarium Textus Codicis Iuris Canonici* (5 vols., Vol. V, Romae: Collegio Angelico, 1924), V, n. 81, p. 124.

CHAPTER II

Exclusion From the Performance of Authorized Ecclesiastical Acts As the Result of Excommunication

"Removetur Excommunicatus Ab Actibus Legitimis Ecclesiasticis Intra Fines Suis In Locis Iure Definitos: . . ."—Canon 2263.

Article I. introductory notions concerning excommunication

Section 1. The Notion of Excommunication

Canon 2263 decrees that one who is excommunicated is to be excluded from the performance of authorized ecclesiastical acts. For the sake of a better understanding of the provisions of this canon, a few fundamental remarks concerning excommunication are in order here.

The word excommunication comes from the words *ex* and *communis,* that is, to place one outside the common condition, the community of others.[1]

Excommunication is a censure by which a person is excluded from the communion of the faithful with the effects which are enumerated in the canons of the Code, which effects cannot be separated from one another.[2] It is a censure, that is, a penalty by which a baptized person who is delinquent and contumacious is deprived of certain spiritual goods, or goods joined to spiritual ones, until upon receding from his contumacy he is absolved.[3] Thus, before a person can have inflicted upon him a censure, he must be baptized, delinquent and contumacious.[4]

Baptism is necessary in that it is the gateway to the Church, and thus to one's subjection to the authority of the Church.[5] One is

[1] Raus, *Institutiones Canonicae* (altera editio, Lugdini-Parisiis: Typis Emmanuelis Vitte, 1931), p. 701.

[2] Canon 2257, § 1.

[3] Canon 2241, § 1.

[4] Cf. canon 2241, § 1.

[5] Cf. canon 87.

delinquent when one has committed a delict, that is, has violated a law to which a canonical sanction, at least an indeterminate one, is attached, has done so in an external manner, and is morally responsible for his act.[6] It is the particular property of censures that before they can be inflicted the subject must be contumacious. The law considers one contumacious in different ways depending on the manner in which the censure is to be imposed. If it is a case of a *ferendae sententiae* censure, the person is considered contumacious when, notwithstanding the admonitions provided for in the law, he fails to desist from his crime or to do penance and make proper reparation for the injury or scandal arising from it. If the censure is imposed as a *latae sententiae* penalty, the mere transgression of the law to which the penalty is attached suffices for one to be considered contumacious, unless of course he is excused in view of some legitimate reason.[7]

This contumacy is postulated as a condition before a censure can be imposed, inasmuch as the primary purpose of the penalty seeks to bring about the emendation of the delinquent. Thus, if he is already sincerely repentant, there is no room for a censure. By the same token the censure is to be removed by way of absolution as soon as the delinquent has receded from his contumacy.[8]

The goods of which the one subject to a censure is deprived are the spiritual goods or the goods annexed to spiritual ones over which the Church has power.

In addition to excommunication there are two other censures, interdict and suspension.[9] An interdict is a censure by which the faithful, while remaining in communion with the Church, are forbidden certain sacred things as recounted in the canons.[10] Suspension is a censure by which a cleric is forbidden the use of his office, his benefice, or both.[11] An interdict can affect both the laity and the clergy, as can excommunication. Suspension can affect only

[6] Canon 2195, § 1.

[7] Cf. canon 2242, § 2.

[8] Cf. canon 2248, § 2.

[9] Canon 2255, § 1, nn. 2 and 3.

[10] Canon 2268, § 1.

[11] Canon 2278, § 1.

clerics. The interdict and suspension as non-censures can be inflicted upon moral persons as well as physical, whereas excommunication can affect only physical persons. Thus, if excommunication is imposed upon a moral person or community, it is to be understood as affecting only those physical persons who cooperated in the delict.[12] The reason for this difference seems to lie in the effects of these penalties. "The effects of excommunication concern personal spiritual benefits and favors, that is, such as touch the soul and salvation of the individual, whereas the privation entailed by suspension or interdict is not of an individual spiritual character." [13] An interdict may also be local, that is, laid upon a place.

Excommunication is always a censure, whereas interdict and suspension can also be vindictive penalties. In a doubtful case, however, the law presumes them to be censures.[14] It is clear that excommunication excludes one from or places one outside of the communion of the faithful. Suspension and interdict, on the other hand, are imposed upon those who remain within this communion.[15]

It is clear from this brief comparison that excommunication is the most severe of the censures and is in fact the gravest of all ecclesiastical punishments. The law of the decretals aptly described it as the ultimate penalty inflicted by the Church.[16] For this reason the Church prescribes that all censures, especially those which are of a *latae sententiae* character, and most of all excommunication, are to be inflicted only after careful and sober consideration of the circumstances involved.[17]

Excommunication, it has been seen, involves an exclusion from the communion of the faithful. This communion may be considered in several ways. In the first place it involves a purely internal union with Christ and the faithful in the possession of grace and charity. Secondly, there is a purely external communion which involves the

[12] 2255, § 2.

[13] Augustine, A Commentary on the New Code of Canon Law, VIII, 165.

[14] Canon 2255, § 2.

[15] Canons 2257, § 1; 2268, § 1; 2278, § 1.

[16] ". . . quum Ecclesia non habeat ultra quid faciat."—C. 10, X, *de iudiciis,* II, 1.

[17] Cf. canon 2241, § 1.

ordinary social relationships with the faithful. Finally, there is what authors refer to as a "mixed" communion, that is, one consisting of certain external rights and acts which are ordained to produce spiritual effects. The Sacrifice of the Mass, the sacraments, the public prayers and suffrages of the Church, ecclesiastical burial, and other ceremonies are contemplated here.[18]

An excommunicated person is excluded from the communion of the faithful. In what sense is one to understand this statement? It is clear that the Church is not able to deprive one of the purely internal union with Christ and his members. Such a loss can only be effected by the will of the individual. Excommunication may be an indication that such a communion no longer exists, but it does not cause such a condition.[19]

The Church is able to exclude one from the purely external and social communion with its members by means of excommunication.[20] The reason for this seems to lie in the fact that all such intercourse: ". . . ought to be directed by the faithful to a spiritual end, and since the refusal of such communication is well calculated to bring the offender to repentance, there is no doubt but that the same can fall under the prohibition of the Church." [21]

A study of the present discipline makes it evident that the communion with the faithful about which the Church is primarily concerned when leveling excommunication is that which is referred to above as "mixed." A brief glance at the effects of excommunication as stated in canons 2259-2267 discloses that the excommunicated are deprived not only of such external rights as the exercise of

[18] Cf. Hyland, *op. cit.*, p. 5; Roberti, *De Delictis et Poenis* (Romae: Apud Aedes Facultatis Iuridicae ad S. Apollinaris, 1938), n. 280, p. 319; Sipos, *Enchiridion Iuris Canonici* (Editionem Sextam Recognovit L. Galos, Romae: Herder, 1954), p. 832, footnote 3; Cipollini, *De Censuris Latae Sententiae* (Taurini: Marietti, 1925), p. 54; Vermeersch-Creusen, *Epitome*, III, n. 459, p. 282.

[19] Hyland, *op. cit.*, p. 5; Roberti, *De Delictis et Poenis*, n. 325, p. 383; Chelodi-Ciprotti, *Ius Canonicum De Delictis et Poenis*, n. 36, p. 47; Raus, *op. cit.*, n. 456, p. 701; Blat, *Commentarium*, V, n. 82, p. 127.

[20] Chelodi, *op cit.*, n. 37, p. 44; Hyland, *op. cit.*, p. 6; Raus, *op. cit.*, n. 456, p. 701; Sipos, *op. cit.*, n. 235, p. 830; footnote 3.

[21] Hyland, *op. cit.*, p. 6.

jurisdiction, the performance of authorized ecclesiastical acts, and the administration of offices and benefices, but also of the sacraments and the sacramentals, the suffrages of the Church and divine offices.[22]

Section 2. The Classes of Excommunicated Persons

Excommunicated persons are considered by the present law as *vitandi,* that is, persons to be shunned, or as *tolerati,* that is, persons who are tolerated.[23] It is not within the province of this study to investigate the history of this distinction. Some of these notions have been pointed out in the previous section. It is sufficient to point out here that the basis of the law of the Code is found in the decretals and was further expounded in the Constitution *Ad evitanda* of 1418, issued by Pope Martin V (1417-1431).[24]

There has been some discussion concerning the proper text of this Constitution. Augustine (1872-1943) pointed out that the Constitution has come down to us in two different readings, that of the Council of Constance (1414-1418) and that preserved in the acts of the V General Council of the Lateran (1512-1517). The difference in these texts is a substantial one in that the Constance text mentions two kinds of *vitandi:* those who have been publicly denounced and those who are notorious beaters of clerics. The Lateran text mentions these and adds to the list those who have so notoriously fallen under sentence of excommunication that it cannot be concealed or excused.

The Code in presenting the present discipline seems to favor the text of Constance.[25] Today no one is a *vitandus* unless he has been by name excommunicated by the Holy See, unless the excommunication has been publicly declared, and also unless it is expressly stated in the decree or sentence that he must be shunned.[26] In addition, one who lays violent hands upon the person of the Roman Pontiff not

[22] Hyland, *op. cit.*, p. 6: Sipos, *op. cit.*, n. 325, p. 830, footnote 3; Raus, *op. cit.*, n. 456, p. 701.

[23] Canon 2258, § 1.

[24] C. 14, X, *de sententia excommunicationis,* V, 39; *Fontes,* n. 45.

[25] Augustine, *op. cit.*, VIII, 173.

[26] Canon 2258, § 2; cf. Roberti, *De Delicitis et Poenis,* n. 326, p. 384.

only contracts a *latae sententiae* excommunication most specially reserved to the Holy See, but also is *ipso facto* a *vitandus*.[27]

In a practical consideration of the effects of excommunication upon the performance of authorized ecclesiastical acts it is necessary to point out further distinctions among the excommunicated. This is necessary because of the fact that the law provides for different effects in line with the different status or class that encompasses the excommunicated person. These differences will be pointed out later in this study. It suffices here to advert to these classifications.

As has been pointed out, there are two general divisions among the excommunicated, that is, the *vitandi* and the *tolerati*. A further distinction must be noted among the *tolerati*. A *toleratus* upon whom there has been inflicted a condemnatory or a declaratory sentence is to be distinguished from the one upon whom no such sentence has been inflicted. The former is a *toleratus* who is notorious by law. The latter may be a *toleratus* who is notorious with a notoriety of fact, or he may lack all notoriety in consequence of an occult delict. These distinctions will be more clearly illustrated later by way of exemplification.[28]

Section 3. The Effects of Excommunication

The primary and principal effect of excommunication is that the censured person is completely segregated or excluded from communion with the faithful. This communion, when enjoyed, embraces a number of rights and obligations. The privation of these rights, in consequence of the severing of the bond of communion,[29] constitutes the several effects of excommunication.[30] It is because these

[27] Canon 2258, § 2; and 2343, § 1, n. 1.

[28] "Tolerati dicuntur omnes, qui non sunt vitandi. Sed ex toleratis alii sunt occulti, alii vero notorii; et ex notoriis, alii sunt tales notorietate facti, alii vero iuris; notorius notorietate iuris quis constituitur post sententiam declaratoriam vel condemnatoriam."—Cerato, *Censurae Vigentes* (Patavii: Typis Seminarii, 1918), n. 36, pp. 46-47.

[29] Cf. canon 87.

[30] Conte a Coronata, IV, n. 1771, p. 207; Augustine, *op. cit.*, VIII, 175; Chelodi-Ciprotti, *Ius Canonicum De Delictis et Poenis* (5. ed., Vicenza: Società Anonima Tipografia, Trento: Liberia Moderna Editrice, 1943), n. 37, p. 48.

effects flow from this exclusion as from their source that they are inseparable from one another.[31] When there is no communion with the faithful these rights simply are not enjoyed.

The effects of excommunication must be considered both objectively and subjectively. Objectively they are enumerated in the canons of the Code and concern the divine offices (canon 2259), the reception and administration of the sacraments and sacramentals (canons 2260-2261), the suffrages of the Church (canon 2262), the authorized ecclesiastical acts (canon 2263), the exercise of jurisdiction (canon 2264), the right of election, presentation and nomination (canon 2265), the acquiring of dignities, benefices, offices in both the strict and, wide sense (canons 2263 and 2265), the reception of orders (canon 2265), the enjoyment of income (canon 2266), civil intercourse (canon 2267), concessions and privileges (canon 2263), the right to be a plaintiff in ecclesiastical causes (canon 2263).

These effects must also be considered subjectively, since they do not follow in the same manner in each individual case. The Code deals differently with the excommunicated in so far as they belong to the various categories explained above. Thus a *vitandus* is affected differently in many cases than a *toleratus* who is under censure through an occult delict.

It is with the specific effect that involves a person's exclusion from the performance of authorized ecclesiastical acts that the present chapter is concerned.

Article II. Historical Development of the Exclusion from the Performance of Authorized Ecclesiastical Acts as the Result of Excommunication

Section 1. Introductory Notions

The notion of excommunication is as old as society itself. It is obvious from the very nature of social life that those who interfere with the common good must as times be separated from the communion of their fellows. In order that a common end be attained by a perfect society it is absolutely necessary that there be authority

31 Canon 2257, § 1.

to legislate, judge and enforce laws which serve as means to the attainment of this end. History clearly reveals that all peoples possess and exercise these powers. Excommunication is only one means of protecting the very existence and the attainment of the end of a society.[32]

It is obvious that the Church as a perfect society possesses this right of inflicting excommunication in order that it may attain its end and perfect its members. This right flows from the intention of the Divine Founder, who established his Church as a perfect society for the salvation of souls. Thus it follows that the Church enjoys all those means which are necessary for the attainment of this end.[33] One of these means is the right of punishing its delinquent members. Excommunication is one of these punishments.

The possession and use of the powers of excommunication by the Church from its earliest days is clear.[34] It is the purpose of the present article to trace the historical evolution of the exclusion, as the result of excommunication, from those actions which the present law designates as authorized ecclesiastical acts.

Section 2. The Law in the Pseudo-Isidorian Decretals

In accordance with their general aim and purpose the false decretals delved into great detail in judicial matters, and were not slow to impose the penalty of excommunication upon those who offended in this regard. Thus according to a letter attributed to Pope Saint Callistus I (217-222), those who conspired against their bishops as well as those who consented to such actions were to be deprived of communion with the Church.[35]

[32] Ottaviani, *Institutiones Iuris Publici Ecclesiastici,* I, 80-128.

[33] Ottaviani, *op. cit.,* I, 194-196.

[34] Cf. St. Matthew, 18:18; 18:15-17; 1 Timothy, 1:18-20; 1 Corinthians, 5:1-5; 1 Corinthians, 5:11 and 13; Romans, 16:17; Titus, 3:10; 1 Corinthians, 16:22.

[35] Pseudo-Callistus, Ep. II, cap. 8—Hinschius, *Decretales Pseudo-Isidorianae et Capitula Angilramni* (Lipsiae, 1863), p. 138 (hereafter cited Hinschius); Jaffé, *Regesta Pontificum Romanorum ab condita Ecclesia ad Annum post Christum natum MCXCVIII* (2. ed. by F. Kaltenbrunner [—to the year 590], P. Ewald [590-882], and S. Löwenfeld [882-1198], Lipsiae, 1885-1888), +86 (hereafter cited Jaffé).

It was one of the principal purposes of the composers of these decretals to make it all but impossible for the bishop to be brought to court. Many preliminary steps were necessary before such action could be taken, and if they were not observed, then excommunication was to be meted out.[36] A like punishment was reserved for those who were unable to prove a charge of crime leveled against bishop, priest, or deacon.[37]

Despite the great amount of time and space the authors of the Pseudo-Isidorian Decretals devoted to judicial matters, they furnished little if any material for tracing the history of the exclusion, as the result of excommunication, from what are now known as authorized ecclesiastical acts. The decretals abound in prohibitions and exclusions, but it is only by way of inference that exclusion from any of the authorized ecclesiastical acts may be included under these restrictions. It is abundantly clear that the excommunicated could not enter suit in court.[38] They were also excluded from being witnesses in many instances.[39]

It seems safe to conclude that, since the excommunicated could not act even in the capacity of a plaintiff or a witness, they certainly were excluded from other judicial offices and capacities. It nevertheless remains true that no text was discovered which directly excluded them from these or other authorized ecclesiastical acts.

Section 3. The Law in the *Corpus Iuris Canonici*

A. THE DECREE OF GRATIAN

Gratian (+ca. 1157) mentioned many cases in which the penalty of excommunication was imposed. Much of this legislation was

36 Sixtus II, Ep. 2, cap. 5—Hinschius, p. 192, Jaffé, n. +134.

37 *Capitula Angilramni,* Cor. Par. V—Hinschius, p. 767.

38 Pseudo-Callistus, Ep. II, cap. 9: "Hi vero in nullius accusatione sunt recipiendi, nec eorum vel anathamatum vox ullum nocere aut accusare potest."—Hinschius, p. 138, Jaffé, n. +86; Stephanus, Ep. II, cap. 7: "Nullius enim anathema suscipiatur. . . ."—Hinschius, p. 184, Jaffé, n. +131; Pseudo-Fabianus, Ep. I, cap. 6—Hinschius, p. 159, Jaffé, n. +92; Pseudo-Eutychianus, Ep. II, cap. 8—Hinschius, p. 211, Jaffé, n. +146; Sixtus II, Ep. II, cap. 8—Hinschius, p. 193, Jaffé, n. +134.

39 *Capitula Angilramni,* Cor. Par. Sal. IX—Hinschius, p. 767.

concerned with the penalty contracted by those who were guilty of association with the excommunicated. The general principle was that those who associated with the excommunicated merited the same censure.[40] Moreover, it seems that this penalty was of a *latae sententiae* character in that it was contracted immediately upon the perpetration of the acts.[42]

Despite much legislation dealing with excommunication, the *Decretum* offers little for the historical development of the exclusion from authorized ecclesiastical acts as a result of the incurring of this censure. The law does seem clear in excluding the excommunicated from the position of judge on the basis that an association certainly could not be tolerated on this level when it was forbidden under such dire penalties in matters of less importance.[43] It seems that this exclusion could be applied to all authorized ecclesiastical acts relating to judicial matters.

B. THE DECRETALS

The various collections of decretals which together complete the *Corpus Iuris Canonici* contain many examples of crimes which were punished with excommunication.

The decretals in general and those of Gregory IX in particular furnish the primary sources for the cases of exclusion, as the result of excommunication from authorized ecclesiastical acts.

Those who had been excommunicated publicly or by name were to be shunned both in judicial and extra-judicial matters, and were to be prevented from exercising law-approved (legitimate) acts.[44] At first glance one could feel tempted to identify these *legitimi actus* with the *actus legitimi ecclesiastici* as listed in canon 2256, n. 2,

[40] Cc. 3, 4, 5, 16, 17, 18, C. XI, q. 3.

[42] Cc. 28, 29, C. XI, q. 3.

[43] C. 37, C. XXIV, q. 1; *glossa ordinaria* ad c. 19, C. XXVII, q. 1, s.v. *Quosque*.

[44] C. 14, *de sententia excommunicationis,* V, 11, in VI°: "Excommunicatus tamen nominatim, vel specialiter et expresse, . . . et nedum in iudicialibus, sed etiam in extra-iudicialibus evitari, ac a legitimis actibus removeri debebit, quousque, quod post appellationem legitimam excommunicatus fuerit, vel alias de ipsius sententiae docuerit nullitate."

and thus believe that there exists some foundation for the all-embracing prescriptions of canon 2263. A closer examination of the text, however, presents certain difficulties. It is very hard to determine just what is to be included within the scope of this expression, for, as was noted, the excommunicated were to be shunned not only in the judicial forum but in extra-judicial matters as well *and* excluded from the performance of these acts. The prohibition in this text without doubt concerns the general area of this study, but to just what acts it pertains is not clear.

Those who were excommunicated for cooperating with or aiding heretics were given a year within which to make satisfaction. If they failed to do so, other penalties were inflicted.[45] Thus these excommunicates were not permitted to act in many judicial capacities, some of which the Code today regards as authorized ecclesiastical acts. Generally, they were not permitted to hold any public office or to give counsel or advice. More specifically, if perhaps they were judges and exercised their office, their sentence *"nullam obtinet firmitatem,"* and no causes were to be brought to them for trial. They were also prohibited from exercising their office as advocates in that *"eius patrocinium nullatenus admittitur."* An excommunicated notary was likewise excluded in that everything drawn up by him *"nullius est momenti."* That those who were excommunicated and who held other judicial positions were likewise excluded from the performance of their duties is clear from this same text.[46]

The decretal law also mentioned in this place that such excommunicates were to be regarded as *intestabiles*. The glossator commented that this group was likewise to be repelled from the performance of any authorized act.[47] The gloss sheds little light on the contents of such acts, however, for the commentator merely added that the *intestabiles* were subject to commercial limitations as well as those already stated.

The excommunicated were not only excluded from the various judicial capacities already mentioned, but were also barred from

[45] C. 13, X, *de haereticis*, V, 7.

[46] "Et in similibus idem praecipimus observari."—c. 13, X, *de haereticis*, V, 7; cf. c. 5, *de poenis*, V, 9, in VI°.

[47] *Glossa ordinaria* ad c. 13, X, *de haereticis*, V, 7, s.v. *sit etiam intestabilis*.

the ecclesiastical courts altogether.[48] They were forbidden to appear in court in person, whether in the capacity of plaintiff or of defendant. To prevent them from benefitting from their punishment, the law provided that they could be sued, but they were to be represented in court by a proxy.[49] This exclusion was later extended to the civil courts as well.[50] The glossators indicated that as a result of this prohibition the excommunicated were forbidden to sue in court, and in fact could not even appear as a defendant.[51] Since they could not appear in their own name, they certainly were not admitted for the purpose of representing another.[52] The prohibition likewise extended to the giving of testimony.[53]

The extent to which the excommunicated were barred from forensic communication with the faithful was dictated by two general principles. It is clear that in the *Decretum* of Gratian all communication with the excommunicated was forbidden.[54] Forensic actions were a very important segment of communication or association among men, and thus the excommunicated were barred from them. The mandatory exclusion was called for also in the secular courts in line with the general principle referred to above.[55]

During the course of the judicial procedure the exception of excommunication could always be brought against those who had contracted this censure.[56] If the person had been publicly excommunicated, the judge was to repel him from judicial action even if the exception had not been raised. There was no need, however, to exclude the *excommunicati tolerati* if no exception was lodged

[48] C. 7, X, *de iudiciis,* II, 1; c. 37, C. XXIV, q. 1.

[49] C. 7, X, *de iudiciis,* II, 1.

[50] C. 8, *de sententia excommunicationis,* V, 11, in VI°.

[51] *Glossa ordinaria* ad c. 8, *de sententia excommunicationis,* V, 11, in VI°, s.v. *ab agendo.*

[52] *Glossa ordinaria* ad c. 8, *eod. tit.,* V, 11, in VI°, s.v. *patrocinado.*

[53] C. 8, *eod. tit.,* V, 11, in VI°; c. 1, X, *de haereticis,* V, 7.

[54] Cc. 3, 4, 5, 16, 17, 18, C. XI, q. 3.

[55] C. 8, *de sententia excommunicationis, suspensionis et interdicti,* V, 11, in VI°.

[56] C. 1, *de exceptionibus,* II, 12, in VI°; c. 12, X, *de exceptionibus,* II, 25.

against them.[57] Sentences rendered by a judge who was himself at the time excommunicated were subject to rescission.[58] But if the exception of the excommunication was raised without the accompaniment of proof then the expenses were to be paid by the false accuser.[59]

The Constitution "*Ad evitanda*" of 1418, issued by Pope Martin V (1417-1431), introduced a new leniency into the question of communication with the excommunicated.[60] Because of the number and magnitude of the problems created by the law forbidding communion with the excommunicated, several mitigations were introduced. In a final effort to assist the faithful in their difficulties, the pope presented this Constitution. Its basic provision consisted in dividing the excommunicated into groups which came to be known as the *tolerati* and the *vitandi.* The former made up the majority of the persons under this censure, and the faithful were no longer obliged to refrain from communication with them. The *vitandi* were still to be shunned, but this group consisted only of those who had contracted the penalty by reason of violence against a cleric in such a notorious manner that the action could not be concealed or excused, and also of those whose censure had been made public by the judge in a special manner.[61] Though this legislation was of great importance in the general study of excommunication, it did not play an essential role for the present consideration, inasmuch as the excommunicated were still bound to remain dissociated from the faithful, for the privileges as stated in the Constitution *Ad evitanda* were extended to the faithful, and not to the excommunicated.

The excommunicated were prohibited from acting as procurators.[62]

57 C. 1, *de exceptionibus,* II, 12, in VI°; c. 21, X, *de officio et potestate iudicis delegati,* I, 29.

58 C. 24, *de sententia et re iudicata,* II, 27.

59 C. 1, *de exceptionibus,* II, 12, in VI°.

60 *Fontes,* n. 45.

61 Cf. A. Boudinhon, "Excommunication," *The Catholic Encyclopedia* (15 vols. and 2 supplements, New York: Appleton, 1907-1922), V, 678.

62 C. 7, X, *de probationibus,* II, 19.

This could well be deduced from the general principles cited above.[63] Further, since they could not be witnesses, it stands to reason that they could not fulfill the role of procurator.[64] If he could not act for himself, how could he do so for another?

The exercise of the office of notary was likewise forbidden to the excommunicate.[65] The law also excluded the excommunicate from the office of advocate.[66] This prohibition was directly in line with the general principles. It must be noted, however, that the rules and distinctions provided by Pope Martin V in the Constitution *Ad evitanda* determined the validity and even the lawfulness of many of these otherwise prohibited acts. It is not the purpose of this study to determine the precise value of these acts at that time. The purpose here is to determine when the excommunicated were excluded from their performance in consequence of the penalty incurred. In order to point to the effect of the Constitution, however, it may be remarked that, if such a person undertook the performance of the office, the exception of excommunication could of course be raised against him. The judge was to repel him whether the exception was raised or not, as long as the excommunication was of a public character. If, however, he was a *toleratus,* there was no need of his exclusion, provided that the persons with vested interests consented to his ministrations.

It can safely be assumed that the excommunicated were likewise deprived of the administration of ecclesiastical property. Although the decretal law did not specifically state this, the conclusion is justified from the very nature of and the privations deriving from the penalty.[67] Further evidence of this is found in a text of the *Liber Sextus* of Boniface VIII.[68]

[63] C. 3, 4, 5, 16, 17, 18, C. XI, q. 3; c. 8, *de sententia excommunicationis, suspensionis et interdicti,* V, 11, in VI°.

[64] C. 8, *de sententia excommunicationis, suspensionis, et interdicti,* V, 11, in VI°.

[65] C. 13, X, *de haereticis,* V, 7; c. 5, *de poenis,* V, 9, in VI°.

[66] C. 13, X, *de haereticis,* V, 7.

[67] Franciscus Suarez, *Disputationes de Censuris in Communi* (Lugduni: Horatius Cardon, 1608), disp. XIII, s. 2, n. 6.

[68] C. 1, *de electione et electi potestate,* 1, 6, in VI°.

The right of suffrage in ecclesiastical elections was denied to the excommunicated. Votes cast by the *vitandi* were invalid, whereas votes cast by the *tolerati* were simply illicit, unless the exception of excommunication had been raised against them. The gloss to the pertinent canon in the decretals pointed out that the excommunicated could neither elect nor be elected.[69]

Section 4. The Law From the Council of Trent to the Code of Canon Law

Cases of excommunication found in the Council of Trent and in subsequent legislation are numerous and well known. The Council of Trent itself very frequently imposed excommunication as a penalty for a variety of crimes and abuses.[70]

The Council of Trent made only one addition to the list of those who were excluded as the result of their status of excommunication from the performance of authorized ecclesiastical acts.

> If any cleric or laic, of whatever rank, even imperial or royal, should be so possessed by avarice, the root of all evil, as to presume to convert to his own use and to usurp *per se vel alios,* by force of fear, or even by means of supposititious persons, whether clerical or lay, or by any fraud or colored pretext whatever, the prerogatives, properties, rents and rights, even those held in fee or under lease, revenues, profits, or any incomes whatsoever, belonging to any church or benefices, secular or regular, eleemosynary institutions or any other pious places, which ought to be used for the needs of the ministers and the poor, or to hinder them from being received by those to whom they by right belong, he shall be anathematized till he shall have restored integrally to the church and to its administrator or beneficiary the prerogatives, properties, effects, rights, fruits and revenues which he has seized or in whatever way they have come to him, even by way of gift

[69] *Glossa ordinaria* ad c. 23, X, *de appellationibus, recusationibus et relationibus,* II, 28, s.v. *excommunicationis;* c. unicum, *ne sede vacante aliquid innovetur,* III, 8, in VI° ; Suarez, *loc. cit.*

[70] Conc. Trident., sess. XIII, *de Eucharistia,* cc. 1-11; sess. XXIII, *de ref.,* c. 11; sess. XXIV, *de ref. matrim.,* c. 6; sess. XXV, *de regularibus,* cc. 5, 11, 12, 18, 19, and many others.

> from a supposititious person, and furthermore, till he shall have obtained absolution from the Roman Pontiff. If he be a patron of that church, he shall in addition to the aforesaid penalties, be *eo ipso* deprived of the right of patronage.[71]

It is obvious that the exclusion from the exercise of the right of patronage was not a direct result of excommunication as it was stated by the Council. Nevertheless the relationship was close enough to warrant mention here. The Council mentioned a similar case in another place.[72]

Legislation contemporary with and subsequent to the Council of Trent listed many causes for the incurring of excommunication. It set a seal of confirmation on many of the exclusions from authorized ecclesiastical acts ritherto considered.

Anyone of whatever rank who meddled in papal elections was to be excommunicated, excluded from the right of patronage, and from all active and passive voice in elections. He was further made incapable of the enjoyment of all dignities, honors and goods. Such a one was also unable to perform law-approved acts.[73] Notaries and judges under the penalty of excommunication were still not permitted to carry out their offices.[74] The excommunicated were further not to be admitted as sponsors at baptism.[75] Since the exclusion from the office of sponsor at baptism is to be dealt with at greater length in a subsequent chapter, the reader is referred to that discussion.

[71] Conc. Trident., sess. XXII, *de ref.*, c. 11—translation by Schroeder, *Canons and Decrees of the Council of Trent* (St. Louis: B. Herder, 1941), p. 158.

[72] Conc. Trident., sess. XXV, *de ref.*, c. 9.

[73] Paulus IV, const. *Cum secundum,* 16 dec. 1558, nn. 2, 3, 5—*Bull. Rom. Taur.*, VI, 545.

[74] Julius III, const. *Cui nuper,* 1 febr. 1554—*Bull. Rom. Taur.*, VI, 476.

[75] I Council of Milan (1565), Par. II, *De Baptismo*: "Caveant vero parochi, ne excommunicatos, . . . admittant ad levandum baptizatum de sacro fonte."—Mansi XXXIV, col. 16; Trombelli, *Tractatus de Sacramentis* (5 vols., Vol. II, Bononiae, 1770), II, diss. VI, n. 11; *Rituale Romanum, Pauli V Pontificis Maximi jussu editum, et Benedicto XIV auctum et castigatum* (Ratisbonae, 1901), tit. II, cap. 1, *De Sacramento Baptismi,* nn. 22-26.

There were many other instances of legislation of a more general character which deprived the excommunicated of all offices, dignities, benefices, honors and the like. Because of the confusion in the meanings of the terms used, there will be no attempt here to particularize the meaning of these decrees. It suffices to cite several of them.[76]

According to a Constitution of Pope Julius III (1550-1555) those who were convicted a third time of blasphemy were deprived of all active and passive voice in elections.[77]

Thus in general the legislation from the Council of Trent to the appearance of the Code confirms what has been discovered previously, and provides some valuable additions to the study of the exclusion from authorized ecclesiastical acts as the result of excommunication.

ARTICLE III. COMMENTARY ON THE PRESENT LAW

Section 1. Statement of the Question

With the general historical development in the exclusion from authorized ecclesiastical acts duly inspected one may proceed to a more detailed consideration of the present law. The Code states in canon 2263: "Removetur excommunicatus ab actibus legitimis ecclesiasticis intra fines suis in locis iure definitos; nequit in causis ecclesiasticis agere, nisi ad normam can. 1654; prohibetur ecclesiasticis officiis seu muneribus fungi, concessisque antea ab Ecclesia privilegiis frui." What is the meaning of this law? Just what exactly does the term "removetur" signify? To what extent are the excommunicated to be excluded from the performance of authorized ecclesiastical acts. For a correct answer to these questions there must be a correct interpretation of the phrase *"intra fines suis in locis iure definitos."* This is the key to the problem.

[76] Paulus III, *Alias felicis,—Bull. Rom. Taur.*, VI, 256; Julius III, const. *Videntes Ecclesiastici*, 21 febr. 1553—*Bull. Rom. Taur.*, VI, 469; Julius III, const. *In multis depravatis*, 1 febr. 1554—*Bull. Rom. Taur.*, VI, 479; Paulus IV, *Postquam divina bonitas*, 20 iul. 1558—*Bull. Rom. Taur.*, VI, 538.

[77] Julius III, const. *In multis depravatis*, 1 febr. 1554—*Bull. Rom. Taur.*, VI, 479.

Section 2. Statement of the Principal Interpretations

There are two interpretations given to these words. One, which may be referred to as a strict interpretation, holds that this phrase refers only to those places in the law which deal specifically with authorized ecclesiastical acts. Thus, the excommunicated are to be removed from authorized ecclesiastical acts only in so far as their removal therefrom is stated in the canons which treat specifically of these acts.

There is also a wider interpretation of these words.[78] This position maintains that not only those canons which deal specifically with authorized ecclesiastical acts are embraced in the phrase *"intra fines suis in locis iure definitos,"* but also other canons which have a definite bearing and relationship, even though no specific mention of authorized ecclesiastical acts is made. This opinion holds that fundamentally (*per se*) an excommunicated person cannot carry out any authorized ecclesiastical act licitly. It is summed up well by Hyland in this manner:

> The clause, *"intra fines suis in locis iure definitos,"* seems to be a guide to determine whether the placing of a legitimate ecclesiastical act by an excommunicate is, besides being illicit, invalid as well. Furthermore, it is to be understood not only concerning the places in law which treat specifically of the legitimate ecclesiastical acts, but likewise with reference to the other canons dealing with the effects of excommunication." [79]

A. STRICT INTERPRETATION

At first glance this problem does not seem to present great difficulty. The obvious solution seems to be that the phrase in question refers only to those places in the law which treat specifically of authorized ecclesiastical acts. Many authors who do not deal extensively with this problem seem to reach this conclusion. Thus Bouscaren in his paraphrase of canon 2263 states:

[78] It is to be noted that the terms "strict" and "wide" used throughout this section are not employed in their technical meaning. They are used merely to designate two interpretations which have the appearance of these extremes.

[79] Hyland, *op. cit.*, p. 128.

> An excommunicated person is excluded from legitimate ecclesiastical acts in the measure which is defined in the parts of the Code which deal respectively with various such acts.[80]

Blat (1870-1943), after remarking that the Code is in accord with the law of the Decretals on this matter, pointed out:

> Removetur excommunicatus quilibet hac de causa ab actibus legitimis ecclesiasticis (can. 2256, 2°), . . . et ab illis intra fines cognoscendos suis in locis Codicis pro illorum diversitate, seu iure scripto definitos, ultra quos non extendatur remotio, . . .[81]

Berutti expresses the same opinion.[82] Regatillo-Zalba state that the excommunicated are not to be removed from all authorized ecclesiastical acts listed by canon 2256, n. 2, but only from those treated specifically in the Code. These places are then listed.[83]

Other authors such as Jone, Sipos (+1949) and Abbo-Hannan, do not deal directly with the problem, but indicate by their general treatment of the matter that they accept what has been termed the strict interpretation.[84]

Certain general principles dealing with the interpretation of law may seem to lend support to this position. There is a twofold principle which must be recalled when there is a question of laws of this kind. This principle is stated in canons 19 and 2219. Canon 19 declares that laws which state a penalty, or restrict the free exercise of rights, or contain an exception to the law are to undergo a strict interpretation.[85] Canon 2219 teaches that in penal matters

80 Bouscaren-Ellis, *op. cit.*, p. 898.

81 *Commentarium,* V, p. 137, n. 90.

82 "Omnes excommunicati singulos actus illicite ponerent qui in can. 2256, 2°, enumerantur, salvis tamen peculiaribus praescriptis quae aliud expresse caveant";—*Institutiones Iuris Canonici,* VI, n. 63, p. 176.

83 Regatillo-Zalba, *Theologia Moralis,* III, n. 1058, p. 926.

84 Jone, *Commentarium,* III, 470; Abbo-Hannan, *The Sacred Canons,* II, p. 839, footnote 9; Sipos, *Enchiridion Iuris Canonici,* n. 235, p. 834.

85 "Leges quae poenam statuunt, aut liberum iurium exercitium coarctant, aut exceptionem a lege continent, strictae subsunt interpretationi."

the more benign interpretation is to be applied.[86] These prescriptions are based upon the time-tested jurisprudence of the past.[87] The first specifically concerns the penal law itself and refers to the fact that it is to receive a narrow rather than an enlarged application. The second concerns the penalty stated by the law, and teaches that, when there is a doubt, the milder interpretation is to be preferred to that which is more severe.[88]

The actual effect of these provisions upon the question at issue will be discussed further in that section, which deals with what the writer believes to be the correct interpretation.

B. WIDE INTERPRETATION

The wide interpretation of the words in question holds that an excommunicated person fundamentally (*per se*) cannot licitly place any authorized ecclesiastical act. The various canons which have a relationship to the placing of these acts, and not only those which specifically mention authorized ecclesiastical acts, determine whether such actions are invalid as well as illicit.

A majority of the authors who deal extensively with the difficulties involved seem to favor this opinion. Hyland thus proposes it as being in conformity both with the nature and the other effects of excommunication.[89] Chelodi (1880-1922) gave a clear exposition of this interpretation when he wrote:

> Quae haec omnia [actus legitimi etc.] excommunicatus *illicite* facit, nisi forte ei quaedam licita fiant sive ex generali principio (can. 2232, § 1) sive ex petitione fidelium; non tamen per se *invalide,* praeter casus a iure specialiter definitos.[90]

Conte a Coronata briefly outlines the problem and proposes this view as the more common and acceptable one.[91] Perhaps the most

[86] "In poenis benignior est interpretatio facienda."

[87] Reg. 15, R.J., in VI°: "Odia restringi, favores convenit ampliari"; Reg. 49, R.J., in VI°: "In poenis benignior est interpretatio facienda."

[88] Cf. Cappello, *op. cit.*, I, n. 585, p. 491.

[89] Hyland, *op. cit.*, p. 127.

[90] Chelodi-Ciprotti, *op. cit.*, n. 37, p. 49.

[91] Conte a Coronata, IV, n. 1776, p. 215.

forceful practical expression of this view is set forth by Roberti. Although he does not state the problem as such, in considering the effects of excommunication he does not list authorized ecclesiastical acts separately, but reduces all of them either to *munera* or *iura.*[92] He then goes on to state his general principle that every excommunicated person exercises these *iura* and *munera* illicitly.[93] This position is based on canons 2263, 2264, 2265, § 1, n. 1 and n. 2. In particular, he teaches that even the excommunicated person with whose condition no notoriety is attached cannot licitly accept or carry out any ecclesiastical *munera*[94] or *iura.*[95] Heylen follows Roberti closely in his treatment of the matter and reaches the same conclusions.[96]

Cappello holds this position also, for in speaking of the *simpliciter* excommunicated, that is, those whose excommunication is not notorious, he teaches: "Actus legitimi ecclesiastici, ab excommunicato positi, sunt quidem illiciti, nisi excuset causa iusta. . . ."[97] Cipollini also seems to follow this wide interpretation, although he does not go into the question in great detail.[98]

[92] Roberti, *De Delictis et Poenis,* I, n. 337, p. 401; "Codex inter effectus excommunicationis loquitur quoque de actibus legitimis ecclesiasticis (c. 2263). Iam vero qui dicuntur actus legitimi ecclesiastici (c. 2256, n. 2) aut sunt munera aut iura; munera quidem stricto sensu sunt iudicis, relatoris, et auditoris; lato sensu vero sunt defensoris vinculi, promotoris iustitiae et fidei, notarii et cancellarii, cursoris et apparitoris, advocati et procuratoris, itemque munus administratoris bonorum ecclesiasticorum e.g. membrum consilii administrativi dioecesani, oeconomus seminarii, administrator cuiusvis operis pii ecclesiastici, nec non patrini in baptismo vel confirmatione. Contra, ad iura reducuntur ius ferendi suffragium in electionibus ecclesiasticis et exercendi ius patronatus de quibus mox (n. 340) loquemur."—*Ibid.,* n. 338, p. 402.

[93] Roberti, *De Delictis et Poenis,* I, n. 327, p. 386.

[94] Canon 2265, § 1, n. 1; Roberti, *De Delictis et Poenis,* I, n. 340, p. 404; canon 2263; Roberti, *De Delictis et Poenis,* I, n. 339, p. 402.

[95] Canon 2265, § 1, n. 1; canon 2256, n. 2; Roberti, *De Delictis et Poenis,* I, n. 340, pp. 405, 406.

[96] Heylen, *De Censuris* (4. ed., Mechliniae: H. Dessain, 1945), pp. 76-77; 86-88.

[97] Cappello, *De Censuris* (4. ed., Taurini, Romae: Marietti, 1950), n. 150, p. 141.

[98] *De Censuris Latae Sententiae,* n. 65, p. 63.

Raus (1881-1943) [99] and Cerato,[100] taught that an excommunicate cannot fundamentally (*per se*) perform an authorized ecclesiastical act licitly. However, they did not sufficiently develop their treatment, so that one could list them as subscribing to the second tenat of the wide interpretation as it has been stated, that is, that the phrase in question is a guide to determining whether these actions are placed not only illicitly but invalidly as well.

Section 3. Influence of Canon 2232, § 1

The frequent repetition of the words *per se* in the treatment of the wide interpretation will have been noted. This interpretation holds that fundamentally or as a rule an excommunicated person cannot licitly perform any authorized ecclesiastical act. This qualification is necessitated by the terms of canon 2232, § 1:

> Poena latae sententiae, sive medicinalis sive vindicativa, delinquentem, qui delicti sibi sit conscius, ipso facto in utroque foro tenet; ante sententiam tamen declaratoriam a poena observanda delinquens excusatur quoties eam servare sine infamia nequit, et in foro externo ab eo eiusdem poenae observantiam exigere nemo potest, nisi delictum sit notorium, firmo praescripto can. 2223, § 4.

The general norm of canon 2232, § 1, is clear. It settles any indefiniteness which may have existed before the Code. The person conscious of his crime is bound to observe the *latae sententiae* penalty for that crime whether it be in the nature of a censure or of a vindictive penalty. He is thus bound in both the internal and the external forum. This is true even before there is a declaratory sentence, and even should the crime be materially or formally occult.

Thus the excommunicated person, when conscious of his status, is bound to observe his penalty and its effects in both the internal and external forum.

The law, however, has mitigated this general norm. In the absence of a declaratory sentence, a delinquent is excused from the

99 *Institutiones Canonicae,* n. 150, p. 703.

100 *Censurae Vigentes,* n. 37, p. 54.

observance of any *latae sententiae* penalty as often as he cannot observe it without the loss of his good name and reputation. Thus one subject to a *latae sententiae* penalty of excommunication is excused from the observance of that penalty when he cannot observe it without such defamation.

This legislation once again testifies to the spirit of mercy of the Church in regard to penal matters. It is not demanded that the delinquent defame himself.

It is clear, however, that the conditions of canon 2232, § 1, must be verified before the delinquent can take advantage of this refuge. Not only must there have been no declaratory sentence, but the situation must be such that the penalty cannot be observed without loss of reputation by the delinquent. The crime, then, must be occult. If it were public or notorious, this loss would already have been suffered, so that the observance of the penalty would not bring it about. The secrecy of the crime must be measured in relation to the circumstances in which the delinquent finds himself. Should it be occult in the place or among the persons with whom he is situated, he may avail himself of the protection offered by this canon.[101]

It is clear, then, that this canon may serve to aid only that class of the excommunicated to whose delict no notoriety is attached. Thus the *vitandi,* the *tolerati* after a condemnatory or declaratory sentence has been given, or also those whose excommunication is notorious by notoriety of fact are not open to the assistance provided in this canon. The reason for this lies in the fact that the persons in the above-mentioned categories have already suffered the loss of their good name in some degree in consequence of the notoriety of their status.

It is difficult to lay down general norms as to just when the observance of a penalty serves to bring about defamation to the delinquent. This judgment must be left to the person involved in each particular case.

Not only is the delinquent excused from the observance of a *latae sententiae* penalty in the circumstances outlined above, but in

[101] Tatarczuk, *Infamy of Law,* p. 93.

the external forum no third party can demand that he observe it unless his delict is notorious. Thus an excommunicated person to whose delict no notoriety attaches may not be forced to observe his penalty and its effects in the external forum. The case mentioned in canon 2223, § 4, is excepted from this general rule. This canon deals with rules by which the judge or superior is to be guided in the imposition of penalties, and states that as a rule it is left to the discretion of the superior to declare a *latae sententiae* penalty. He must issue the sentence, however, if an interested party demands it or the public good requires it.

Section 4. Comparison of Interpretations

In an effort to reach the correct interpretation of this canon recourse to the rules set down in canons 18 and 19 is indicated. As an aid to the application of these rules it will be most helpful to take the interpretations outlined above and draw them out to their logical conclusions as they apply to the prohibition and exclusion of the excommunicated from authorized ecclesiastical acts. In this way the correct interpretation will more easily appear.

A. Administration of Ecclesiastical Property

(1) *Strict Interpretation*

The first authorized ecclesiastical act referred to in canon 2256, n. 2, is that of the administration of ecclesiastical property, "*munus administratoris gerere bonorum ecclesiasticorum.*" In following what has been termed the strict interpretation one must look to those canons in the Code which deal specifically with this authorized ecclesiastical act if one is to determine whether an excommunicated person is to be excluded from the performance of such a function. Such an investigation brings to light no legislation which forbids any excommunicate to perform this function. Canons 1520 and 1521 do state certain qualifications necessary in certain cases. Thus those who serve on the board of administrators to be set up by the ordinary are to be qualified ("*idonei*") and not related to the ordinary by affinity or consanguinity within the second degree.[102] In addition to this diocesan board, other administrators appointed by the ordinary for the administration of the goods of churches or of pious institutions are to be prudent and qualified men of good reputation.[103] These are very general qualifications, and whereas indeed it seems evident that they do not contemplate the admission of an excommunicated person to this office, such a conclusion is not reached through a rigorous application of the strict interpretation.

Thus, a strict interpretation of the phrase *"intra fines suis in locis iure definitos"* leads one to the conclusion that an excommunicated person may carry out this function.[104]

(2) *Wide Interpretation*

The general principle of the broad or wide interpretation as pertaining to this particular authorized ecclesiastical act maintains that no excommunicated person may licitly exercise the function of administrator of ecclesiastical goods.

The law repeatedly refers to the capacity of the administrator of ecclesiastical property as a *munus*.[105] Thus in determining the limits within which the excommunicated may perform this authorized ecclesiastical act, those sections of the law which deal with *munera* must be referred to. Those excommunicated persons who are already in possession of this office must be distinguished from those who seek to obtain it. Those who already possess the office shall be considered first.

All excommunicated persons, no matter of what category, exercise this function illicitly.[106] The law goes on to point out that the *vitandi* exercise their office invalidly. This results from the fact

[102] Canon 1520.

[103] Canon 1521: ". . . ordinarius loci . . . assumat viros providos, idoneos et boni testimonii, . . ."

[104] Cf. Hyland, *op. cit.*, p. 127.

[105] Canon 2256, n. 2; canon 1520, § 1; canon 1522.

[106] Canon 2263.

that once sentence has been rendered they lose the office itself. Thus, any exercise of an office which one has lost must be invalid.[107]

As the analysis of the effects of excommunication upon the performance of authorized ecclesiastical acts will reveal, the law generally equates the positions, on the one hand, of the *vitandi* as such, and, on the other hand, of the *tolerati* upon a declaratory or condemnatory sentence. The foregoing prescription, then, is in the line of an exception to the general trend, for it points only to the invalidity of the acts placed by the *vitandi*.

Consideration must now be given to the problem of the obtaining of the *munus* of administrator of ecclesiastical property. Once again the general principle states that no excommunicated person can licitly obtain this position.[108] In addition, the *vitandi* and the *tolerati post sententiam* cannot do so validly.[109] It may be noted here that the general qualifications demanded by canons 1520 and 1521 for administrators of church property are hardly consistent with the notion of an excommunicated person.

B. JUDICIAL PROCEDURE

The next twelve authorized ecclesiastical acts as listed in canon 2256, n. 2, are concerned in some way with judicial procedure. The office of the chancellor may be excluded from this category, but, since the same general rules apply to it, it will be considered along with that of the judge, the auditor, the referee, the defender of the bond, the promoter of justice, the promoter of the faith, the notary, the messenger, the apparitor, the advocate and the procurator.

The judge, the auditor and the referee each has an office in the strict sense of the term,[110] which as a function corresponds to the law's definition of an office as a position established in a fixed manner, either by divine or by ecclesiastical law, conferred in accord with the norms of the sacred canons, and entailing some participation

107 ". . . vitandus . . . manet privatus . . . ipsamet dignitate, officio, beneficio, pensione, munere."—Canon 2266.

108 Canon 2265, § 1, n. 2.

109 Canon 2265, § 2.

110 Hyland, *op. cit.*, p. 129; Roberti, *De Delictis et Poenis*, I, n. 328, p. 387.

in ecclesiastical power, whether of orders or of jurisdiction.[111] The other authorized ecclesiastical acts which are dealt with in this section reflect offices at least in the wide sense, that is, functions legitimately carried out for a spiritual purpose.[112] In view of this basic distinction, these two classes of authorized ecclesiastical acts call for a separate treatment in the consideration to be given to the strict and the wide interpretations.

(1) *Strict Interpretation*

In those sections of the Code which deal with the offices of the judge (*officialis*), the auditor, and the referee (*relator*) certain qualifications for these positions are set down. The judge is to be a priest of irreproachable reputation, a doctor of canon law or a person at least well versed in this science. He is to be at least thirty years of age.[113] The deputy judge is to be a priest of good character and an expert in canon law.[114] The auditor should possess the same qualities since he is to be selected from among the deputy judges.[115] The referee (*relator*) should likewise be thus qualified.[116] While the canons make no specific reference to the exclusion of the excommunicated, the provisions of canon 1628, § 3, must also be kept in mind. This canon refers to the exception that may be raised against an excommunicated judge at any period or stage of the trial, provided this be done before the final sentence. The *vitandi* as such and the *tolerati* upon a condemnatory or a declaratory sentence must always be excluded *ex officio*.

The remaining authorized ecclesiastical acts connected in some way with judicial procedure likewise presuppose in their agents certain qualifications. The promoter of justice and the defender of the bond are to be priests of good reputation, doctors or at least experts

[111] Canon 145, § 1.

[112] Canon 145, § 1; Roberti, *De Processibus,* I, n. 338, p. 402; Heylen, *op. cit.,* p. 86; Berutti, *op. cit.,* VI, n. 63, p. 177.

[113] Canon 1573, § 4.

[114] Canon 1574, § 1.

[115] Canon 1581.

[116] Canon 1584.

in canon law, men of prudence and of zeal for justice.[117] The *cursor* or messenger and the *apparitor* or constable are to be men, usually laymen, of good life and of a character beyond all suspicion.[118] The chancellor and the notary are to be priests of good life and men who rise above all suspicion.[119] Advocates and procurators are to be Catholics of good reputation and at least 21 years of age. The advocate must likewise be a doctor of canon law or at least an expert in it.[120]

Once again no specific reference to the excommunicated is noted. The provisions of canon 1628, § 3, regarding the possible raising of the exception of excommunication is to be noted, however.

Thus in rigorously adhering to the strict view, one has thus consulted the canons which treat of the individual authorized ecclesiastical acts. In these canons one has found nothing that specifically forbids excommunicated persons to act. One has noted only certain provisions dealing with the possible exception of excommunication that can be raised. These provisions effectively remove the *vitandus* and the *toleratus post sententiam* from the performance of these actions. Other excommunicated persons may be objected to at any stage of the proceedings short of the final sentence.

It seems that the canons stating the necessary qualifications for the incumbents of the positions in question may perhaps indirectly prohibit the excommunicated from so acting. They do not, however, do so directly.

(2) *Wide Interpretation*

The judge, the auditor, and the referee possess offices in the strict sense of the term and exercise jurisdiction.[121]

Once again the distinction must be made between those who already possess these offices and those who seek to obtain them. First, those who are in possession of one of these offices will be considered. No excommunicated person can licitly carry out such an office.

[117] Canon 1589, § 1.

[118] Canons 1592 and 373, § 4.

[119] Canon 373, § 4.

[120] Canon 1657, § 1, § 2.

[121] Hyland, *op. cit.*, p. 129; Roberti, *De Delictis et Poenis*, I, n. 328, p. 387.

This is true not only because of the provisions of canon 2263,[122] which forbids them to exercise an ecclesiastical office, but also in virtue of canon 2264, which states that acts of jurisdiction placed by them are illicit.[123] The exercise of these offices is invalid when performed by a *vitandus* or by a *toleratus* upon a condemnatory or declaratory sentence. This is clear from the provisions of canon 2264: "...; *et, si lata fuerit sententia condemnatoria vel declaratoria, etiam invalidus,* . . ." Canon 2266 strengthens this position when it specifies that a *vitandus* is deprived of the office itself.[124] Thus any exercise of it is invalid.

The general statement of the wide interpretation regarding these offices must be modified by the provision of canon 2264, which permits the *toleratus* upon whom a sentence has not been inflicted to perform these authorized ecclesiastical acts licitly should his services be sought.[125] This is an important provision of law, because it is clear that these officers are always requested by the faithful to exercise their office.[126]

An excommunicated person cannot licitly obtain the office of judge, of auditor or of referee. This is based on the provision of canon 2265,

122 ". . . prohibetur ecclesiasticis officiis seu muneribus fungi, . . ."—Canon 2263.

123 "Actus iurisdictionis tam fori externi quam fori interni positus ab excommunicato est illicitus; . . ."—Canon 2264; cf. Roberti, *De Delictis et Poenis,* n. 339, p. 403.

124 "Post sententiam condemnatoriam vel declaratoriam excommunicatus manet privatus fructibus dignitatis, officii, beneficii, pensionis, muneris, si quod habeat in Ecclesia; et vitandus ipsamet dignitate, officio, beneficio, pensione, munere."—Canon 2266.

125 "Actus iurisdictionis tam fori externi quam fori interni positus ab excommunicato est illicitus; et si lata fuerit sententia condemnatoria vel declaratoria, etiam invalidus, salvo praescripto can. 2261, § 3; secus est validus, imo etiam licitus, si a fidelibus petitus sit ad normam mem. can. 2261, § 2." Cf. Jone, *Commentarium,* III, 470; Vermeersch-Creusen, *Epitome,* III, n. 466, p. 287; Regatillo-Zalba, *Theologia Moralis,* III, n. 1058, p. 926; Conte a Coronata, IV, n. 1777, p. 216; Cappello, *Summa Iuris Canonici,* III, n. 646, p. 536; Augustine, *A Commentary,* VIII, 189-190; Berutti, *Institutiones Iuris Canonici,* VI, n. 63, p. 176; Hyland, *op. cit.,* pp. 130; 147-148; Prümmer, *Manuale Iuris Canonici* (editio quarta et quinta, Friburgi: Herder, 1927), p. 666.

126 Cf. Roberti, *De Processibus,* I, n. 178, p. 443.

§ 1, n. 2.[127] In addition, the *vitandus* and the *toleratus* upon a declaratory or a condemnatory sentence cannot do so even validly. Canon 2265, § 2, points this out clearly.[128]

Canon 1628, § 3, treats of the exception raised against excommunicates. Its provisions have been discussed in connection with the strict interpretation. This law is understood as a confirmation of the principles outlined in the presentation of the wide interpretation, for it provides for the raising of the exception of excommunication at any stage of the trial before the final sentence. It clearly provides that the *vitandi* and the *tolerati post sententiam* must always be excluded *ex officio*.

No excommunicated person can licitly perform the functions of the defender of the bond, the promoter of justice or of the faith, the notary, the chancellor, the messenger, the constable, the advocate, or the procurator. The basic reason for this lies in the fact that these positions, while not being ecclesiastical offices in the strict sense, are *munera* or offices in the wide sense.[129] As such, their exercise is forbidden to the excommunicated.

Those who already are in possession of such a position are excluded from the licit exercise of it in consequence of the very ruling contained in canon 2263 itself.[130] Since these positions do not entail the use of the power of jurisdiction, there is some difficulty in determining just when their exercise is invalid. Certainly the *vitandus* cannot perform them validly, since he loses his very position as a result of his status.[132] There is no express provision which declares the action of a *toleratus post sententiam* invalid. It is clear, however, that this class of excommunicated persons must always be *ex officio* excluded from the judicial trial along with the *vitandus*.[133]

127 "Quilibet excommunicatus: 2°—Nequit consequi dignitates, officia, beneficia, pensiones ecclesiasticas aliudve munus in Ecclesia."

128 "Actus tamen positus contra praescriptum § 1, nn. 1, 2, non est nullus, nisi positus fuerit ab excommunicato vitando vel ab alio excommunicato post sententiam declaratoriam vel condemnatoriam."

129 Canon 145, § 1; Berutti, *op. cit.*, VI, n. 63, p. 177; Roberti, *De Delictis et Poenis*, I, n. 338, p. 402; Heylen, *De Censuris*, p. 85.

130 ". . . prohibetur ecclesiasticis officiis seu muneribus fungi. . . ."

132 Canon 2266.

133 Canon 1628, § 3.

No excommunicated person can licitly obtain one of these positions. This is the clear teaching of canon 2265, § 1, n. 2.[134] Further, the *vitandi* as such and the *tolerati* upon a condemnatory or a declaratory sentence do so invalidly. The second paragraph of canon 2265 points this out.[135]

C. SPONSOR AT BAPTISM AND CONFIRMATION

The exercise of the role of sponsor at baptism or also at confirmation is another authorized ecclesiastical act. The law regarding this position is identical for both sacraments in what is of interest here, and accordingly they are treated as a unit. What is said of the generic "sponsor" applies equally to the exercise of this action at the administration of either sacrament.

(1) *Strict Interpretation*

Canon 765 lists the qualifications and conditions necessary before one can validly be admitted to the authorized ecclesiastical act of being a sponsor at the recepton of baptism. Canon 795 is its counterpart as regards sponsorship at confirmation. There can be no doubt that these canons deal with and contemplate the valid exercise of this act. The introductory words of the canons make this clear: *"Ut quis sit patrinus, oportet*: . . ."[136] Further, the following canon in each section clearly refers to those things which are necessary for the licit performance of this function. *"Ut autem quis licite patrinus admittatur, oportet: . . ."*[137]

Canons 765 and 795 point out that this authorized ecclesiastical act is performed invalidly by any excommunicated person who is a *vitandus* as such or a *toleratus* upon a condemnatory or a de-

[134] "Quilibet excommunicatus: 2°—Nequit consequi dignitates, officia, beneficia, pensiones ecclesiasticas aliudve munus in Ecclesia; . . ."

[135] "Actus tamen positus contra praescriptum § 1, nn. 1, 2, non est nullus, nisi positus fuerit ab excommunicato vitando vel ab alio excommunicato post sententiam declaratoriam vel condemnatoriam; . . ."

[136] Canons 765; 795.

[137] Canons 766 and 796; cf. Kearney, *Sponsors at Baptism,* p. 76. All commentators seem most readily to agree on this.

claratory sentence.[138] Those who are excommunicated in consequence of a notorious delict cannot licitly be admitted to the performance of this act.[139]

These canons make it clear that the *vitandus* as such and the *toleratus* whose excommunication is notorious at law (*de iure*) cannot be admitted validly to the performance of these authorized ecclesiastical acts. The *toleratus* whose excommunication is notorious in fact alone (*de facto*) is admitted illicitly. By implication, the *toleratus simpliciter*, that is, the person whose excommunication is the result of an occult delict, can be admitted to the role of sponsor at both baptism and confirmation. The strict interpretation thus provides for licit action on the part of one class of the excommunicated.[140]

(2) *Wide Interpretation*

The position of sponsor at baptism and confirmation is repeatedly referred to by the Code as a *munus*.[141] It is an ecclesiastical office in the wide sense.[142]

Thus, by way of general rule, every excommunicated person carries out this authorized ecclesiastical act illicitly. This prohibition follows from the text of canon 2263, which forbids the excommunicated to exercise any ecclesiastical office in the wide or the strict sense of the term.[143]

The inability of the *vitandus* to perform this function validly is illustrated through the provisions of canon 2265, § 2, which point to the fact that he cannot even qualify for the act of sponsorship.

138 Canon 795, n. 2; "Ad nullum pertineat haereticam aut schismaticam sectam, nec sententia condemnatoria vel declaratoria sit excommunicatus. . . ."—Canon 765, n. 2.

139 "Ut autem quis licite patrinus admittatur, oportet: Non sit propter notorium delictum excommunicatus . . ., quin tamen sententia intercesserit . . ."—Canon 766, n. 2. Cf. canon 796, n. 3.

140 Cf. Cerato, *Censurae Vigentes*, n. 36, pp. 46-47; Conte a Coronata, IV, n. 1771, p. 207.

141 Canons 2256, n. 2; 765, n. 1; 766; 769; 795, n. 1; 796.

142 "Officium ecclesiasticum lato sensu est quodlibet munus quod in spiritualem finem legitime exercetur";—Canon 145, § 1.

143 "Prohibetur ecclesiasticis officiis seu muneribus fungi, . . ."

Joined with him in this incapacity is the *toleratus post sententiam*. Thus any sponsorship by a person of either of these groups is invalid.[144] Canons 765, n. 2, and 795, n. 2, which have been discussed above, confirm this view in no uncertain terms.

In spite of the above-mentioned provisions of law, it seems one must acknowledge the exception provided in canons 766 n. 2, and 796, n. 3, in favor of the *simpliciter tolerati*. There is at least a tacit support in these canons for their lawful admission to sponsorship. Thus it seems that the *simpliciter tolerati* may be licitly admitted to the performance of this authorized ecclesiastical act.

D. VOTE IN ECCLESIASTICAL ELECTIONS

The act of voting in an ecclesiastical election is an authorized ecclesiastical act.[145] The law protects this very important function by means of a series of regulations and disqualifications. It is a pertinent matter of interest here to determine to what extent excommunicated persons are to be removed from the enjoyment of this right or excluded from its exercise.

The Code of Canon Law deals with elections in canons 160-182. These canons deal primarily with elections to ecclesiastical offices in the strict sense. This is clear when it is noted that Title IV of Book II of the Code treats of offices in the strict sense, and of election as one of the means of filling these offices. Provision is made, however, in other parts of the Code for the application of these norms to other elections as well.[146] Thus ecclesiastical elections in their great majority fall under these provisions. It is clear, however, that the election of the Roman Pontiff is governed exclusively by the Constitution of Pope Pius XII, *Vacantis Apostolicae Sedis*, of December 25, 1945.[147] This Constitution supersedes the Constitution of Pope St. Pius X, *Vacante Sede Apostolica*, of December

144 Canon 2265, § 2.

145 Canon 2256, n. 2.

146 Cf. canons 507, § 1; 697, 2; Mock, *Disqualification of Electors in Ecclesiastical Elections*, p. 75.

147 *AAS*, XXXVIII (1946), 65-99.

25, 1904,[148] and also the amendments made by Pope Pius XI in his *motu proprio Cum proxime,* of March 1, 1922.[149]

(1) *Strict Interpretation*

Any person who is excommunicated upon a condemnatory or a declaratory sentence cannot vote validly in an ecclesiastical election. This is true, since canon 167 states that persons under censure after a sentence cannot cast a vote.[150] Excommunication is most certainly a censure.[151] That a vote cast in defiance of this prohibition is invalid is equally certain from the words of canon 167, § 2: *"Si quis ex praedictis admittatur, eius suffragium est nullum. . . ."* This is verified by canon 2265, § 1, n. 1, and § 2. Every excommunicated person is forbidden to make use of the right of election.[152] A vote cast contrary to this prescription is invalid when cast by a *vitandus* as such or by a *toleratus post sententiam.*[153]

The strict interpretation also holds that no excommunicated person may licitly perform this particular authorized ecclesiastical act. This is clear from the wording of canon 2265, § 1, n. 1, referred to above: *"Quilibet excommunicatus: 1°—Prohibetur iure eligendi. . . ."*

Thus, a strict interpretation of the phrase of canon 2263 in question excludes all excommunicated persons from casting a vote in an ecclesiastical election.

(2) *Wide Interpretation*

Once again the wide interpretation states that no excommunicated person may licitly carry out this authorized ecclesiastical act. This results from the prohibition of canon 2265, § 1, n. 1. The *vitandus* as such and the *toleratus post sententiam* do so invalidly in the light

[148] *Fontes,* n. 633; cf. *Codex Iuris Canonici,* Docum. I.

[149] *AAS,* XIV (1922), 145.

[150] "Nequeunt suffragium ferre: 3°—Censura vel infamia iuris affecti, post sententiam tamen declaratoriam vel condemnatoriam";—Canon 167, § 1, n. 3.

[151] Canon 2255, § 1.

[152] Canon 2265, § 1, n. 1.

[153] Canon 2265, § 2.

of the regulations enacted in canon 167, § 1, n. 3, § 2, and canon 2265, § 2.

It is to be noted that, even when a *vitandus* or a *toleratus post sententiam* casts his ballot invalidly, the election itself is not thereby rendered invalid. Such an election would be null only when it was certain that the person elected would not have received the required number of votes without such ballots, or when such a vote was cast by a *vitandus* or by a *toleratus post sententiam* who was known to be such and yet was admitted in spite of this.[154]

It is interesting to note that in this instance the strict and wide interpretations reach the same results in practice. Both recognize the same class of excommunicates as acting invalidly when the strict view joins the wide in forbidding the performance of this authorized ecclesiastical act to all other excommunicates.

E. THE RIGHT OF PATRONAGE

The exercise of the right of patronage is an authorized ecclesiastical act.[155] The Code defines this right as a group of privileges, accompanied with certain obligations, which through the concession of the Church belong to the Catholic founders of a church, a chapel or a benefice, or to those whose title derives from the founder.[156] The principal privilege inherent in the right of patronage is that of presentation.[157] It is with the exercise of this privilege that this study is primarily concerned.

(1) *Strict Interpretation*

The strict interpretation of canon 2263 indicates that the *vitandi* as such and the *tolerati post sententiam* cannot validly exercise the right of patronage. This position is based on the words of canon 1470, § 4: "Censura aut infamia iuris innodati post sententiam condemnatoriam vel declaratoriam, usque dum censura vel infamia perdurant, nequeunt ius patronatus exercere eiusque privilegiis uti."

[154] Canon 167, § 2.
[155] Canon 2256, n. 2.
[156] Canon 1448.
[157] Canon 1455, n. 1.

The excommunicated are of course to be numbered among the censured.[158]

Canon 1453, § 1, further points out that a personal right of patronage cannot be validly passed on to a *vitandus* or *toleratus post sententiam*.[159] Should a thing to which a real right of patronage is attached come into their possession, the right of patronage is suspended.[160]

Other excommunicated persons are not restricted from the performance of this authorized ecclesiastical act.

(2) *Wide Interpretation*

No excommunicated person can licitly exercise the right of patronage. This follows from the fact that every excommunicated person is generally forbidden to enjoy privileges previously granted to him by the Church.[161] In particular, he is forbidden to exercise the right of presentation.[162]

Those persons who are excommunicated as *vitandi* or as *tolerati post sententiam* cannot perform this authorized ecclesiastical act validly. This is clear from canon 2265, § 2, and seems to be confirmed by the provisions of canon 1470, § 4, referred to above.

The above-mentioned prescriptions of canon 1453, § 1, and of canon 1453, § 3, are also to be noted.

Section 5. Conclusions

The first principle to be observed in the interpretation of ecclesiastical laws is that these laws are to be understood according to the proper meaning of their words considered both in their text and context.[163] Thus as Schmidt points out:

158 Canon 2255, § 1, n. 1.

159 "Ius patronus personale transmitti valide nequit ad . . ., nec ad quoslibet excommunicatos post sententiam declaratoriam vel condemnatoriam."

160 Canon 1453, § 3.

161 Canon 2263.

162 Canon 2265, § 1, n. 1.

163 "Leges ecclesiasticae intelligendae sunt secundum propriam verborum significationem in textu et contextu consideratam; . . ."—Canon 18.

> The text and context together conspire to convey the proper meaning of the words and consequently, the intention of their author, because ideas are not shackled by words, but rather words are to be subservient to thought. Thus the result of the examination of the context—which process takes precedence over any of those to be described in the remainder of canon 18—may be the immediate revelation of the mind of the legislator as contained in the law under investigation. The law is thus clear and "in se certa." [164]

The correct interpretation of the phrase *"intra fines suis in locis iure definitos"* can be obtained by means of this first principle. The law simply means that an excommunicated person is generically to be removed from the performance of authorized ecclesiastical acts. This removal is to be governed by the limits defined by the law in those places in the Code which are pertinent and have reference to the matter at hand. These passages will determine more specifically the quality of the removal prescribed by canon 2264. In some cases this will refer merely to the unlawfulness of an authorized ecclesiastical act when performed in opposition to the rule stated in this canon. In others it will declare the performance of the act to be invalid. The term *"removetur"* is a general one. Its exact meaning is determined in each particular case through the application of the pertinent principles of law. The wider interpretation seems, in the writer's opinion, to be the correct one.

The provisions for the interpretation of the law as provided in canons 19 and 2219 do not conflict with this conclusion. A law is strictly interpreted in the sense of canon 19 when in explaining the sense of the law, one indeed employs the proper meaning of the words, but in so far as it is possible within this framework embraces or comprehends a smaller number of cases or subjects within the law. The interpretation is wide when the words of the law, while retaining their proper meaning, are used in an extensive sense in

164 *The Principles of Authentic Interpretation in Canon 17 of the Code of Canon Law,* The Catholic University of America Canon Law Studies, n. 141 (Washington, D. C.: The Catholic University of America Press, 1941), p. 133.

so far as this is possible, so that the words extend to or comprehend a larger number of cases or subjects.[165]

The important thing to be remembered here is that first and foremost the proper meaning of the words is to be retained. It is only when more than one meaning is proper to the words themselves that these variant interpretations come into play.[166] The rule of canon 19 is supplementary and subordinate to the general rules of interpretation and in no way derogates from them.[167] It is to be used as an aid in the interpretation of a particular species of law. When the meaning of the words of these laws is certain from text and context, this canon has nothing to add to the interpretation.[168]

The principle enunciated in canon 2219 does not have immediate pertinence in this discussion. It is properly concerned with a penalty in an individual case in which there may be some doubt either of law or fact.[169]

By way of summary it may be stated that the phrase in question has been understood in two ways. One of these has been described as a strict interpretation, the other as a wide interpretation. There exist certain principles of law which seem to favor the latter of these interpretations, and accordingly the writer supports the wide interpretation. He does so, first of all, because he believes that it reflects the clear meaning of the words in their text and context, and secondly, because a comparison of the results of the application of these interpretations in practice reveals that the wide interpretation is more in conformity with the nature and effects of the censure of excommunication.

[165] Cf. Jone, *Commentarium,* I, 38; Conte a Coronata, I, n. 25, p. 40.

[166] "Numquam quidem lex ita late sumi potest ut ultra sensum proprium sive usualem sive iuridicum verborum extendatur; nec strictius quam fert iustitia legis et proprietas verborum, una cum legis ratione, quae etiam conservanda est. Sed quando, salva verborum proprietate, verba duplici usu sumi possunt, amplior usus latam, restrictus usus strictam interpretationem efficit."—Vermeersch-Creusen, *Epitome,* I, 118-119; Jone, *op. cit.,* III, 420.

[167] Cf. Schmidt, *op. cit.,* p. 123, footnote 18.

[168] Cf. Beste, *Introductio in Codicem,* p. 86; Abbo-Hannan, *The Sacred Canons,* II, 802; Ayrinhac-Lydon, *Penal Legislation,* p. 29; Regatillo-Zalba, *Theologia Moralis,* III, n. 1027, p. 896.

[169] Cf. Woywod, *A Practical Commentary,* II, n. 2054, p. 415; Abbo-Hannan, *op. cit.,* II, p. 802; Regatillo-Zalba, *op. cit.,* III, n. 1027, p. 896.

Certain other canonical principles must also be considered in this question, principles which are not consonant with the so called strict view.

An ecclesiastical office cannot be validly obtained without canonical appointment.[170] By the term, canonical appointment, is meant the granting of an ecclesiastical office by the competent ecclesiastical authority in accordance with the sacred canons.[171] Thus there are three conditions which are required for the valid appointment to an ecclesiastical office:

> (1) The granting or conferring of the office;
> (2) The granting by the competent ecclesiastical authority;
> (3) The observance of the norms of the general law or duly approved particular law involved. The nature of these laws must be carefully considered, since some concern the validity of the appointment, others only its lawfulness.[172]

The person to be promoted to a vacant office[173] must be a cleric and possess all the qualities that are required for that office by the universal or the particular law, or by the law of its foundation,[174] When the one appointed does not possess the required qualifications, the appointment is invalid if this effect is predicated in the universal or the particular law, or in the law of the foundation; otherwise the appointment is valid, but it is rescinded through the sentence of the legitimate superior.[175]

The fitness of candidates is established by way of both positive and negative qualifications as required in those who aspire to ecclesiastical offices.[176] Negative qualities involve immunity from penal disability such as that spoken of in canons 2298, n. 5; 2345; 2346;

170 Canon 147, § 1.

171 Canon 147, § 2.

172 Abbo-Hannan, *op. cit.*, I, 211.

173 "In iure officium ecclesiasticum accipitur stricto sensu, nisi aliud ex contextu sermonis appareat."—Canon 145, § 2.

174 Canon 153, § 1.

175 Canon 153, § 3.

176 Abbo-Hannan, *op. cit.*, I, 213.

2390; 2394. Immunity from certain censures which entail a juridic incapacity also comes under negative qualities. Thus, the excommunicated are included under certain conditions[177] as are those who are under personal interdict[178] and suspension.[179]

The positive qualities which indicate fitness for the ecclesiastical office involved include the clerical state and, in some cases, the order of priesthood;[180] a definite age when fixed by law;[181] irreproachable morals and a good reputation;[182] the knowledge postulated for the office.[183]

It is evident that in line with these principles the excommunicated are not fit candidates for the offices in question. In addition to the foregoing argumentation it hardly seems probable that one who is excommunicated meets the qualifications specified by law in regard to those authorized ecclesiastical acts the performance of which reflects an office in the strict sense. Certainly the excommunicated person is not "*integrae famae,*"[184] or "*probatae vitae.*"[185] It seems also that, since similar qualifications are required for those authorized ecclesiastical acts the performance of which reflects an ecclesiastical office in simply the wide sense of the term,[186] these principles may be applied to them as well.[187]

It is true that none of the qualifications referred to involves the invalid appointment of the office or position in question in itself; nevertheless it hardly seems tenable that the excommunicated can

[177] Cf. canon 2265.

[178] Cf. canon 2275, n. 3.

[179] Cf. canon 2283.

[180] Cf. canon 154.

[181] Cf. canons 320, § 2; 367, § 1; 331, § 1, n. 4; 399, § 1; 559, §§ 1 and 2.

[182] Cf. canons 232, § 2, n. 1; 331, § 1, n. 4.

[183] Cf. canons 331, § 1, n. 5; 367, § 1; 399, § 1; 434, § 2; 1573, § 4; 1598, § 2; 2017; 2018.

[184] As demanded by canon 1573, § 4, in the case of the *officialis* and *vice officialis*.

[185] Cf. canon 1574, § 1.

[186] "Officium ecclesiasticum lato sensu est quodlibet munus quod in spiritualem finem legitime exercetur."—Canon 145, § 1.

[187] Cf., e.g., the qualifications demanded by the law in canons 1589, § 1; 1592; 373, § 4; 1657, §§ 1 and 2.

be licitly appointed even when the sole involvement is that of the censure itself. Thus the strict interpretation seems untenable in the matter of its practical application.

Article IV. The cessation of the exclusion from the performance of authorized ecclesiastical acts as the result of excommunication

The meaning and the extent of the exclusion from the performance of authorized ecclesiastical acts has been noted. The question that now arises looks to the time when and the manner in which these restrictions cease. When may one feel free to again perform authorized ecclesiastical acts validly and licitly?

A censure is a penalty by which a baptized person, as delinquent and contumacious, is deprived of certain spiritual goods, or of goods connected with spiritual ones, until upon receding from his contumacy he is absolved.[188] Since excommunication is a censure,[189] this law presents the key to the solution of the problem. The object of a censure is the deprivation of certain spiritual goods or of goods connected with spiritual goods. It is clear that these must be goods over which the Church has jurisdiction.[190] In this particular case these goods are the ones outlined in canons 2257-2267, 985, n. 7, and 2340. They flow from the exclusion from the communion of the faithful, and among them is the performance of authorized ecclesiastical acts along with other pertinent capacities already referred to. Since the deprivation of these goods comes about as a result of the censure of excommunication,[191] it is only reasonable that the deprivation of them ceases when the censure itself no longer exists. In other words, when one has been restored to the communion of the faithful, those rights which belong to him in virtue of this communion, but of which he was deprived when this bond was broken, are restored to him. How does this come about?

188 Canon 2241.

189 Canons 2255, § 1, n. 1, and 2257, § 1.

190 Abbo-Hannan, *The Sacred Canons,* II, 821; Roberti, *De Delictis et Poenis,* n. 280, p. 319; Jone, *Commentarium,* III, 465.

191 Canon 2257, § 1.

Canon 2241 points out that as the result of a censure a baptized person is deprived of certain goods *until upon receding from his contumacy he is absolved.*[192] Thus once the censured person has receded from his state of contumacy and has been absolved, these goods are restored. In the case of excommunication the good involved is really only one, that is, the total exclusion from the communion of the faithful. In this communion, however, many rights and privileges may be distinguished, and thus they constitute, as it were, several effects and deprivations.[193]

It has been noted that the law considers a person to be contumacious in different ways in line with the manner of infliction of the penalty in question. Thus when it is a question of a *ferendae sententiae* censure, the person is contumacious when he fails to give up his crime or refuses to do penance and make the proper amends for the injury and scandal caused by it. In the case of a *latae sententiae* censure, the person is contumacious when he simply transgresses the law or the precept to which the penalty is attached, unless he is excused by some legitimate reason. In these cases there is no need for a formal admonition, since the law itself in threatening the penalty to be *ipso facto* incurred contains an admonition.[194]

The manner in which a delinquent recedes from his contumacy must now be considered, the delinquent's recession is necessary in order that he may obtain absolution. Contumacy is said to be terminated when the delinquent person has truly repented of the delict he committed and at the same time has given adequate satisfaction for the injury and scandal caused, or has at least seriously promised to do so. It remains for the one from whom the absolution is sought to decide whether the repentence is sincere, the satisfaction adequate, and the promise sincerely made.[195]

Once the censured person has truly receded from his contumacy,

192 "Censura est poena qua homo baptizatus, delinquens et contumax, quibusdam bonis spiritualibus vel spiritualibus adnexis privatur, donec, a contumacia recedens, absolvatur."—Canon 2241.

193 Chelodi-Ciprotti, *De Delictis et Poenis,* n. 37, p. 48; Augustine, *A Commentary,* VIII, 175.

194 Canon 2242, § 2; Augustine, *op. cit.*, VIII, 118.

195 Canon 2242, § 3.

there is no place for the censure. He has a right to its removal.[196] This principle flows from the very nature of a censure in that its primary purpose is the amendment and reformation of the delinquent person.[197] Thus, once the party has receded from his contumacy, this purpose has been achieved, and the removal of the censure is to be granted.

The act by which the censure is terminated, and as a result of which the right to perform authorized ecclesiastical acts is restored, is absolution. Once a censure has been contracted it can be removed only within the legitimate framework of absolution.[198] The fifth book of the Code of Canon Law contains various regulations which concern the granting of this absolution. It is beyond the scope of this work to go into this matter here. The important thing to be noted here is this: the censure of excommunication is removed by way of the absolution for which the law provides. Oncc this absolution has been obtained by him, the erstwhile delinquent is restored to the communion of the faithful, with the result that no longer is he to be excluded from the performance of the authorized ecclesiastical acts with relation to which his earlier status of excommunication had erected a barrier or hindrance.

196 "Absolutio denegari nequit cum primum delinquens a contumacia recesserit ad normam can. 2242, § 3; . . ."—Canon 2248, § 2.

197 Abbo-Hannan, *op. cit.*, II, 815-816, p. 850; Roberti, *De Delictis et Poenis*, n. 279, p. 318, and n. 280; Augustine, *op. cit.*, VIII, 114; Vermeersch-Creusen, *Epitome*, III, n. 436, p. 262; Regatillo-Zalba, *Theologia Moralis*, III, n. 1041, p. 908.

198 Canon 2248, § 1.

CHAPTER III

The Incapacity for the Performance of Authorized Ecclesiastical Acts on the Part of the Infamous At Law

Article I. introductory notions concerning infamy of law

Section 1. The Notion of Infamy of Law

The good name, honor and reputation of a man are among his most prized possessions. Each man has a strict right to enjoy his good name among his fellows until such time as by his own actions he has forfeited it. This lack of honor, reputation and good name is known as infamy, and is referred to as infamy of law or of fact in line with the proximate cause from which it is derived. Should this loss of reputation exist in the minds of prudent men simply because of one's misdeeds, it is called infamy of fact. Infamy of law is present when one has lost his good name or reputation legally, either upon the perpetration of some deed the law considers defaming, or in consequence of the determination inherent in a judicial sentence.[1]

Infamy of Law is listed in canon 2291, n. 4, as one of the common vindictive penalties inflicted by the Church. A penalty is a deprivation of some good inflicted by legitimate authority on the delinquent for his correction and in punishment of the offense.[2] It is vindictive when it tends directly toward the expiation of the offense so that its remission does not depend on the cessation of the delinquent's contumacy.[3]

As was noted in the previous chapter, excommunication is a species of censure. Its principal purpose is the correction of the delinquent. Infamy of law differs from it in that it is a vindictive penalty and thus has as its chief purpose, not the correction of the delinquent, but the punishment of the offense. It is for this reason

[1] Cf. canon 2293, §§ 1-3.

[2] Canon 2215.

[3] Canon 2286.

that the repentance and the receding from contumacy on the part of the delinquent do not necessitate the remission of a vindictive penalty.

The fact that infamy of law is a penalty means that before it can be inflicted on a person he must be guilty of a delict, that is, an external and morally imputable violation of a law to which a canonical sanction, at least an indeterminate one, is attached.[4]

Section 2. The Source of Infamy of Law

It is clear that at the present time infamy of law arises only from those cases in which the law of the Code makes specific mention of it.[5] This penalty can exist either as a *latae sententiae* or as a *ferendae sententiae* punishment.

There is general agreement that the delinquent in the following cases is subject to *latae sententiae* infamy of law: [6]

> (1) All apostates from the Christian faith and each and every heretic or schismatic incur infamy of law if they have joined a non-Catholic sect or have publicly adhered to it.[7]
>
> (2) Anyone who desecrates the Sacred Species by throwing them away, or who carries them off or retains them for an evil purpose; [8]
>
> (3) One who violates the bodies or graves of the dead for the purpose of theft or for some other evil aim; [9]
>
> (4) Those who lay violent hands on the person of the Roman Pontiff, of a cardinal, or of a legate of the Holy See; [10]

[4] Canon 2195, § 1.

[5] Canon 2293, 2; Gasparri, *Tractatus Canonicus de Sacra Ordinatione* (2 vols., Vol. I, Parisiis, Lugduni, 1893) I, n. 289, p. 187.

[6] Cf. Augustine, *A Commentary,* VIII, 246; Conte a Coronata, IV, n. 826, p. 273, footnote 2; Ayrinhac-Lydon, *Penal Legislation,* p. 121; Berutti, *Institutiones,* VI, n. 87, p. 219; Prummer, *Manuale Iuris Canonici,* pp. 666-667; Cerato, *Censurae Vigentes,* n. 143, p. 217; Tatarczuk, *Infamy of Law,* pp. 38-65; Christ, *Dispensation from Vindicative Penalties,* The Catholic University of America Canon Law Studies, n. 174 (Washington, D. C.: The Catholic University of America Press, 1943), pp. 159-160.

[7] Canon 2314, § 1, n. 3.

[8] Canon 2320.

[9] Canon 2328.

[10] Canon 2343, § 1, n. 2, § 2, n. 2.

(5) The principals and their seconds in a duel; [11]

(6) Bigamists, that is, those who attempt marriage, even only civilly, while a previous bond of marriage impedes this attempt; [12]

(7) Lay persons who by law have become convicted of committing crimes against the sixth commandment with minors below the age of sixteen, or of committing rape, sodomy, incest, or pandering; [13]

Canon 2358 mentions that clerics in minor orders who are condemned for the crimes mentioned above also incur *ipso facto* legal infamy.

It is clear that the following are subject to a *ferendae sententiae* infamy of law:

(1) All apostates from the Christian faith and each and every heretic or schismatic who have been admonished but do not repent; [14] If they have joined or publicly adhered to a non-Catholic sect they fall victim to the *latae sententiae* penalty as noted above.

(2) Those who are suspect of heresy and who have been punished with the prohibition to exercise authorized ecclesiastical acts and with suspension *a divinis*, if they be clerics, but who still do not amend within six months of the imposition of these penalties are considered as heretics and liable to the penalties for heresy, one of which is the *ferendae sententiae* infamy of law.[15]

(3) Clerics in sacred orders, be they seculars or religious, who commit a crime against the sixth commandment with minors under sixteen years of age, or who are guilty of adultery, rape, bestiality, sodomy, pandering, or incest with blood relatives or relations by marriage in the first degree.[16]

[11] Canon 2351, § 2.

[12] Canon 2356.

[13] Canon 2357, § 1.

[14] Canon 2314, § 1, n. 2.

[15] Canons 2315 and 2314, § 1, n. 2.

[16] Canon 2359, § 2.

Section 3. The Effects of Infamy of Law

One who has incurred infamy of law is subject to certain incapacities and impediments which flow as effects from this penalty.[17] In the first place, such a one suffers an irregularity *ex defectu* regarding the reception of holy orders.[18]

An irregularity is a perpetual disqualification with the effect of directly and primarily forbidding the receiving of ecclesiastical orders and, as a further effect of this, the exercise of the orders already received. It is established by way of positive law in view of the reverence due the divine ministry.[19] Irregularities may arise from some defect in the candidate or from some crime he has committed. The former are designated as arising *ex defectu,* and the latter as arising *ex delicto.*

The infamous at law are furthermore incapable of obtaining ecclesiastical benefices, pensions, offices, and dignities; they likewise are barred from exercising any ecclesiastical right or function. They are to be forbidden to exercise the sacred functions of the ministry. They are also incapable of performing authorized ecclesiastical acts.

The seriousness of this penalty of infamy of law is evident from its grave consequences. While not impeding the bond of communion with the Church or the use of its sacramental and spiritual aids, it completely deprives one of the opportunity of obtaining and exercising practically all ecclesiastical rights and offices.

Article II. Historical Development of the Incapacity for the Performance of Authorized Ecclesiastical Acts on the Part of the Infamous at Law

Section 1. Origin In Roman Law

Although it is certain that the notion of legal infamy as found in ecclesiastical law was borrowed from Roman jurisprudence [20]

17 Cf. canon 2294, § 1.

18 Canon 984, n. 5.

19 Abbo-Hannan, *The Sacred Canons,* II, 119.

20 Tatarczuk, *Infamy of Law,* p. 13.

a survey of modern scholarship regarding the origin of this concept in the Roman law itself leads to the conclusion that its exact origin simply is not known.[21] Most of the authors are content to attach the earliest traces of the institute to the *intestabiles* mentioned in the *Twelve Tables*.[22] This group consisted of those persons who had indeed consented to give testimony but later refused to do so. In consequence of this refusal they became incapable of witnessing a will, and, at a later date, of even making one.[23] The connection between this group and the infamous is a rather remote one, however, and is based primarily on the fact that the prohibition of being a witness is found as an effect of infamy at a later date.[24]

A clearer indication of a condition similar to infamy of law is found in the status of those who suffered the *notatio* of the censor.[25] From a time as early as 443 B. C. a census was taken every five years.[26] It was the prerogative of the censor to place a mark or *nota* under the name of anyone whom he knew to be guilty of a serious misdeed, or to be carrying on a discreditable trade or practice. This right flowed from the duty of the censor to be the protector of the public morals. In this regard his *notatio* was a greatly feared sanction.

The chief effects of this mark were in the disqualifications of the party for action in the *comitia*, for enrollment in the army and for service to the state. It also involved various changes in one's state of life.[27]

It is only in the edicts of both the *praetor urbanus* and the *praetor peregrinus* that the first lists of defaming causes and the first concise

[21] Greenidge, *Infamia: Its Place in Roman Public and Private Law* (Oxford: Clarendon Press, 1894), p. 3.

[22] Buckland, *Manual of Roman Private Law* (London: Cambridge University Press, 1925), p. 53.

[23] Greenidge, *op. cit.*, pp. 168-169; D. (28. 1) 18; Inst. (2. 10) 6.

[24] Tatarczuk, *op. cit.*, p. 1.

[25] Buckland, *op. cit.*, p. 53; Leage, *Roman Private Law* (2. ed., by C. H. Ziegler, London: MacMillan and Co., 1930; reprinted in 1948), pp. 29-30.

[26] Roby, *Roman Private Law in the Times of Cicero and the Antonines* (2 vols., Vol. II, London: Cambridge University Press, 1902), II, App. D., CCLXXIV.

[27] Greenidge, *op. cit.*, pp. 109-110.

determination of infamy's effects are found.[28] But even here the term "infamy" was not used. Gaius (2nd century, A. D.), however, remarked that those whom the praetor placed under such disabilities were called infamous.[29]

These lists were later reorganized and stabilized under the Emperor Hadrian (117-138). The notion of infamy of law became a fixed one, so that any further expansion of its scope was the result of imperial decrees.[30]

As noted above, the principal effects of infamy under the censor were exclusion from the army, from public service, from the exercise of some public rights, and above all, from the office of judge.

Under the praetorian *edicta* the infamous were denied the *ius suffragii,* the *ius honorum,* and the *ius postulandi.* At one time the *ius connubii* was likewise withheld.[31] Thus one so restricted lost the right of voting, of holding office, as well as that of representing another in judicial matters. He could neither act as a procurator nor appoint one.[32] His right to marry a freeborn person was also restricted for a time.

In the course of time several of these restrictions lost their full significance in consequence of the change in the political structure of the state. The infamous continued to be restricted in judicial matters in that they could not bring accusation in a criminal court.[33] Further, they were capable of representing in court only those to whom they were bound by agnatic ties.[34] There were further disqualifications in reference to the making of wills.

[28] Leage, *op. cit.,* p. 150.

[29] Cf. Sohm, *The Institutes* (3. ed., Oxford: Clarendon Press, 1907), p. 183; Gaius, *Institutionum Iuris Civilis Commentarii Quattuor* (5. ed., 4 vols., Lipsiae: 1886), IV, 182, note 6.

[30] Tatarczuk, *op. cit.,* p. 6.

[31] Greenidge, *op. cit.,* pp. 155-156; Leage, *op. cit.,* pp. 75 and 130; Buckland, *Textbook of Roman Law from Augustus to Justinian* (2. ed., London: Cambridge University Press, 1932), pp. 9, 93, 96; Schulz, *Classical Roman Law* (Oxford: Clarendon Press, 1954), p. 45.

[32] Greenidge, *op. cit.,* pp. 158-160.

[33] It is not certain that this restriction was invoked precisely because of infamy.

[34] Buckland, *Textbook,* p. 91; Leage, *op. cit.,* p. 131; C. (3.28) 7; D. (4.3) 11.

Section 2. The Law in the Pseudo-Isidorian Decretals

In the pursuit of their general aims the Pseudo-Isidorian Decretals listed a number of crimes the perpetration of which brought infamy to the agent. In the vast majority of cases this penalty resulted *ipso facto* or as a *latae sententiae* stigma, that is, the penalty was incurred through the very fact that the law was violated.

A long list of those who were to be considered *ipso facto* infamous was provided in a letter attributed to Pope Stephen I (254-257).[35] This catalogue includes: those who abandon the norm of Christian law; those who condemn ecclesiastical statutes; thieves; those who have committed sacrilege; those who are ensnared in capital crimes; violaters of graves; those who have taken up arms against their fathers; those who have committed incest, homicide and perjury; those who are guilty of abduction, and many more. There were also many other instances wherein this penalty was meted out.[36]

The effects of infamy of law as delineated in the Pseudo-Isidorian Decretals were similar to the effects mentioned in Roman Law. For the most part they concerned judicial incapacities; only slight traces can be found of the inability to perform the acts now known as authorized ecclesiastical acts. The decretals are quite clear in denying the infamous all right to give testimony or to enter a judicial action or suit.[37]

The decretals were also explicit in making the infamous incapable of acting as procurator or advocate. *"Infamis persona, nec procurator*

[35] Pseudo-Stephanus, Ep. I and II, cap. 2—Hinschius, p. 182, Jaffé, n. +130.

[36] Pseudo-Callistus, Ep. II, cap. 16—Hinschius, p. 140. Jaffé, n. +86. Pseudo-Pius, I, Ep. II, cap. 4—Hinschius, p. 117, Jaffé, n. +43. Pseudo-Stephanus, Ep. II, cap. 12—Hinschius, p. 186, Jaffé, n. +131; Pseudo-Fabianus, Ep. II, cap. 21—Hinschius, p. 165, Jaffé, n. +93; Pseudo-Callistus, Ep. II, cap. 8—Hinschius, p. 138, Jaffé, n. +86; Pseudo-Alexander, Ep. I, cap. 5—Hinschius, p. 96, Jaffé, n. +24; Pseudo-Fabianus, Ep. II, cap. 18—Hinschius, p. 164, Jaffé, n. +93; Pseudo-Gaius, Ep. unica, cap. 4—Hinschius, p. 214, Jaffé, n. +157; Cor. Par. Sal. XXI—Hinschius, p. 762; Cor. Par. XLVIII—Hinschius, p. 766.

[37] Pseudo-Eusebius, Ep. III, cap. 18—Hinschius, p. 239, Jaffé, n. +165; Pseudo-Eutychianua, Ep. II, cap. 8—Hinschius, p. 211, Jaffé, n. +146; *Capitula Angilramni,* Cor. Par. XVIII—Hinschius, p. 762.

esse potest nec cognitor." [38] In this legislation are found few, if any, other explicit exclusions from authorized ecclesiastical acts as resulting directly from the incurring of infamy of law.

Section 3. The Law in the *Corpus Iuris Canonici*

A. THE DECREE OF GRATIAN

Gratian incorporated in his work a great many of the causes of infamy of law listed in the Pseudo-Isidore. He also added others to this number.

Gratian listed a number of crimes the commission of which rendered the culprit *ipso facto* infamous. Those who apostatized or who transgressed the commands of the Holy See suffered this penalty.[39] The act of conspiracy against one's bishop, whether committed by a layman or by a cleric, rendered the guilty one infamous.[40] Many other examples were listed.[41]

The study of Gratian, however, adds little in the search regarding the development of the effects of infamy of law in so far as they concerned what are now understood to be authorized ecclesiastical acts. It was clear, however, that the infamous were not able to function in the capacity of a judge. *"Infames, iudices esse non possunt."* [42] They were likewise unable to carry out the function of the procurator and advocate, at least in normal circumstances.[43]

[38] *Capitula Angilramni,* Par. IV—Hinschius, p. 759.

[39] Pseudo-Pius I, Ep. II, cap. 4—Hinschius, p. 117; Jaffé, n. +43; c. 3, C. III, q. 4.

[40] Ps. Stephanus I, Ep. II, cap. 12—Hinschius, p. 186, Jaffé, n. +131; c. 8, C. II, q. 7.

[41] Ps. Alexander I, Ep. I, cap. 5—Hinschius, p. 96, Jaffé, n. +24; c. 9, C. III, q. 4; c. 15, C. I, q. 3; II General Council of the Lateran (1139), c. 2—Mansi, XXI, col. 526; Innocent II (1130-1143), Ep. of March 29, 1139—Migne, *Patrologiae Cursus Completus, Series Latina* (221 vols., Parisiis, 1844-1855), CLXXIX, 415; Jaffé, n. 7960; c. 4, C. XXV, q. 6; Council of Troia (1093), c. 1—Mansi, XX, col. 790; c. 9, C. III, q. 5; Ps. Stephanus I, Ep. I and II, cap. 2—Hinschius, p. 182, Jaffé, n. +130; Ps. Eusebius, Ep. III, cap. 18—Hinschius, p. 239, Jaffé, n. +165; c. 17, C. VI, q. 1; c. 2, C. XXXV, q. 2; c. 9, C. III, q. 5.

[42] *Proemium* ad c. 1, C. III, q. 7; c. 2, C. III, q. 7.

[43] C. 2, C. III, q. 7.

"Infames non possunt esse procuratores, vel patroni causarum." [44] The fact that they were prevented from performing the closely allied tasks of accuser and witness in judicial processes was also pointed out.[45]

Thus one notes that the exclusions from authoried ecclesiastical acts were basically the same at the time of Gratian as in the days when they were dictated by the Roman Law. The process reflected a more definite statement and a closer application to ecclesiastical procedure rather than a startling development and expansion.

B. THE DECRETALS

The decretals added new reasons for the incurring of infamy, and effected a further development for others already mentioned in previous collections. Those who suffered excommunication either because they professed heresy or were an aid to heretics by sheltering or defending them were given a year in which to repent and make satisfaction. If they failed to do so they were *ipso facto* infamous.[46] All those Christians who returned to or were converted to Judaism became subject to the same penalty.[47] There were many other examples.[48]

The period of the decretals sheds considerable light upon the present study. There have been few important additions to the list of exclusions from authorized ecclesiastical acts from that time until the promulgation of the Code of Canon Law itself. Many of the prohibitions and exclusions listed in the previous legislation are likewise found in the decretals. Thus the infamous at law were prohibited from acting in the capacity of judge.[49] The offices of

[44] C. 1, 2, C. III, q. 7; *Capitula Angilramni,* Par. IV—Hinschius, p. 759.

[45] C. 18, C. II, q. 7; c. 7, C. XXII, q. 5.

[46] C. 13, X, *de haereticis,* V, 7; Mansi, XXII, 986.

[47] C. 13, *de haereticis,* V, 2, in VI°.

[48] C. 11, X, *de haereticis,* V, 7; c. 5, *de poenis,* V, 9, in VI°; c. un., *de poenis,* V, 7, in Extravag. Com.; c. 4, X, *de bigamis non ordinandis,* I, 21; c. 1, *de simonia,* V, 1, in Extravag. Ioan. XXII; c. 23, X, *de sententia et re iudicata,* II, 27; Potthast, *Regesta Pontificum Romanorum inde ab anno post Christum natum MCXCVIII ad annum MCCCIV* (2 vols., Berlin, 1874-1875), n. 4587.

[49] C. 54, X, *de testibus et attestationibus,* II, 20; c. 7, X, *de testibus cogendis*

procurator and advocate were likewise out of bounds for them.[50] This ruling was modified, however, by the glossator in his comment on Rule 87 of the *Regulae Juris in VI°*. Whereas this rule was general in nature: "*infamibus portae non pateant dignitatum, . . .*" the commentator defended the position that, whereas they could not act as judge, they could act as arbiter. "*. . . Infamis, licet non possit esse iudex: tamen (ut dictum est) potest esse arbiter, cum arbitrium non sit dignitas. . . .*"[51] This was also true regarding the position of procurator. "*. . . Idem in ministerio procuratoris, . . .*"[52] In fact, these positions were to be considered burdens rather than dignities. Such an interpretation, however, was not in accord with the general trend of the legislation as it has been witnessed.

The decretal law likewise called for the exclusion of the infamous at law from the position of judicial notary.[53] They were also deprived of the allied capacities of bringing accusation and of giving testimony, and they continued to be included among the *intestabiles*.[54]

It is during this period that one first comes across those regulations that forbade or invalidated the performance of authorized (or law-approved) acts, as discussed in the first chapter of this dissertation. Some of the texts discussed there have direct reference to the infamous.[55] It is the writer's purpose, then, to examine these texts in order to determine if possible just what the content of these law-approved acts was. It will be recalled that in the first chapter the general conclusion was reached that perhaps the former law simply did not make clear the content of this term. Further investigation lets one reach this conclusion once again. It is true that

vel non, II, 21; c. 1, X, *de exceptionibus*, II, 25; c. un., *de poenis*, XII, 12 in Extravag. Ioan. XXII; c. 5, *de poenis*, V, 9, in VI°.

[50] C. 5, *de poenis*, V, 9, in VI°.

[51] *Glossa ordinaria* ad Reg. 87, R.J., in VI°.

[52] *Glossa ordinaria* ad Reg. 87, R.J., in VI°.

[53] C. 5, *de poenis*, V, 9, in VI°.

[54] C. 5, *de poenis*, V, 9, in VI°.

[55] C. un., *de poenis*, XII, in Extravag. Ioan. XXII; c. 47, X, *de testibus et attestationibus*, II, 20; Council of Milan (1287), c. 18—Mansi, XXIV, 878; *glossa ordinaria* ad c. un., *de poenis*, XII, in Extravag. Ioan. XXII, s.v. *perpetuo sit infamis;* Paulus IV, const. *Cum secundum*, 16 dec. 1558, nn. 2, 3, 5—*Bull. Rom Taur.*, VI, 545; c. 5, *de poenis*, V, 9, in VI°.

at times the text seems to indicate penalties which deprive the guilty party of acting in various fields, and thus one is given some idea of the general category into which law-approved acts could be fitted. Thus the decretals of Boniface VIII pointed out that those who were guilty in any way of an attack on a cardinal were punished by being denied access to three distinct categories of actions or offices, namely, benefices, ecclesiastical offices and law-approved acts.[56] This indeed narrowed down the content of the term to some extent. A canon of the Council of Milan also pointed to a general division when it commanded bishops to let it be known that the infamous were to be repelled from ruling in the Church, and also from law-approved acts.[57] Thus two wide classifications were delineated.

When one tries to narrow down the concept of law-approved or authorized acts any more than these general classifications indicate, one receives little help from the texts themselves. The first impression garnered from a penal canon of the *Extravagantes* of John XXII is that the law-approved or authorized acts of the former law referred to judicial matters exclusively; closer study indicates, however, that added reference to other offices which stood in contradistinction cancels out this initial impression.[58]

This same comment may be made about the other pertinent texts, some giving a bit more indication of some real distinction than others.[59] Thus one must conclude that when the decretal law excluded the infamous from *actus legitimi*, one does not know exactly what specific acts were included within the content of this term.

Thus it is seen that the decretal law contributed to the search regarding exclusions from the performance of authorized ecclesiastical acts as a result of the incurring of infamy of law by making the previous legislation more distinct and by making greater use of, if not also introducing, the term *actus legitimi*.

[56] C. 5, *de poenis*, V, 9, in VI°.

[57] Council of Milan (1287), c. 18—Mansi, XXIV, 878.

[58] C. un., *de poenis*, XII, in Extravag. Ioan. XXII.

[59] Cf. c. 47, X, *de testibus et attestationibus*, II, 20; Paulus IV, const. *Cum secundum*, 16 dec. 1558, n. 2, 3, 5—*Bull. Rom. Taur.*, VI, 545; *glossa ordinaria* ad c. un., *de poenis*, XII, in Extravag. Ioan. XXII, s.v. *perpetuo sit infamis*.

Section 4. The Law From the Council of Trent to the Code of Canon Law

In general the cases of infamy of law remained identical in this period with the ones previously established. Nevertheless, a few extensions and restrictions obtained.

The Council of Trent added the crime of dueling to the list of crimes that *ipso facto* brought infamy of law in their wake. Those who engaged in the actual action as well as their seconds incurred excommunication, the confiscation of all their property, and perpetual infamy. Rulers who provided a place in their domain for this practice were likewise punished with excommunication.[60] This legislation, pre-Tridentine in its origin, was frequently repeated in laws enacted after the Council of Trent.[62]

The law of this period extended penalties previously established in that those who cooperated with the principal agent came frequently to be considered infamous along with him.[63] There were many other cases of infamy established by the law also.[64]

The effects of infamy of law regarding the inability to perform what are now known as authorized ecclesiastical acts remained unchanged for the most part in this period from the Council of Trent to the Code of Canon Law. These effects were given new force and clarification, however, by official pronouncements and approved commentary.

The primary note of interest for this study was the reiteration of the legislation that the infamous were to be excluded from all

60 Conc. Trident., sess. XXV, *de ref.*, c. 19.

62 Leo X, const. *Quam Deo,* 23 iul. 1519, § 3—*Fontes,* n. 75; Pius IV, const. *Ea quae a praedecessoribus,* 13 nov. 1560, § 4—*Fontes,* n. 101; Council of Avignon (1592), c. 40—Mansi, XXXIV, 1365.

63 Conc. Trident., sess. XXIV, *de ref. matrim.*, cap. 6; Pius V, const. *Infelicis,* 19 dec. 1569, § 7—*Bull. Rom. Taur.*, VII, 792.

64 Pius, V, const. *In earum rerum,* 19 maii 1569, n. 3—*Bull. Rom. Taur.*, VII, 753; Paul IV, const. *Cum secundum,* 16 dec. 1558, nn. 2, 3, 5—*Bull. Rom. Taur.*, VI, 545; Pius IV, const. *In elegendis,* 2 oct. 1562, n. 18—*Bull. Rom. Taur.*, VII, pars I, 234; Julius III, const. *In multis,* 1 febr. 1554, nn. 2, 3, 8—*Bull. Rom. Taur.*, VI, 478.

ecclesiastical dignities, honors and offices in general.[65] This exclusion, coupled with those already cited[66] as embracing law-approved acts, proved pivotal in the present study.[67]

Pope Paul IV (1555-1559) repeated the regulation that heretics contracted infamy.[68] In this regard they were excluded from several other authorized ecclesiastical acts. It is not easy to determine, however, that their inability to perform these acts was precisely the result of having incurred infamy of law. The text does not make this perfectly clear.

It is in this period from the Council of Trent to the Code of Canon Law that one encounters for the first time the notions of sponsorship at baptism and confirmation as falling within the concept of *actus legitimi.* From the earliest days of the Church it was understood that persons of good life and reputation should be selected for these positions because of the great duties and responsibilities which were assumed. Legislation on the point is found in the I Provincial Council of Milan in 1565. The Council warned parents to choose as sponsors those who by reason of their way of life would be capable of carrying out the role of spiritual father or mother to the new Christian.

> *Fideles in baptizandis filiis eos potius eligant compatres qui eorum animae consulere, quam qui inopiae subvenire, possint. Cuius officii saepius eos parochus admonebit; curabitque ut compatres tales deligantur, qui fidei et morum ratione suscipiendo muneri satisfacere possint.*[69]

It is evident what the Church intended with this legislation; it would be stretching things a bit too far, however, were one to imply

[65] Reg. 87, R.J., in VI°.

[66] C. 47, X, *de testibus et attestationibus,* II, 20; c. 14, *de sententia excommunicationibus, suspensionis et interdicti,* V, 11, in VI°; Council of Milan (1287), c. 18—Mansi, XXIV, 878; c. un., *de poenis,* XII, in Extravag. Ioan. XXII.

[67] Cf. discussion in Chapter 1.

[68] Paulus IV, const. *Cum ex apostolatus,* 15 febr. 1559, § 5—*Fontes,* n. 94.

[69] I Council of Milan (1565), Pars II, *De Baptismo*—Mansi, XXXIV, col. 16.

that with the phrase *ratione morum* the absence of infamy of law was demanded.

The Milan Ritual was more explicit however in outlawing the infamous at law from the capacity of sponsorship at baptism.[70] The Roman Ritual repeated this prohibition in the following way:

> *Sciant praeterea Parochi, ad hoc munus non esse admittendos infideles, aut hereticos, non publice excommunicatos, aut interdictos, non publice criminosos, aut infames. . . .*[71]

It is clear that this legislation did not invalidate the act when undertaken by one who was infamous. Subsequent instructions and replies lead to the same conclusion. It is to be remarked here that from the texts of the Rituals one cannot derive a clear-cut case of infamy of law. The basic position of ecclesiastical legislation at the time was simply this: while the infamous did not assume this office invalidly, they could not do so licitly.

In summary, it seems warranted to hold that although one is unable to determine the precise content of the *actus legitimi* of the former law, it is clear, in consequence both of the general exclusion expressed in the *Regulae Iuris* [72] and also of other more specific citations, that the infamous at law were excluded from all those actions which are now described by the Code of Canon Law as authorized ecclesiastical acts.[73]

Article III. Commentary on the Present Law

Section 1. The General Statement of the Law

> *Qui infamia iuris laborat, non solum est irregularis ad normam can. 984, n. 5, sed in super est inhabilis ad obtinenda beneficia, pensiones, officia et dignitates ecclesiasticas, ad actus legitimos ecclesiasticos perficiendos, ad exercitium*

[70] Cf. Trombelli, *Tractatus de Sacramentis,* II, diss. VI, n. 11.

[71] Rituale Romanus, *Pauli V Pontificis Maximi jussu editum, et a Benedicto XIV auctum et castigatum* (Ratisbonae, 1901), tit. II, cap. 1, *De Sacramento Baptismi,* nn. 22-26.

[72] Reg. 87, R.J., in VI°.

[73] Cf. Tatarczuk, *op. cit.,* p. 28.

> *iuris aut muneris ecclesiastici, et tandem arceri debet a ministerio in sacris functionibus exercendo. . . . Vide etiam can.* 167, § 1, n. 3, § 2; 373, § 4; 765, n. 2; 766, n. 2; 795, n. 2; 796, n. 3; 1470, § 4; 1589, § 1; 1657, § 1.[74]

Canon 2294, § 1, states that one who has incurred infamy of law is not only irregular but furthermore is incapable of obtaining ecclesiastical benefices, pensions, offices and dignities. He is also incapable of performing authorized ecclesiastical acts, of exercising any ecclesiastical right or function, and must also be restrained from exercising the sacred functions of the ministry. The portions of this legislation with which the present study is primarily concerned are: ". . . *sed super est inhabilis ad obtinenda . . . officia . . . ecclesiasticas, ad actus legitimos ecclesiasticos perficiendos, ad exercitium iuris aut muneris ecclesiastici,* . . ."

There is no doubt that the law here refers to the radical incapacity and inability of the one suffering infamy of law to obtain, perform or exercise the functions referred to. This is an example of a disqualifying law as described in canon 11.[75] It simply is not within the power of one under infamy of law to perform these functions in a valid manner. The text of canon 2294, § 1, leaves no room for doubt on this point.[76]

Thus it is that one who suffers infamy of law is not able to validly obtain an office (in the strict sense), perform any authorized ecclesiastical act, or exercise any ecclesiastical right or function. Offices, rights and functions (*munera*) are mentioned here together with authorized ecclesiastical acts because, as was noted above, all authorized ecclesiastical acts can be reduced to offices, functions and rights.[77]

One may well recall here the differences to which expression is given in these various prohibitions. One under legal infamy is in-

[74] Canon 2294, § 1, and footnote.

[75] "Irritantes aut inhabilitantes eae tantum leges habendae sunt, quibus aut actum esse nullum aut inhabilem esse personam expresse vel acquivalenter statuitur."—Canon 11.

[76] Cf. Conte a Coronata, IV, n. 1827, p. 274: "In rebus in quibus infamis fit inhabilis de validitate quaestio est"; Chelodi, *De Delictis et Poenis,* n. 50, p. 62; Jone, *Commentarium,* III, 485.

[77] Cf. Roberti, *De Delictis et Poenis,* n. 338, p. 402; Heylen, *De Censuris,* p. 85.

capable of *obtaining* or *securing* any ecclesiastical office. This refers to an office in the strict sense of this term.[78] Thus he could not acquire any rightful claim to those authorized ecclesiastical acts which reflect offices in the strict sense. He cannot *exercise* any ecclesiastical right or function. This prohibition strengthens his inability to perform authorized ecclesiastical acts in general, since the remaining acts can be reduced to rights or functions.

The Code's annotation to paragraph 1 of canon 2294 is most interesting; it seems practically essential to any full commentary on this canon. In addition to the historical references the annotation refers the reader to nine other canons of the Code, involving altogether ten authorized ecclesiastical acts.[79]

Three of these citations seem to be in the nature of a confirmation of the legislation of canon 2294, § 1, itself, for they refer to the qualifications demanded by the law in those who are to carry out certain authorized ecclesiastical acts.[80] These canons point out that the chancellor, the notary, the promoter of justice, the defender of the bond, the procurator and the advocate in addition to other qualifications must be men possessed of a good reputation.[81]

The annotation could equally well have contained parallel references to the good reputation required of others who perform authorized ecclesiastical acts.[82] Certainly these canons point up and elucidate the legislation of canon 2294, § 1. It is easier to understand that the infamous at law are incapable of performing authorized ecclesiastical acts when we realize that the possession of a good name is requisite for acquiring the office, or for exercising the function

78 Canon 145, § 2.

79 Canons 167, § 1, n. 3, § 2; 373, § 4; 765, n. 2; 766, n. 2; 795, n. 2; 796, n. 3; 1470, § 4; 1589, § 1; 1657, § 1.

80 Canons 373, § 4; 1589, § 1; 1657, § 1.

81 ". . . integrae famae et omni suspicione maiores."—Canon 373, § 4; ". . . integrae famae"—Canon 1589, § 1; ". . . bonae famae";—Canon 1657, § 1.

82 *Officialis* and *vice-officialis*: ". . . integrae famae . . ."—Canon 1573, § 4; Synodal and pro-synodal judges: ". . . probatae vitae . . ."—Canon 1574, § 1; Messenger and apparitor: ". . . integrae famae . . ."—Canons 1592 and 373, § 4; Administrator of ecclesiastical property: ". . . boni testimonii, . . ."—Canon 1521, § 1.

or right which constitutes or forms the basis for the exercise of such acts.

The other canonical references in the footnote of canon 2294, § 1, are of more importance. They provide the key to a correct interpretation of this paragraph. They point out that despite the very strong wording of this law, which makes it clear that the infamous at law are incapable of performing authorized ecclesiastical acts, there are some exceptions. Were it not for these citations, there could seem to be a conflict between the law, in its nature of a general norm as expressed in canon 2294, § 1, and other sections of the Code.

Section 2. Mitigations of the Law

A. STATEMENT OF INTERPRETATION

The other six canonical references in the footnote to canon 2294, § 1, point to mitigations affecting the law in its nature of a general norm. They reveal situations wherein one under infamy of law is capable of the performance of authorized ecclesiastical acts.[83]

Canon 167, § 1, n. 3, points out that a vote cast in an ecclesiastical election by one under infamy of law is invalid only after a condemnatory or a declaratory sentence has been issued. Thus, prior to such a sentence, such a vote is valid. This is an exception to the general norm which states that any person suffering from infamy of law is incapable of performing any authorized ecclesiastical act. The second paragraph of canon 167, which is also referred to, points out just when the election itself is valid or invalid.

Canon 1470, § 4, refers to the exercise of the right of patronage and points out that one who is infamous at law cannot exercise the rights or use the privileges of patronage once there has been a declaratory or a condemnatory sentence. This inability remains for as long as the infamy perdures. Thus, prior to such a sentence, the rights and privileges of patronage may be exercised validly.

The remaining references concern the position of sponsorship at baptism and confirmation. Canons 765, n. 2, and 795, n. 2, point out that one who is infamous at law attempts sponsorship invalidly

[83] Canons 167, § 1, n. 3, § 2; 1470, § 4; 765, n. 2; 766, n. 2; 795, n. 2; 796, n. 3.

only after a condemnatory or a declaratory sentence. Thus, prior to this sentence, sponsorship by such a person is valid. The general norm is further mitigated by the provisions of canons 766, n. 2, and 796, n. 3. There it is made clear that sponsorship at baptism and confirmation is illicit only when the delict which is the basis for the infamy of law is notorious. Thus, if the crime is not notorious, the infamous person can not only be a valid sponsor but acts licitly as well. This certainly constitutes a considerable mitigation of the general norm—"*Qui infamia iuris laborat . . . est inhabilis . . . ad actus legitimos ecclesiasticos perficiendos. . . .*"

Although this interpretation seems justified and correct according to the text of the law and the norms of interpretation, it is by no means unanimously approved by the authors. Many authors seem to give no treatment to the possibility that the canon itself provides exceptions to the general norm. They are content with a statement of the law or a paraphrase of its content.[84] Others make reference to the canons listed in the footnote of canon 2294, § 1, but do not become more explicit as to the nature of the correlation between the general norm and these canons.[85]

Some authors seem to be opposed to the interpretation presented above. They seem to take the references in the footnote as pointing up rather than mitigating the general norm. Thus they emphasize the canons cited in the footnote as illustrations of the general norm. Thus Augustine (1872-1943) remarked: "It (legal infamy) disqualifies the infamous person from performing any legal ecclesiastical act of the kind mentioned in can. 2256, n. 2, especially sponsorship."[86] Prümmer (1866-1931) reasoned along the same lines.[87] Cocchi seems to consider the citations as specific examples of the general norm rather than as mitigations of it.[88]

[84] Cf. Cerato, *Censurae Vigentes,* n. 143, pp. 216-218; Blat, *Commentarium,* V, n. 126, p. 177; Chelodi, *De Delictis et Poenis,* n. 50, p. 62.

[85] Cf. Conte a Coronata, IV, n. 1827, p. 274.

[86] Augustine, *A Commentary,* VIII, 246.

[87] "Inhabiles ad actus legitimos ecclesiasticos e. gr. ad munus patrini, ad suffragium ferendum in electionibus ecclesiasticis."—Prümmer, *Manuale,* p. 667.

[88] ". . . exercitium actus legitimi ecclesiastici . . . sunt nullius valoris; . . . confer exempla in cc. 167, § 1, 3°, et § 2 quoad electores; 373, § 4 quoad Curiae notarios; 765, 766, 795, 796, quoad baptismum et confirmationem;

Certain authors seem to grasp the problem more clearly than others. Even among these, however, there are differences as to the correct interpretation. Thus Regatillo-Zalba hold that not only the exceptions pointed to should be upheld, but that any act placed by or upon one infamous at law, but before a condemnatory or a declaratory sentence, is indeed illicit but still valid. They reason from the pertinent canons mentioned in the footnote of canon 2294, § 1,[89] and from an analogy with excommunication, suspension and interdict, whereby certain acts are rendered invalid *post sententiam,* but only illicit before sentence.[90] This seems to be going too far in a direction opposite to the authors referred to above. The cases treated of in canons 167, § 1, n. 3; 765, n. 2; 766, n. 2; 795, n. 2; 796, n. 3 and 1470, § 4, are exceptions to the general norm expressed in canon 2294, § 1, and in virtue of canon 19 are subject to a strict interpretation.[91] The annotation to canon 2294, § 1, contains a complete and exhaustive list of exceptions to the general norm.

The interpretation outlined above as the proper one is not without support from the authors. Jone, realizing that the law does make exceptions, states that there are times when authorized ecclesiastical acts placed by the infamous at law are not invalid but merely illicit.[92] Ayrinhac (1867-1930)-Lydon agree, for after stating the general norm of the law, they add: "After sentence of the court a person who is infamous by law cannot vote in canonical elections (167), nor stand as god-father in baptism or confirmation (765-795); nor exercise the right of patronage (1470, § 4)"; [93]

The clearest exposition of this interpretation is presented by Tatarczuk. After commenting that infamy of law invalidates the performance of "most" of the authorized ecclesiastical acts he goes on to point out:

1470, § 4, quoad ius patronatus; 1589, § 1, 1657, § 1, . . . quoad diversa munera iudicialia."

[89] Canons 167, § 1, n. 3; 765, n. 2; 766, n. 2; 795, n. 2; 796, n. 3; 1740, § 4.

[90] Regatillo-Zalba, *Theologia Moralis,* III, n. 1077, p. 938.

[91] "Leges quae poenam statuunt, aut liberum iurium exercitium coarctant, aut exceptionem a lege continent, strictae subsunt interpretationi."—Canon 19.

[92] *Commentarium,* III, 485.

[93] *Penal Legislation,* p. 122.

"The Code, however, in a few special cases, has partially mitigated this normal consequence of *infamia iuris,* inasmuch as it renders the exercise of the rights of sponsorship, of voting, and of patronage invalid only when a proper declaratory or condemnatory decree of infamy has intervened. These exceptions, as specified in law, cannot be extended to the remaining authorized ecclesiastical acts which have not been removed from the general scope of canon 2294, § 1, by the expressed determination of the pertinent canons dealing with these official functions." [94]

The proposed interpretation is further substantiated when it is recalled that the former law likewise made exceptions in this regard. It is clear from the historical investigation of canon 2294, § 1, that although it had always been the desire of the Church that worthy persons of good reputation be selected to act as sponsors at baptism, the infamous were not excluded in such a way as to invalidate their attempt to act in this capacity. As was pointed out above, the legislation of the I Provincial Council of Milan (1565),[95] the Milan Ritual [96] and the Roman Ritual [97] make this clear. The basic position of ecclesiastical legislation under the former law was this: while the infamous person did not assume the office of sponsor at baptism invalidly, he could not do so licitly.

B. PRACTICAL EFFECTS OF THIS LEGISLATION

In virtue of canon 2294, § 1, then, one who is infamous at law is incapable of performing authorized ecclesiastical acts with the exceptions explained above. A brief glimpse at what this legislation implies in practice will aid in the true understanding of the law.

Any person infamous at law is not capable of carrying out the administration of ecclesiastical property. This incapacity must be applied however only to those acts of administration which constitute the authorized ecclesiastical act spoken of in canon 2256,

[94] Tatarczuk, *Infamy of Law,* p. 81.

[95] Pars II, *De Baptismo*—Mansi, XXXIV, col. 16.

[96] Cf. Trombelli, *Tractatus de Sacramentis,* II, diss. VI, n. 11.

[97] Rituale Romanum, *Pauli V Pontificis Maximi jussu editum, et a Benedicto XIV auctum et castigatum* (Ratisbonae, 1901), tit. II, cap. 1, *De Sacramento Baptismi,* nn. 22-26.

n. 2, that it, the administration lawfully exercised over property held by the Church or by moral persons juridically constituted within the Church.

The infamous are incapable of carrying out those judicial functions which constitute authorized ecclesiastical acts, that is, those of the judge, the notary, the auditor, the referee, the promoter of justice, the promoter of the faith, the chancellor, the messenger, the apparitor, the defender of the bond, the advocate and the procurator.

Thus, no one under infamy of law could validly act as *officialis*, or as a synodal or pro-synodal judge. Should an infamous person attempt to do so, his actions are invalid and the sentence absolutely null.[98]

Should an infamous person attempt to carry out the function of the auditor by exercising any of the duties of this office as outlined above, such actions are invalid. This action does not vitiate the entire judicial process however.[99]

The functions of the referee are likewise carried out invalidly by one infamous at law. The influence of his incapacity upon the entire process is slight when he is considered *qua* referee. Most often, however, this office is carried out by one of the judges of the collegiate tribunal, and his inability in this respect would affect the validity of the proceedings.[100]

Not only is one infamous at law incapable of performing functions proper to these positions should he be already invested with them at the time of his infamy, he is unable also to acquire the right of exercising them in the first place since they are offices in the strict sense.[102]

One infamous at law further is not capable of acting as the promoter of justice or as the defender of the bond. An attempt to so

[98] Cf. canons 1829, n. 1; 1680, § 1; 205, § 3; Noone, *Nullity in Judicial Acts*, The Catholic University of America Canon Law Studies, n. 297 (Washington, D. C.: The Catholic University of America Press, 1950), p. 39.

[99] Canon 1680, § 2.

[100] Canon 1680, § 1.

[102] Cf. Roberti, *De Delictis et Poenis*, n. 338, p. 402; Canon 2294, § 1.

act on his part would invalidate the process in those cases in which his presence is required.[103]

The function of the notary is essential to the execution of the judicial process.[104] One who is infamous at law cannot validly carry out the functions assigned to this office.[105] The acts of a cause cannot be validly drawn up or signed by such a person,[106] and other documents drawn up by him do not have the value of public documents, since he is incapable of being a qualified witness.[107]

The functions of the messenger and the apparitor are likewise invalidly performed by one who is infamous at law. Such incapability is of little practical significance today, since these offices have all but been dispensed with by our tribunals in favor of other means. Nevertheless, should an infamous person attempt to act in either or both of these capacities, the acts which he might write would not serve as public documents and legal proof of what they directly assert.[108] Further complications could arise in relation to the serving of the summons.[109]

One who is infamous at law cannot act validly as an advocate or as a procurator. The attempted activity by such a person in the role of the procurator would cause the sentence to be irremediably null, since he is incapable of receiving the legitimate mandate which is necessary for the validity of the sentence.[110]

Section 3. The Influence of Canon 2232, § 1

As in the case of excommunication, so also in the consideration of legal infamy, the possible effect of canon 2232, § 1, must be considered. It will be recalled from the previous chapter that this

[103] Cf. canon 1587.

[104] Roberti, *De Processibus,* I, p. 284, n. 130; Conte a Coronata, III, n. 1123, p. 44.

[105] Canons 373; 374; 1813, § 1, n. 2; *Provida,* Art. 73—*AAS,* XXVIII (1936), 330.

[106] Canon 1581, § 1.

[107] Canons 1581; 1813 § 1, n. 2; *Provida,* Art. 156, n. 2—*AAS,* XXVIII (1936), 344.

[108] Cf. canon 1593.

[109] Cf. canons 1711-1719.

[110] Cf. canon 1892, n. 3.

law makes it evident that one who has incurred a *latae sententiae* penalty of which he is conscious is bound to observe it in both the external and the internal forum. He is, however, excused from its observance before there has been a declaratory sentence, namely in those circumstances in which it could not be observed without the loss of his reputation. No one can demand his observance of such a penalty in the external forum unless the crime underlying the penalty is notorious.

Thus, in general, those who suffer infamy of law as a result of the commission of the crimes listed in canons 2314, § 1, n. 3; 2320; 2328; 2343, § 1; 2353, § 2; 2356 and 2357, § 1, are bound to observe the effects of this penalty as outlined in canon 2294, § 1. They are, then, incapable of performing authorized ecclesiastical acts with the exceptions explained above.

The mitigations of canon 2232, § 1, as mentioned here and as explained in the previous chapter, may be used by the infamous at law when all the postulated circumstances are present. Thus, one under this penalty as long as no declaratory sentence has been pronounced is not bound to observe it in the external forum when he cannot do so without loss to his reputation. In order that this be the case, his crime must be at least relatively occult. If it were public or notorious the condition of preserving his reputation would not militate in his favor, and the refuge which this canon provides would not be available to him. Whether there be present a danger to one's good name through the observance of the penalty must be judged and determined in each individual case.

It is to be noted here, however, that the provisions of canon 2223, § 4, are to be observed. Thus, the superior involved must issue a declaratory sentence with reference to the *latae sententiae* incurred penalty if an interested party demands it, or when common good requires it.

Section 4. The Cessation of the Incapacity for the Performance of Authorized Ecclesiastical Acts on the Part of the Infamous at Law

Canon 2294, § 1, lists the effects of infamy of law. Thus one who is marked with legal infamy is not only irregular *ex defectu,* but he is also incapable of obtaining ecclesiastical benefices, pensions, offices and dignities, of performing authorized ecclesiastical acts, and from exercising any ecclesiastical right or function. He also is forbidden the exercise of the sacred functions of the ministry. These inabilities and restrictions come to one precisely because he is infamous at law.

There is, then, a relationship of cause and effect between legal infamy and these incapacities. It stands to reason, then, that when the cause of these punishments is removed, the punishments themselves also perish. Thus, when one is no longer infamous in the sight of the law, he no longer suffers the disabilities that legal infamy brings with it. When legal infamy is removed, one is no longer incapable of performing authorized ecclesiastical acts, at least under this heading. In order then to determine when the incapacity for the performance of authorized ecclesiastical acts spoken of in canon 2294, § 1 ceases, one must determine when the legal infamy which is the cause of this incapacity ceases.

In general, the remission of a penalty, whether through absolution in the case of a censure or by way of a dispensation in the case of a vindictive penalty, may be granted only by the one who inflicted it, his competent superior or successor, or by one to whom this power has been committed.[111] The difference in method for the remission of censures and vindictive penalties is necessitated by the very nature of these penalties.

> Unlike a censure, which is medicinal and intended to quicken the amendment of a delinquent, a *vindictive penalty*, as the term implies, serves primarily to expiate an injury done to society and to vindicate the violated authority of the Church. Consequently its cessation depends not upon the reformation of the offender, but entirely upon the discretion of ecclesiastical authority. It is accomplished either on the lapse of the time and the fulfillment of the conditions specified in the law for the observance of the penalty, or upon the granting of a favorable dispensation by the proper authority who established the sanction, or by his superior, or their lawful delegate.[112]

[111] Canon 2236, § 1.

[112] Tatarczuk, *Infamy of Law*, p. 97; cf. Woywod, *A Practical Commentary*, II, n. 2076, p. 424; Canon 2289; Christ, *Dispensation From Vindicative Penalties*, p. 65.

Infamy of law is not imposed for a specific period of time; it is in the nature of things (*per se*) perpetual.[113] In general, it ceases only upon a dispensation granted by the Apostolic See.[114] The law as expressed in canon 2295 seems quite absolute on this point.[115] Further investigation, however, reveals several mitigations of this rule.[116] Canon 2237 grants certain powers to the ordinary concerning the remission of *latae sententiae* penalties established by the law of the Code. *Latae sententiae* infamy of law comes within this category, and thus within these powers. The provisions of canons 81 and 2290, § 2, must also be considered in this regard.

It is a disputed point whether the dispensation from vindictive penalties spoken of in canon 2236, § 1, and 2289 is to be considered as equivalent to that defined in canon 80.[117] If such an equivalence is asserted, canon 81 may be brought into play. According to this norm, the ordinary may dispense from the law which obtains in general throughout the Church, not only in those cases wherein this power is explicitly or implicitly granted, but also when there is difficulty in having recourse to the Holy See, when simultaneously there is danger of grave harm in the delay of such recourse, and when at the same time the dispensation is one which the Holy See is accustomed to grant. This would enable the ordinary to dispense from legal infamy whenever these conditions are fulfilled, even in cases which are not occult.

The ordinary [118] is empowered by law to remit the *latae sententiae* penalties enacted in the law of the Code even in public cases, though with certain exceptions.[119] One of these exceptions is infamy of law. This grant of power to ordinaries is an exemplication of the words of canon 2236: "*Remissio poenae . . . concedi . . . ab eo cui*

[113] Cf. Vermeersch-Creusen, *Epitome,* III, n. 495, p. 305; Regatillo-Zalba, *Theologia Moralis,* III, n. 1078, p. 939; Cocchi, *Commentarium,* n. 112, p. 194; Christ, *op. cit.,* p. 55.

[114] Canons 2295 and 2289.

[115] "Infamia iuris desinit sola dispensatione a Sede Apostolica concessa; . . ."—Canon 2295.

[116] Cf. Christ, *op. cit.,* p. 166; Tatarczuk, *op. cit.,* p. 97.

[117] Cf. Tatarczuk, *op. cit.,* pp. 100-103; Christ, *op. cit.,* pp. 66-70.

[118] Cf. canon 198, § 1.

[119] Canon 2237, § 1.

haec potestas commissa est." [120] It can be exercised in public cases, that is, cases which involve a formally public crime, [121] or a public vindictive penalty, or both. Infamy of law, however, is expected from the possible use of this power.

In occult cases, without prejudice to canons 2254 and 2290, the ordinary may remit, either personally or through another, the *latae sententiae* penalties enacted in the law of the Code, with the exception of censures reserved *specialissimo modo or speciali modo* to the Apostolic See.[122]

An occult case involves two elements, a crime and the vindictive penalty that results from it. The crime or delict is occult when it is not public, that is, when it has not already been divulged and when its divulgement is to be considered as not readily or easily occurring.[123] A delict must be at least formally occult in order that there be an occult case as contemplated by canon 2237, § 2. Vindictive penalties likewise may be considered occult or public depending on the particular circumstances involved. An occult case, then, as envisioned by this canon consists of a crime which is at least formally occult, or an occult vindictive penalty, or both.[124]

It seems that this power of the ordinary may be exercised only in the internal forum. Canon 202, § 3, declares that, if the forum for which a power is given is not expressed, the power is to be understood as granted for both forums, unless the nature of the case should dictate otherwise. The power granted to the ordinary in canon 2237, § 2, is to be exercised only in occult cases which pertain to the internal forum by reason the occult delicts involved. Thus it is clear that the nature of these cases dictates the use of this power only in the internal forum.[125]

The power of suspending the observance of *latae sententiae* vindictive penalties, and therefore also of infamy of law, is granted

120 Cf. Christ, *op. cit.*, p. 127.

121 Canon 2197, n. 1.

122 Canon 2237, § 2.

123 Canon 2197, nn. 1 and 4.

124 Christ, *op. cit.*, p. 164.

125 Blat, *Commentarium,* V, n. 59, pp. 84-85; Berutti, *Institutiones,* VI, n. 38, p. 106; Christ, *op. cit.*, pp. 165-166.

by canon 2290, § 1. In virtue of this legislation, in the more urgent occult cases wherein the guilty party would betray himself with resulting infamy and scandal by observing the penalty, any confessor may suspend the penalty in the sacramental forum under the following conditions: the confessor is to oblige the penitent to have recourse to the Sacred Penitentiary, or to a bishop with the faculty of dispensing. This recourse is to be made within one month by letter or through the confessor, if it can be done without grave inconvenience. The name of the delinquent is not to be mentioned, and the instructions of the superior to whom the recourse was made are to be carried out.[126] If in some extraordinary case this recourse is impossible, the confessor himself can grant the dispensation according to the norm of canon 2254, § 3.[127]

Authors are not in agreement as to just exactly what constitutes the more urgent cases referred to in canon 2290, § 1. It is evident that the law itself describes these cases in the words: ". . . *reus seipsum proderet cum infamia et scandalo,* . . ." It is not clear, however, whether both these elements must be present before this canon comes into play, or whether even one of them suffices. The Code seems by its wording to combine both elements within a given case. It seems to require that there be infamy to the party under the penalty, and scandal to others. Some authors of note understand the law precisely in this way. Thus Conte a Coronata, in comparing the provisions of this canon with those of canon 2254 concerning absolution from *latae sententiae* censures, points out that the law is more strict in the former case, since it demands the presence of both infamy and scandal, whereas either one of them suffices in the case of censures.[128] Blat (1870-1943) had come to the same conclusion,[129] as did Vermeersch-Creusen [130] and Augustine,[131] and in a more recent day also Berutti.[132]

[126] Canon 2290, § 1.

[127] Canon 2290, § 2.

[128] *Institutiones Iuris Canonici,* IV, n. 1823, p. 268.

[129] *Commentarium,* V, n. 120, p. 171.

[130] *Epitome Iuris Canonici,* III, n. 491, p. 300.

[131] *A Commentary,* VIII, 240.

[132] *Institutiones,* VI, n. 86, p. 216.

Others, however, maintain that the provisions of this canon come into play when either infamy alone or also scandal alone is present. They thus understand *"et"* in the disjunctive sense of *"aut."* Their argument is based upon the analogy with canon 2254, § 1, which deals with the *"periculum gravis scandali vel infamiae."* Thus Jone points out:

> *Norma secundam quam urgentior habetur si reus poenam observare non potest sine infamia et scandalo, ita intelligenda videtur, ut—sicut in can. 2254, § 1—sufficiat si ex observatione poenae aut infamia aut scandalum oriatur.*[133]

Christ agrees and goes on to point out that this very canon (2290, § 1) uses the word *"et"* in the disjunctive sense of *"vel"* in another place when it speaks of having recourse *"per epistolam et per confessarium."* The word is to receive the same interpretation here because of the analogy with canon 2254, § 1, and thus the danger either of infamy or of scandal suffices.[134] Abbo-Hannan[135] and Bouscaren-Ellis concur in this doctrine.[136]

It seems that in practice these elements will nearly always be present simultaneously, so that this problem of interpretation will scarcely ever arise.

Ultimately, it is up to the confessor to decide whether the problem at hand is actually to be considered one of the "more urgent" cases. It is, however, the testimony of the penitent which is to form the basis for this judgment.[137]

It is rather generally agreed that the copula *"et"* is used in the sense of *"aut," "vel"* or *"sive,"* so that the recourse may be made either by the penitent or by the confessor.[138]

If the recourse spoken of above is impossible, the confessor may then actually dispense from the penalty in accordance with the norms

133 *Commentarium,* III, 483.

134 Christ, *op. cit.*, p. 169.

135 *The Sacred Canons,* II, 851.

136 *Canon Law,* p. 912.

137 Christ, *op. cit.*, p. 181.

138 Conte a Coronata, IV, n. 1824, p. 269, footnote 1; Chelodi, *De Delictis et Poenis,* n. 47, p. 60, footnote 1; Christ, *op. cit.*, p. 169.

of canon 2254, § 3, which deals with the remission of censures. Thus, in some extraordinary case when the recourse is morally impossible, the confessor may grant absolution without the obligation of recourse. The confessor is to impose on the penitent what the law requires (for example, restitution) and impose an appropriate penance and satisfaction under the condition that the penitent shall fall back under the penalty if he does not perform the penance and make satisfaction within the time specified by the confessor.[139] In this case the confessor does not merely suspend, but he actually dispenses from, the penalty.

The law lists certain crimes the commission of which automatically renders the delinquent infamous at law or at least subject to a condemnatory sentence of infamy. This penalty of infamy causes certain incapacities and restrictions, one of which is the inability to perform authorized ecclesiastical acts. When the penalty of infamy is removed by way of dispensation, these effects are no longer present. When and while the infamy is suspended, the effects are likewise suspended. Thus the incapacity for the performance of authorized ecclesiastical acts on the part of the infamous at law ceases when the penalty of infamy is dispensed from. It is suspended when and for the length of time the infamy is suspended.

139 Canons 2290, § 2, and 2254, § 3.

CHAPTER IV

The Exclusion From the Performance of Authorized Ecclesiastical Acts On the Part of the Infamous In Fact

Article I. introductory notions concerning infamy of fact

Section 1. The Notion of Infamy of Fact

As was pointed out in the previous chapter, the good name, honor and reputation of a man are among his most prized possessions.[1] Each man has a right to enjoy his good name among his fellow men until such time that he forfeits it by his own actions. This loss of honor and reputation results in a state referred to as infamy. This term is derived from the preposition *"in,"* which denotes a privation, and the noun *"fama,"* meaning good name or reputation. The term thus implies a lack of good name or a loss of reputation.[2] It is called infamy of law when one has lost his good name legally. It is designated infamy of fact when the loss of reputation exists in the minds of prudent men simply because of one's misdeeds. It is with this latter consideration that the present chapter is concerned.

It was noted that infamy of law is a vindictive penalty. Infamy of fact, on the other hand, is not a penalty in the strict sense of the term. It is rather a natural consequence of a crime or of a penalty. It is a recognition on the part of the law of the existence of this natural reaction on the part of the good and prudent men to the misconduct of their fellows.[3] It is, then, a punishment or a penalty only in a broad sense. It is more a reflection of status than the sustaining of a penalty.

[1] ". . . potentiae a natura tributae cuilibet quia homo est. homo enim est dignior omni creatura . . . omnis creatura ei serviat . . ."—*Glossa* ad D. (50.13) 5, s.v. *dignitatis.*

[2] Gasparri, *De Sacra Ordinatione,* I, n. 284, p. 183.

[3] Gasparri, *op. cit.,* I, n. 305, p. 196; Cocchi, *Commentarium,* VIII, n. 112, p. 193; Regatillo-Zalba, *Theologia Moralis,* III, n. 1077, p. 938; Chelodi-Ciprotti, *op. cit.*, n. 50, p. 66; Rodimer, *The Canonical Effects of Infamy of Fact,* p. ix.

It is not difficult to understand that the notion of infamy of fact is as old as society itself. It is simply a description of the natural reaction of good and prudent men to the misconduct of one of their fellows. All systems of law must then have provision for it. It is the duty of the legislator not only to safeguard the right men have to their good name, but also to see to it that offices and positions of importance are not filled by those who are unworthy of them when they have lost their good name.

As will be pointed out in the following article, the notion of infamy of fact has not always been understood in precisely the same way as it is understood today in the Code of Canon Law. Canon 2293, § 3, gives a clear description of this state:

> *Infamia facti contrahitur, quando quis, ob patratum delictum vel ob pravos mores, bonam existimationem apud fideles probos et graves amisit, de quo iudicium spectat ad Ordinarium.*

Infamy of fact may be contracted by any person, man or woman, lay, clerical or religious.[4] It is said to be contracted rather than imposed or inflicted, for it is not a penalty in the technical sense. It is true that infamy of fact may result from the sentence of a court, be it ecclesiastical or civil. This result, however, is not due to the sentence as such, but rather to the reaction of good and prudent men to the condemnation and the crime involved.[5]

The law lists two ways in which one may contract infamy of fact. The first involves the commission of a delict or crime. Canon 2195 points out that a delict is an external and morally imputable violation of a law to which a canonical sanction, at least an indeterminate one, is attached. It is this definition that must be actualized for the act in question before there can result any infamy of fact by reason of a delict.[6] It was noted in the previous chapter that the commission of a crime was likewise necessary before infamy of law could be inflicted. It is only in consequence of certain deter-

[4] Blat, *Commentarium,* V, n. 125, p. 176; Rodimer, *op. cit.,* p. 38.

[5] Cf. Cocchi, *op. cit.,* VIII, n. 112; p. 193; Berutti, *Institutiones,* VI, n. 87, p. 220.

[6] Blat, *op. cit.,* V, n. 125, p. 176.

mined and very grave crimes that this penalty follows, however. It is self-evident that the crime contemplated must be public before it can be the cause of infamy of fact.[7]

The observance of a penalty inflicted as the result of a crime may also give rise to infamy of fact. The Code alludes to this in several places, as has been noted above. The danger of infamy of fact to the delinquent is listed by canon 2232, § 1, as a reason which excuses the delinquent from the observance of a *latae sententiae* penalty, provided there has been no sentence and the delict is occult. Canon 2254, § 1, and 2290, § 1, consider this danger as giving rise to the urgent case in which the confessor can absolve from a censure and suspend the obligation of observing a vindictive penalty.

The state of infamy of fact is also contracted *"ob pravos mores,"* that is, by immoral conduct. This second means of becoming infamous in fact is distinguished from the first in that it looks to a habitual manner of acting whereas the phrase *"patratum delictum"* concerns some particular crime or delict. Here it is a question of those who "repeatedly and openly commit serious sin or who remain in the near occasion of serious sin, and who make no noticeable amendment and are, therefore, observed to be impenitent."[8]

It is clear that infamous in fact are those who are guilty of public, serious and continuous sins. The question then arises whether this group is to be identified with the public sinners spoken of by the Code in other places.[9] Although the Code does not specify just who are to be regarded as public sinners, the lists provided by the authors seem to include also those people who must be regarded as suffering

[7] "Necesse autem est quod causa huius infamiae sit publica, quia actualis diffamatio apud graves et honestos ex causa occulta ne intelligi quidem potest."—Gasparri, *op. cit.*, n. 306, p. 196; Reiffenstuel, *Ius Canonicum Universum* (5 vols. in 7, Parisiis, 1864-1870), VI, Lib. V, n. 57, p. 558; Laymann, *Theologia Moralis* (2 vols. in 1, Venetiis, 1630), Lib. I, Tract V, Pars. V, Cap. IV, n. 3, p. 173; Rodimer, *op. cit.*, p. 44; Vogelpohl, *The Simple Impediments to Holy Orders,* The Catholic University of America Canon Law Studies, n. 224 (Washington, D. C.: The Catholic University of America Press, 1945), p. 150.

[8] Rodimer, *op. cit.*, p. 52; cf. Vogelpohl, *op. cit.*, pp. 151-152.

[9] Cf. canons 693, § 1; 1066; 1240, § 1, n. 6.

infamy of fact.[10] Nevertheless, canon 855, § 1, in speaking of those who are forbidden to receive the Holy Eucharist, seems to distinguish the groups when it includes the infamous of fact among a more generic group of the unworthy.[11] Thus the expression "public sinners" of the Code connotes a more generic classification than the group which is made up of those who are infamous in fact as the result of immoral conduct.[12]

It must also be noted that infamy of fact arising from what is termed "immoral conduct" is a relative thing. It very often depends to a great extent upon the time, locality and persons involved.[13]

The loss suffered by one who is infamous in fact is that of his good name, honor and reputation. This loss must be suffered among the faithful, that is, those who are subjects of the Church.[14] This is only just since this status brings with it the exclusion from various ecclesiastical rights, offices, dignities and acts. There is no reason why the judgment of others should play a part in these matters internal to the Church. It is evident that this loss of reputation must be among good and serious persons. This qualification has existed as long as the notion of infamy of fact itself.[15]

Canon 2293, § 3, further states that the judgment of the ordinary is to play a part in the determination of the presence of infamy of fact. The term ordinary here includes abbots and prelates *nullius*, vicars general, diocesan administrators, vicars apostolic, prefects apostolic, the legitimate successors during the vacancies of these offices, and major superiors of clerical exempt religious.[16] The very

[10] Conte a Coronata, II, n. 816, p. 134; Jone, *Commentarium*, II, 436; Vermeersch-Creusen, *Epitome*, II, n. 549, p. 389.

[11] "Arcendi sunt ab Eucharistia publice indigni, quales sunt excommunicati, interdicti manifestoque infames, . . ."—Canon 855, § 1.

[12] Rodimer, *op. cit.*, p. 52.

[13] Gasparri, *op. cit.*, I, n. 306, p. 196; n. 308, pp. 198, 199; Laymann, *op. cit.*, Lib. I, Tract. V, Pars. V, Cap. IV, n. 4, p. 173.

[14] Blat, *op. cit.*, V, n. 125, p. 176.

[15] Reiffenstuel, *op. cit.*, VI, Lib. V, n. 53, p. 557; Laymann, *op. cit.*, Lib. I, Tract. V, Pars. V, Cap. IV, n. 4, p. 173; Blat, *op. cit.*, V, n. 125, p. 176; Gasparri, *op. cit.*, I, n. 305, p. 196; Rodimer, *op. cit.*, pp. 58-59.

[16] Canon 198, § 1.

position of the ordinary lends itself to the forming of the judgment whether the delinquent has lost his good reputation among good and serious Catholics because of a delict or some immoral conduct. He is to determine whether these conditions exist in fact.[17]

The law seems to demand an expressing of this judgment by the ordinary before infamy of fact is strictly present. Conte a Coronata understands it in this way.[18] At any rate, such a declaration is necessary in practice in order that the presence of infamy of fact be established and the subsequent effects of this juridical status be enforced.

Section 2. The Effects of Infamy of Fact

One who is infamous in fact is subject to certain exclusions which follow as effects of this status. Thus canon 2294, § 2, points out that the infamous in fact are simply impeded from the reception or the exercise of orders for as long as the status of infamy perdures. The ordinary is to make his judgment regarding this duration.[19] They are also to be repelled from the reception of ecclesiastical dignities, benefices, and offices. The exercise of the sacred ministry and the performance of authorized ecclesiastical acts are likewise forbidden to them.[20]

Canons 766, n. 2, and 796, n. 3, indicate that the infamous in fact cannot licitly be admitted as sponsor at baptism or at confirmation. This prescription strengthens that of canon 2294, § 2, which forbids them to exercise authorized ecclesiastical acts.

Canon 855, § 1, lists those who are manifestly infamous as among those who are unworthy of receiving the Holy Eucharist. It is clear that infamy of fact is included in this concept.[21]

17 Ayrinhac-Lydon, *op. cit.*, p. 121; Augustine, *A Commentary,* VIII, p. 246; Cocchi, *op. cit.*, VIII, n. 112, p. 193; Chelodi-Ciprotti, *op. cit.*, n. 50, p. 66; Berutti, *op. cit.*, VI, n. 87, p. 220.

18 "Declaratio autem Ordinarii necessaria omnino videtur ita ut nunquam quis infamia facti laborare censendus sit nisi haec declaratio praecesserit."—*Institutiones Iuris Canonici,* IV, n. 1826, p. 273.

19 Canon 987, n. 7.

20 Canon 2294, § 2.

21 Stadler, *Frequent Holy Communion,* The Catholic University of America Canon Law Studies, n. 263 (Washington, D. C.: The Catholic University of

The infamous are further declared suspect as witnesses in judicial matters by canon 1757, § 2, n. 1. The authors are not in complete agreement whether this refers to the infamous in fact as well as to the infamous at law.[22] A similar situation exists regarding the eligibility of the infamous to serve as judicial experts.[23]

ARTICLE II. THE HISTORICAL DEVELOPMENT OF THE EXCLUSION FROM THE PERFORMANCE OF AUTHORIZED ECCLESIASTICAL ACTS ON THE PART OF THE INFAMOUS IN FACT

Section 1. Survey of Roman Law

As was pointed out in the previous chapter, the legislation of the Code of Canon Law concerning infamy has its origin in Roman Law.[24] This historical development as outlined above concerns infamy of law. Infamy of fact, as has been noted, is not so much a legal institute as a natural reaction on the part of men to the misdeeds of their fellows, and as such has existed as long as society itself. Thus it is that in Roman Law, as in all systems of law, provisions for infamy of fact are found. The law itself does not mention infamy of fact. This state is alluded to, however, in the text of the legislation and identified by the glossators. Thus, the law states that reputation or good name is the condition of unimpaired dignity approved by law and custom, which is diminished or destroyed by legal authority on account of some offense.[25] The loss or deprivation of this good name approved by both law and custom is infamy.[26]

America Press, 1947), p. 58; Rodimer, *op. cit.*, p. 95; Vermeersch-Creusen, *op. cit.*, II, n. 117, p. 79; Regatillo-Zalba, *op. cit.*, III, n. 317, p. 233.

[22] Rodimer, *op. cit.*, p. 136.

[23] Cf. canon 1795, § 2.

[24] Cocchi, *op. cit.*, VIII, n. 112, p. 192; Chelodi-Ciprotti, *op. cit.*, n. 50, p. 66; Gasparri, *op. cit.*, I, n. 285, p. 183; Conte a Coronata, IV, n. 1825, p. 272; Vermeersch-Creusen, *op. cit.*, III, n. 493, p. 304.

[25] "Existimatio est dignitatis illaesae status, legibus ac moribus comprobatus: qui ex delicto nostro authoritate legum aut minuitur, aut consumitur."—D. (50.13) (5.1).

[26] ". . . id est fama sive opinio . . . unde dicitur infamia. id est famae privatio."—*Glossa* ad D. (50.13) 5, s.v. *existimatio est.*

An investigation of Roman Law reveals many cases of infamy of fact. These are most clearly discernible in those cases in which the law declared that the infamy resulting from a crime or misdeed was not legal infamy. It was, therefore, infamy of fact.[27]

Thus it is noted that one who had been forcibly ousted from his land or house had legal recourse by means of the restitutory interdict *"Unde vi."* [28] This interdict ordered the restitution of the possession of the property involved. The one against whom this or any other interdict was leveled was not infamous at law, however. This is evident from the law itself: *"Neque Unde vi neque aliud interdictum famosum est."* [29] The rubric to this legislation leaves no doubt about this:

> Damnatus interdicto Unde vi vel quolibet alio interdicto, infamis non fit scilicet infamia iuris.

The infamy or loss of reputation that naturally followed such a disgrace was then infamy of fact. The glossator pointed this out.[30]

An even clearer example of infamy of fact in Roman Law derives from the case of sons who have been criticized in their father's will. Such disparaging testimony did not render them infamous at law, but it did cause good and serious men to have a poor opinion of them.[31]

This loss of reputation was infamy of fact.

Another cause of infamy of fact was the reprimand given one by the judge during the course of a trial.[32]

[27] Cf. *Glossa* ad C. (12.1) 2, s.v. *Neque famosa.*

[28] Cf. Buckland, *Manual of Roman Law,* p. 412; Leage, *Roman Private Law,* p. 437.

[29] D. (43.16) 13; It is to be noted that the terms *infamis* and *famosus* are used interchangeably in Roman Law. Cf. Buckland, *op. cit.,* p. 54.

[30] ". . . id est non efficitur infamis infamia iuris damnatus aliquo interdicto: de facto tamen infamant quaedam: ut unde vi."—*Glossa* ad D. (43.15) 13, s.v. *famosum.*

[31] "Ea quae pater testimento suo filios increpans scripsit, infames quidem filios iure non faciunt, sed apud bonos et graves opinionem eius, qui patri displicuit, onerant."—C. (2.11) 13.

[32] C. (2.12) 19.

Those who were infamous by infamy of fact inasmuch as they were under accusation suffered certain exclusions. It is in these exclusions that one finds the basis for the law of the Code.[33] Thus they were not permitted to act as an attorney for another until their own innocence was established. The rubric to the law in question pointed out: *"Accusatus de crimine, quousque processus pendet, alterius procurator esse non potest."* [34]

The infamous in fact were likewise excluded from all dignities. That this exclusion applied to the infamous in fact as well as to those who suffered legal infamy is evident both from the law and the commentary.[35] This broad exclusion served as the basis for later ecclesiastical legislation.[36] Its exact comprehension is difficult to determine. The glossator indicated, however, that the dignities referred to pertained primarily to judicial matters [37] and other positions of ecclesiastical administration.[38] It seems, then, that at least in the view of the glossator, most of our present authorized ecclesiastical acts were included.

Section 2. Infamy of Fact in the Early Church

Although it is evident that the Church is indebted to Roman Law for the institute of legal infamy, this adoption was not made in the early days of its history. It was centuries before this institute was in use within the ecclesiastical legal framework.[39] Infamy of fact,

[33] "Reos criminis postulatos novos honores appetere non debere, antequam purgarent innocentiam suam. . . ."—C. (10.58) 1.

[34] "Reum criminis constitutum defensionem causae suscipere non posse, antequam purgarit innocentiam suam, incognitum non est."—C. (2.13) 6.

[35] "Neque famosis, et notatis, et quos scelus, aut vitae turpitudo inquinat, et quos infamia ab honestorum coetu segregat, dignitatis portae patebunt."—C. (12.1) 2; C. (10.57) 1; "Infamia facti a dignitate repellit."—Marginal gloss ad C. (12.1) 2; cf. *Glossa* ad C. (12.1) 2, s.v. *Neque famosa.*

[36] "Infamibus portae non pateant dignitatum."—Reg. 87, R.J., in VI°.

[37] *Glossa* ad C. (12.1) 2, s.v. *Neque famosa.*

[38] Reiffenstuel, *Ius Canonicum Universum,* VI, Lib. V, tit. 37, n. 60, p. 558.

[39] "Although the notion of legal infamy certainly was borrowed from Roman jurisprudence, it was but infrequently mentioned as an ecclesiastical penal sanction until the ninth century."—Tatarczuk, *Infamy of Law,* p. 13; Vermeersch-Creusen, *Epitome,* III, n. 493, p. 304; Conte a Coronata, IV, n. 1825, p. 272; Chelodi-Ciprotti, *op. cit.,* n. 50, p. 66.

however, being not an institute of law but rather the result of a natural reaction of prudent men, was found in the Church from its earliest days.

Evidence for the presence of infamy of fact in the early Church is abundant. This presence is most clearly manifested, however, when there was question of those who were candidates for holy orders, especially the priesthood and the episcopate. Such candidates were to be free from infamy of fact in that their reputations were to be spotless. This is illustrated not only in the words of Sacred Scripture [40] but in the non-inspired sources as well.[41]

In the early centuries of the Church the notion of infamy of fact was closely associated with that of public penance. In fact, it seems that the attitude of the Church toward the infamous in fact was to be determined from its legislation concerning the public penitents. Public penance was always an indication of a grave crime, and thus resulted in a certain defamation or loss of reputation.[42] This status brought with it certain restrictions and limitations. The primary effect of this infamy was the exclusion from the clerical state. Pope Siricius (384-398) stated this exclusion,[43] which was repeated in subsequent legislation.[44]

The infamous in fact were subject to other restrictions as well. The only one which seems to have specific bearing upon the historical analysis in question is that which barred them from the ecclesiastical courts.[45]

Section 3. The Law in the Pseudo-Isidorian Decretals

The presence of infamy of fact is easily discernible in the Pseudo-Isidorian Decretals and related legislation. As was noted in the previous chapter, most of the cases of infamy there cited pertained to infamy of law as is clear from the texts themselves. Nevertheless,

[40] Acts, 6:3; 16:1 and 2; I Timothy, 3:7 and 10; Titus, 1:7.

[41] Cf. Kirsch, *Enchiridion Fontium Historiae Ecclesiasticae Antiquae* (6 ed., quam curavit Leo Ueding, Barcelona: Herder, 1947), n. 6, p. 6; n. 13, p. 12.

[42] Gasparri, *op. cit.*, I, n. 186, p. 113; Rodimer, *op. cit.*, p. 11.

[43] Mansi, III, col. 660, n. 14.

[44] Cf. Mansi, VII, col. 961, n. 3.

[45] Pope Leo I (440-461), Ep. 167—*Bull. Rom. Taur.*, I, 45.

other texts made a clear distinction between the two species of infamy, and then outlined the effects of infamy of fact. Thus the law spoke of those *"qui . . . non rectae conversationis vitam ducunt . . .,"* [46] *"qui non sunt recte conversationis . . . viles personae . . .,"* [47] *"qui non sunt bonae conversationis. . . ."* [48] It is clear that the persons alluded to in these texts were to be regarded as distinct and separate from those who had suffered legal infamy. Thus, the law stated in regard to the bringing of a case to court:

> *. . . ad hoc admitti non debent, nisi bonae conversationis et rectae fidei viri et hi qui omni suspicione careant.*[49]

The infamous in fact were likewise excluded from being witnesses.[50]

Although the presence of infamy of fact was evident in this period, its effects added little to the historical development of the exclusion from what are now known as authorized ecclesiastical acts. Only the exclusions from bringing an accusation, from acting in court, and from serving as a witness approached the nature of these acts. It is to be noted, however, that in addition to these restrictions, the Capitularies of the Frankish Kings also excluded the infamous in fact from the position of judge.[51]

[46] *Capitula Angilramni,* Cor. Sal. Par. III—Hinschius, *op. cit.*, p. 758.

[47] Pseudo Callistus I (218-223), Ep. II, cap. 16—Hinschius, *op. cit.*, pp. 140-141; Jaffé, n. +69.

[48] Ps. Pelagius II (579-590)—Hinschius, *op. cit.*, p. 730; Jaffé, n. +229; c. 6, C. III, q. 5.

[49] *Capitula Angilramni,* Cor. Sal. Par. IV—Hinschius, *op. cit.*, p. 759; ". . . omnes infames . . . et qui non sunt bonas conversationis . . . ab omni accusatione episcoporum funditus submovemus."—Pseudo Pelagius II (579-590)—Hinschius, *op. cit.*, p. 730; Jaffé, n. +229; c. 6, C. III, q. 5.

[50] Pseudo Damasus I (366-384)—Hinschius, *op. cit.*, p. 503; Jaffé, n. +112.

[51] Capitula Hludowico vel Hlothario Adscripta, n. 167: "Hoc sancimus, ut in palatiis nostris ad accusandum et iudicandum et testimonium faciendum non se exhibeant viles personae et infames, . . ."—*Monumenta Germaniae Historica,* Legum Sectio II, *Capitularia,* Tomus I, *Capitularia Regum Francorum* Pars I (ed. A. Boretius, Hannoverae, 1883), p. 334.

Section 4. The Law in the *Corpus Iuris Canonici*

A. PRELIMINARY NOTIONS

The legislation of the *Corpus Iuris Canonici* likewise took cognizance of infamy of fact. It remains true that the law itself made no specific reference to this juridical status, nevertheless those who commented upon the law were clear in making reference to it. It was during this period that the term *"infamia facti"* was first used. The glossators and later commentators on both the *Decretum* of Gratian and the decretals introduced this term in their explanations of the laws which dealt with infamy in general.

The distinction between infamy of law and infamy of fact was clearly made in the gloss to a canon in the second part of the *Decree* of Gratian:

> *Dicunt tamen quidam, quod infamia, quae est irrogata per sententiam, vel quae contrahitur ipso facto, ut cum aliqua deprehenditur in adulterio, vel cum aliquis contrahit binas nuptias. . . . Alia est infamia facti, et melius dicitur infamatio quae inducit purgationem.*[52]

The same gloss added still another species of infamy, which was termed "canonical" and which resulted from the commission of mortal sin.[53] The basic distinction between infamy of law and infamy of fact was again clearly drawn by the glossator in another place in this same part of the *Decree* when he stated: *"Infamia alia iuris: alia facti. . . ."* [54]

The glossator noted that these types of infamy were further distinguished in that infamy of law could not be removed by means of penance, whereas infamy of fact was to be taken away by means of a purgation. Penance was necessary to abolish the so-called canonical infamy.[55]

[52] *Glossa ordinaria* ad c. 2, C. VI, q. 1, s.v. *leges.*

[53] ". . . Est etiam quaedam infamia canonica, quae irrogatur ex quolibet peccato mortali . . ."—*Glossa ordinaria* ad c. 2, C. VI, q. 1, s.v. *leges.*

[54] *Glossa ordinaria* ad c. 2, C. III, q. 7, s.v. *infamia;* cf. *Glossa ordinaria* ad c. 5, D. 51 s.v. *infamiae.*

[55] *Glossa ordinaria* ad c. 2, C. VI, q. 1, s.v. *leges.*

The identification of *infamia facti* and *infamatio* as made in the gloss cited above [56] sheds considerable light upon the concept of infamy of fact as it was viewed by the commentators of this period. They seemed to concentrate on one aspect or source of infamy of fact, namely, that defamation which resulted from the accusation of a crime. Such infamy was to be removed by canonical purgation.[57] This purgation actually involved nothing more than a proof of innocence on the part of the defamed person. It consisted basically in the taking of an oath to his innocence coupled with the testimony of several good witnesses to this effect.[58] This purgation, then, was the test whether the loss of reputation suffered by one who was accused of crime was justified or not, the test whether he labored under infamy of law or not. ". . . *per purgationem demonstratur infamiam sive accusationem fuisse falsam. . .*" [59]

The concept of infamy of fact seems to have been further limited by the commentators in that they made it applicable simply to that loss of reputation which resulted from a false accusation of crime. This seems clear from the reference of the glossator to a canon in Gratian which exemplifies the status of *infamia facti.*[60] This canon explained that God permits the just to suffer detractions and rebuffs in order that they may not succumb to the praise which they often receive. It is to be noted, however, that as in the present law this loss of reputation had to be acknowledged among good and prudent men,[61] of whom there had to be a good number.[62]

[56] *Glossa ordinaria* ad c. 2, C. VI, q. 1, s.v. *leges.*

[57] "Alia est infamia facti, et melius dicitur infamatio . . . et illa aboletur purgatione praestita . . ."—*Glossa ordinaria* ad c. 2, C. VI, q. 1, s.v. *leges;* cf. c. 12, C. II, q. 5; c. 15, C. II, q. 5; c. 13, X, *de purgatione canonica,* V, 34.

[58] Card. Hostiensis, *Summa Aurea* (Lugduni, 1568), pp. 396-397.

[59] Guido a Baisio, *Commentarium in Decretorum Volumen* (Venetiis, 1577), p. 142.

[60] *Glossa ordinaria* ad c. 2, C. VI, q. 1, s.v. *leges* to c. 11, C. VI, q. 1.

[61] ". . . Si vero nullus apparuerit legitimus accusator, et ipsum inveneritis apud bonos et graves super praedictis criminibus, vel ipsorum altero infamatum, purgationem ei canonicam indicatis . . ."—c. 15, X, *de purgatione canonica,* V, 34.

[62] "Qui [iudex] propter dicta paucorum eum infamatum reputare non debet, cuius apud bonos et graves laesa opinio non exsistit."—C. 21, X, *de accusationibus, inquisitionibus et denunciationibus,* V, 1.

The notion of infamy of fact was not completely restricted, however, to those who were accused of a crime. There were many clear provisions in the law itself which called for restrictions to be placed on those who now could come within the comprehension of the concept of infamy of fact as it is known in the Code of today.[63]

B. EXCLUSIONS

Those who were infamous in fact were forbidden the use of certain rights in regard to judicial matters. Because of their status they were unable to make an accusation against another in court or to act as a witness. In order to be a legitimate accuser one had to be in possession of a good reputation.[64]

It is of primary importance to note here that the infamous in fact were forbidden to exercise the legitimate acts, as the former law labelled them. As was pointed out in the previous chapter, it is evident that those who labored under infamy of law suffered this exclusion.[65] That the infamous in fact were likewise affected was indicated by the remark of the commentator in his explanation of this law.[66] The exact content of these acts remains nebulous. The glossator felt, however, that only those actions to which a certain preeminence or honor was attached were to be included within this category.[67]

The infamous in fact were also unable to function as an advocate

[63] Cf. C. 10, C. III, q. 5; c. 17, C. VI, q. 7; c. 2, C. III, q. 7; c. 3, C. VI, q. 1; c. 54, X, *de testibus et attestationibus,* II, 20.

[64] ". . . Debet enim esse sine crimine, non inimicus, bonae famae et opinionis, qui alium accusat, alias non est legitimus accusator."—*Glossa ordinaria* ad c. 1, X, *de accusationibus inquisitionibus et denunciationibus,* V, 1; c. 39, C. II, q. 7; c. 8, C. III, q. 5; cc. 9-10, C. III, q. 5; c. 17, C. VI, q. 7; c. 2, C. VI, q. 1; c. 54, X, *de testibus et attestationibus,* II, 20; c. 56, X, *de testibus et attestationibus,* II, 20.

[65] ". . . actus legitimi sint infamibus interdicti."—C. 47, X, *de testibus et attestationibus,* II, 20.

[66] ". . . quia personas vilibus et indignis portae dignitatis non debent patere."—*Glossa ordinaria* ad c. 47, X, *de testibus et attestationibus,* II, 20, s.v. *actus legitimi.*

[67] *Glossa ordinaria* ad c. un., *de poenis,* XII, in Extravag. Ioan. XXII, s.v. *legitimos.*

or lawyer.[68] They further were not regarded as fit to act as advocates for their bishop in ecclesiastical or personal matters.[69]

The generic exclusion of the infamous from all positions of honor and dignity was summed up in terse form by Rule 87 of the *Regulae Iuris*: *"Infamibus portae non pateant dignitatum."* [70] This sweeping restriction applied to the infamous in fact as well as to those who suffered legal infamy,[71] and barred them from many of the present authorized ecclesiastical acts, not the least of which was the capacity for holding the office of judge.[72]

The law, in further providing that the bishop was always to have clerics of good reputation around him, was implicitly banning the infamous in fact from positions of importance within the curia.[73]

68 "Infames non possunt esse procuratores, vel patroni causarum . . . propter notam turpitudinis."—c. 2, C. III, q. 7.

69 ". . . debet unusquisque eorum [scil. episcopi et sacerdotes] tam pro ecclesiasticis, quam etiam pro suis actionibus . . . habere advocatum non malae famae suspectum, sed bonae opinionis, et laudabilis artis inventum . . ."—c. 3, C. V, q. 3.

70 Reg. 87, R.J., in VI°.

71 "Dicitur hic, quod si aliquis infamatur, non debet ad honores promoveri, donec de hoc inquiratur, vel inde se *purgaverit* . . ."—Casus ad c. 4, X, *de accusationibus,* V, 1; "... dicit Dynus de infamia iuris et facti, de quibus dico hanc regulam intelligi: cum dignitatibus participare non debeant infames quacunque infamia."—*Glossa ordinaria* ad Reg. 87, R.J., in VI°, s.v. *dignitatem;* ". . . neque famosis, et notatis, et quos scelus, et vitae turpitudo inquinat, et quos infamia ab honestorum coetu segregat, dignitatis portae patebunt."—*Glossa ordinaria* ad Reg. 87, R.J., in VI°, s.v. *infamibus;* c. 4, X, *de accusationibus inquisitionibus et denunciationibus,* V, 1; c. 11, X, *de excessibus praelatorum et subditorum,* V, 31; Sylvester, *Summa Silvestrina* (2 vols., Venetiis, 1601), II, p. 25, n. 4; *Joannes Andreae, In Titulum de Regulis Iuris Novella,* p. 30; "Infamia tam ex turpitudine facti, quam a iure proveniens excludit a dignitatibus et honoribus praesertim ecclesiasticis iuxta Regul. 85 [sic], jur. in 6. . . ."—Reiffenstuel, *op. cit.,* VI, Lib. V, Tit. 37, n. 60, p. 558; "Porro infamia facti eadem impedimenta ex iure canonico producit ac infamia iuris. Nimirum arcet a dignitatibus, ex *cit. reg. 87 juris, in 6°,* quae etiam infames infamia facti comprehendit. . . ."—Gasparri, *Tractatus de Sacra Ordinatione,* I, n. 309, p. 199.

72 ". . . infamis enim iudex esse non potest . . ."—*Glossa ordinaria* ad Reg. 87, R.J., in VI°, s.v. *infamibus.*

73 "Episcopi . . . semper secum presbiteros et diaconos, aut alios boni testamenti clericos habeant . . ."—c. 60, C. II, q. 7.

A serious loss of reputation could also occasion the loss of an ecclesiastical office.[74]

Section 5. The Law From the Council of Trent to the Code of Canon Law

In the period following the decretals the concept of infamy of fact remained for the most part as explained above. A return to the primitive notion of this status as held in Roman Law, and similar to the notion of the present Code of Canon Law, was not long in coming however. Some commentators recognized other causes of this status in addition to the *infamatio* of the *Corpus Iuris.*

The cases mentioned in the Roman Law itself were referred to as sources or causes of infamy of fact. Thus, those who were guilty of a crime to which the law did not attach infamy, those who were imprisoned, those whose testimony was refused because of a crime committed by them, those who had been criticized in their father's will, and others also were considered to labor under infamy of fact along with those who had been accused of a crime.[75] This infamy had the same general effects as that recognized in the *Corpus Iuris.*[76] These interpretations were substantiated by later decisions of the Sacred Roman Rota and of the Sacred Congregation of the Council, which pointed out that infamy of fact resulted not only from the accusation of crimes but from the actual commission of crimes as well.[77]

The principal addition to the study of the exclusion from authorized ecclesiastical acts as the result of infamy of fact in this period concerns the position of sponsorship at baptism and confirmation.

As was pointed out in the previous chapter, it was understood from the early days of the Church that those persons who undertook the role of sponsor at the administration of these sacraments were to be of good life and reputation. The reason for this understanding is obvious when the nature of the office is considered. The sponsor

[74] C. 10, X, *de purgatione canonica,* V, 34.

[75] Cf. Sylvester, *op. cit.,* II, n. 3, p. 25; Joannes Andreae, *op. cit.,* p. 30.

[76] Sylvester, *op. cit.,* II, nn. 4-6, p. 25.

[77] Cf. Gasparri, *op. cit.,* I, p. 197; Rodimer, *op. cit.,* p. 32.

is to see to the spiritual welfare of his spiritual child, to aid him by exhortation and above all by example to attain that purpose for which he was created. Certainly one who has suffered the loss of his good name through negligence in regard to his own life could hardly hope to live up to such obligations. The seriousness of the role of the sponsor has been pointed out in both the former and the present law.[78]

This common understanding has found expression in the legislation of the Church dating from this period and even prior to it. Thus, the VIII Council of Paris (829) excluded from this position not only the excommunicated but also those who were undergoing public penance.[79]

As was noted in the previous chapter, the I Provincial Council of Milan (1565) warned parents to choose as sponsors those who by their way of life would be capable of carrying out the role of spiritual parent to the newly baptized Christian.[80] Whereas it is not clear that infamy of law is referred to here, it is evident that those laboring under infamy of fact were meant to be excluded by this legislation.

The Milan Ritual of 1613 was more explicit in forbidding this function when it stated: *"Ne excommunicatos, interdictos, publice*

[78] "Vos ante omnia, tam mulieres quam viros, qui filios in baptismo suscepistis, moneo, ut vos cognoscatis fideiussores apud Deum exstitisse pro illis, quos visi estis de sacro fonte suscipere. Ideoque semper eos admonete, ut castitatem custodiant, iustitiam diligant, charitatem teneant." . . .—c. 105, D. IV, *de cons.*; "Patrinorum est, ex suscepto munere, spiritualem filium perpetuo sibi commendatum habere, atque in iis quae ad christianae vitae institutionem spectant, curare diligenter ut ille talem in tota vita se praebeat qualem futurum esse sollemni caeremonia spoponderunt."—Canon 769.

[79] *Monumenta Germaniae Historica,* Legum Sectio II, *Capitularia Regum Francorum,* (Vol. II, Pars. 1, denuo ediderunt A. Boetius et V. Krause, Hannoverae, 1890), c. 35, p. 39.

[80] I Provincial Council of Milan (1565), Pars II, *de bapismo*: "Fideles in baptizandis filiis eos potius eligant compatres qui eorum animae consulere, quam qui inopiae subvenire, possint. Cuius officii saepius eos parochus admonebit; curabitque ut compatres tales deligantur, qui fidei et *morum ratione* suscipiendo muneri satisfacere possint."—Mansi, XXXIV, col. 16.

criminosos, infamesque . . . ad infantem de Baptismo suscipiendum adhiberi sunt." [81]

The Roman Ritual of 1614 solidified this previous legislation by charging the pastor to determine the qualifications of prospective sponsors, and in so doing formed the proximate basis for the present law of the Code.[82]

It was during this period that the office of the defender of the matrimonial bond was instituted by Pope Benedict XIV in his Constitution *"Dei miseratione"* of 3 November, 1741. It is clear from this legislation that the infamous in fact were to be excluded from this position.[83]

Article III. Commentary on the Present Law

Section 1. Statement of the Law

Canon 2294, § 2, lists the principal effects of infamy of fact, among which is included the statement that the infamous in fact are to be excluded from the performance of authorized ecclesiastical acts.

> *Qui laborat infamia facti, repelli debet tum a recipiendis ordinibus ad normam can. 987, n. 7, dignitatibus, beneficiis, officiis ecclesiasticis, tum ab exercendo sacro ministerio et ab actibus legitimis ecclesiasticis.*

Thus, those persons who labor under infamy of fact as explained above are to be excluded from the performance or exercise of authorized ecclesiastical acts. This exclusion, however, does not involve

[81] Trombelli, *op. cit.*, II, diss. VI, n. 11.

[82] "Sciant praeterea Parochi, ad hos munus non esse admittendos infideles, aut hereticos, non publice excommunicatos, aut interdictos, non publice criminosos, aut infames . . ."—*Rituale Romanum,* tit. II, cap. 1, *De Sacramento Baptismi,* nn. 22-26.

[83] Benedictus XIV, const. *"Dei miseratione,"* 3 nov. 1741, § 5: ". . . decernimus, in suis iubems, ut ab omnibus, et singulis Locorum Ordinariis in suis respective Diocesibus persona aliqua idonea eligatur, et si fieri potest ex Ecclesiastico coetu, iuris scientia pariter, et vitae probitate praedita quae Matrimoniorum Defensor nominabitur . . ."—*Fontes,* n. 318.

invalidity,[84] and in this lies the principal difference between those who are infamous at law and those who are infamous in fact regarding the performance of authorized ecclesiastical acts. As was noted in the previous chapter, with certain mitigations indicated by the law itself, the infamous at law are legally incapable [85] of the performance of authorized ecclesiastical acts. Any attempt to perform an authorized ecclesiastical act is invalid. Those who are infamous in fact are to be repelled from the performance of these acts. They are not permitted to carry them out. It is obvious from the text of the law itself, however, that any performance in contravention of this precept does not bring with it invalidity.[86] The authors are quick to mark this difference in the effect of the two species of infamy. Thus Berutti remarks:

> *Ceteri effectus infamiae facti iidem sunt qui ex infamia iuris oriuntur, cum hac tamen diversitate: quod nempe infamis infamia iuris invalide prorsus actus poneret sibi prohibitos, dum e contra infamis infamia facti illicite tantum eiusmodi actus poneret.*[87]

Section 2. The Exclusion of the Infamous in Fact From Ecclesiastical Offices and Dignities

It is to be noted that the infamous in fact are forbidden the reception of ecclesiastical offices and dignities. Canon 2294 concerns itself exclusively with the reception or the obtaining of ecclesiastical

84 "Animadvertas illum qui inhabilis est agere obtinere invalide, qui repellendus illicite tantum."—Chelodi-Ciprotti, *op. cit.*, n. 50, p. 62; Beste, *Introductio in Codicem,* p. 1018.

85 ". . . est inhabilis . . . ad actus legitimos ecclesiasticos perficiendos . . ."—Canon 2294, § 1.

86 "Irritantes aut inhabilitantes eae tantum leges habendae sunt, quibus aut actum esse nullum aut inhabilem esse personam expresse vel aequivalenter statuitur."—Canon 11.

87 Berutti, *Institutiones,* VI, n. 88, p. 226; cf. also Jone, *Commentarium,* III, 486; Vermeersch-Creusen, *Epitome,* n. 495, p. 305; Beste, *op. cit.*, p. 1018; Woywod, *A Practical Commentary,* II, n. 2135, p. 458; Conte a Coronata, IV, n. 1827, p. 274; Blat, *Commentarium,* V, n. 126, p. 178; Augustine, *A Commentary,* VIII, 247; Cocchi, *Commentarium,* VIII, n. 112, p. 194; Sipos, *Enchiridion,* n. 239, p. 847; Rodimer, *op. cit.*, p. 120.

offices and dignities. It does not deal with the loss of these positions. Thus the infamous at law are declared legally incapable of obtaining them while the infamous in fact are forbidden to do so.

An ecclesiastical office is defined in both a broad and a strict sense in canon 145. In the broad sense it is any function legitimately exercised for a spiritual purpose.[88] In the strict sense it is a function stably constituted by ecclesiastical or divine ordinance, conferred according to the norms of the sacred canons, and entailing at least some participation in the ecclesiastical power of orders or of jurisdiction.[89] In the law the term ecclesiastical office is to be understood in the strict sense unless the contrary is apparent from the context.[90] Thus it is to be understood in the strict sense in canon 2294. The performance of several authorized ecclesiastical acts is intimately bound up with the possession of an office in the strict sense, and thus their execution is forbidden under this heading also.[91]

The reception of ecclesiastical dignities is likewise forbidden to the infamous in fact. This exclusion has been witnessed throughout the history of canonical legislation,[92] and likewise is closely related to the exclusion from authorized ecclesiastical acts. The commentary on the exclusion of the infamous in fact from dignities in both the Roman and the earlier ecclesiastical law pointed to the presence of several authorized ecclesiastical acts within the comprehension of this term.

The term "ecclesiastical dignities" may be understood in several ways within the context of the present law. In the most restricted sense it refers to that group of clerics who together with the canons makes up a collegiate or cathedral chapter.[93] The various offices of

[88] Canon 145, § 1.

[89] Canon 145, § 1.

[90] Canon 145, § 2.

[91] E.g., that of the judge, referee and auditor. Cf. Roberti, *De Delictis et Poenis*, n. 338, p. 402.

[92] C. (12.1) 2; Reg. 87, R.J., in VI°.

[93] "In qualibet ecclesia capitulari sint dignitates et canonici inter quos varia officia distribuantur; . . ."—Canon 393, § 1; "Capitulum constat dignitatibus et canonicis, nisi, ad dignitates quod attinet, aliud ex capitularibus constitutionibus eruatur; . . ."—Canon 393, § 2.

the chapter are to be distributed among the clerics of these two groups.[94]

It is evident from both the pre-Code law and the present legislation that the term "ecclesiastical dignities" need not be restricted to this technical meaning. The glossator pointed out in reference to the exclusion of the infamous in fact from dignities that they therefore could not serve as a judge. They could, however, carry out the function of the *arbiter,* since this position was considered to be a burden rather than a dignity.[95] Commentators on the present law refer to the dignities from which various groups of the penalized are excluded as referring to certain positions of precedence and honor which may or may not be endowed with the power of jurisdiction.[96] Ecclesiastical dignities in the strict sense as mentioned above would most certainly be included within the scope of dignities in the wide sense. Others who might well be included are: the diocesan consultors, members of the pontifical household, possessors of ecclesiastical degrees of the doctorate or licentiate, certain diocesan officials such as the *officialis,* synodal and pro-synodal judges, synodal and pro-synodal examiners, etc.[97] It is clear then that the infamous in fact are excluded from some authorized ecclesiastical acts on the basis of this provision regarding exclusion from dignities.

Section 3. Corroborative Canonical Citations

The footnotes in the Code to canon 2294, § 2, refer the reader to several other canons in an effort to bring out more forcefully the true meaning of this canon itself.[98] Canons 373, § 4, 1589, § 1, and 1657, § 1, confirm the general legislation of canon 2294, § 2, by means of a negative approach. Whereas canon 2294, § 2, states

94 Canon 393, § 1.

95 ". . . Infamis, licet non possit esse iudex: tum (ut dictum est) potest esse arbiter, cum arbitrium non sit dignitas . . ."—*Glossa ordinaria* ad Reg. 87, R.J., in VI°, s.v. *dignitatum.*

96 Cf. Beste, *Introductio in Codicem,* p. 1009; Vermeersch-Creusen, *Epitome,* III, n. 467, p. 287; Blat, *Commentarium,* V, n. 92, p. 139.

97 Rodimer, *op. cit.,* p. 125.

98 Canons 373, § 4; 766, n. 2; 796, n. 3; 1589, § 1; 1657, § 1.

that the infamous of fact are to be excluded from the performance of authorized ecclesiastical acts, these canons state qualifications which are necessary before one may attain certain positions which involve the performance of authorized ecclesiastical acts. The very statement of these requisites makes it clear that the infamous in fact are not qualified for the positions in question. Thus, rather than stating outright that the infamous in fact are not qualified for the position of the chancellor or the notary, canon 373, § 4, declares that these positions must be filled by those who are of unblemished reputation and rise above all suspicion.[99] Canon 1589, § 1, employs the same approach in regard to the promoter of justice and the defender of the bond, who are likewise to be of unblemished reputation.[100] The position of the judicial procurator and advocate is likewise not open to the infamous in fact, since only those who are of good reputation are eligible.[101] The Code provides similar examples of this negative approach in regard to other authorized ecclesiastical acts which are not cited in the footnote to canon 2294, § 2.[102]

Canons 766, n. 2, and 796, n. 3, refer to sponsorship at baptism and confirmation. They likewise confirm the general legislation of canon 2294, § 2. The first point to be noted in this regard is that the same rules apply to both the sponsor at baptism and the sponsor at confirmation as regards infamy of fact. The basic principle is stated in canon 766, n. 2, concerning sponsors at baptism, and is adopted by canon 796, n. 3, for sponsors at confirmation. The rule simply states that one who is infamous in fact cannot licitly be admitted as a sponsor at baptism or at confirmation:

> *Non sit propter notorium delictum excommunicatus vel exclusus ab actibus legitimis vel infamis infamia iuris, quin tamen sententia intercesserit, nec sit interdictus aut alias publice criminosus vel infamis infamia facti;* [103]

99 "Cancellarius aliique notarii debent esse integrae famae et omni suspicione maiores."—Canon 373, § 4.

100 ". . . qui sint sacerdotes integrae famae . . ."—Canon 1589, § 1.

101 ". . . bonae famae; . . ."—Canon 1657, § 1.

102 Cf. canons 1573, § 4; 1574, § 1; 1592; 1521, § 1.

103 Canon 766, n. 2; cf. canon 796, n. 3.

There is some question whether the infamy of fact spoken of in the second part of this number must be such by reason of a notorius delict. The question is then whether the phrase *"propter notorium delictum"* refers to *"infamia facti"* as well as *"excommunicatus vel exclusus ab actibus legitimis vel infamis infamia iuris."* In practice the problem can be reduced to this: must the delict in virtue of which one suffers infamy of fact be notorious or merely public before one is excluded from sponsorship at baptism and confirmation?

The difference between a notorious delict and one which is public is pointed out in canon 2197. A delict is public when it is already divulged or if it was committed under or attended by such circumstances that its divulgement may and must be prudently judged to ensue quite readily.[104] It is notorious by notoriety of law after a competent judge's sentence which has become irrevocable (*res iudicata*), or after a confession of the delinquent made in court in the manner described in canon 1750.[105] It is notorious by notoriety of fact if it is publicly known and if it was committed under such circumstances that it cannot be concealed by way of any subterfuge or excused by way of any warrantable legal claim.[106] It is, therefore, obvious that there are more crimes which are public by nature than there are crimes which are notorious in this strict sense. If it is held that the delict of the person who is infamous in fact must be notorious and not merely public, then fewer infamous persons will be excluded from the function of sponsorship at baptism and at confirmation.

It seems that the question posed above must be answered in this manner: the delict in consequence of which one is infamous in fact need not be notorious.[107] It needs simply to be public. The phrase

[104] Canon 2197, n. 1.

[105] Canon 2197, n. 2.

[106] Canon 2197, n. 3.

[107] *Contra,* Prümmer: "Infamia *facti* contrahitur, quando quis ob patratum delictum vel ob pravos mores bonam existimationem apud fideles probos et graves amisit; de quo iudicium spectat ad Ordinarium, e.gr. episcopum vel superiorem maiorem religiosum. Sufficit quidem unum delictum probosum, dummodo id sit notorium et tam grave, ut iuxta iudicium Ordinarii (non alius hominis) destruat bonam existimationem apud fideles probos et graves."—Prümmer, *Manuale*, p. 667.

"propter notorium delictum" does not refer to *"infamia facti."* Thus, any person who suffers factual infamy is excluded from the authorized ecclesiastical acts of sponsorship at baptism and confirmation.

This answer is based in the first place upon the text and context of canon 766, n. 2. The grammatical structure of the text itself points to a separation of concepts. The first part of the number concerns itself with one who is excommunicated, one who is excluded from the performance of authorized ecclesiastical acts as a result of the particular vindictive penalty spoken of in canon 2291, n. 8,[108] or one who is subjected to legal infamy. Canon 765, n. 2, declares such persons unable to be validly admitted to this position when a condemnatory or a declaratory sentence has been passed.[109] Canon 766, n. 2, states that, even when no such sentence has been passed, they cannot be licitly admitted when the delict because of which they are infamous, excommunicated or excluded from the exercise of authorized ecclesiastical acts is a notorious delict. Other more specific details relating to these canons have already been pointed out in the earlier chapters which deal with excommunication and infamy of law.

The law then goes on to consider three other types of delinquent, that is, the one who is under interdict, the one who is infamous in fact, and the one who in other ways bears the stigma of public crime. This second consideration, introduced with the expression *"nec sit,"* is entirely separate from the first, and hence not modified by the phrase *"propter notorium delictum."*

The text, then, states that those who are marked with infamy of fact are to be excluded from the function of sponsorship. It was noted above in the discussion of the notion of infamy of fact as it appears in the present Code of Canon Law that the delict which gives rise to the infamy of fact must be public. The very nature of the state of infamy of fact calls for this. Infamy of fact is contracted when one loses his good name among good and serious Cath-

108 "Poenae vindicativae quae omnes fideles pro delictorum gravitate afficere possunt, in Ecclesia praesertim sunt: . . . 8°—Remotio ab actibus legitimis ecclesiasticis exercendis";—Canon 2291, n. 8.

109 Canon 765, n. 2.

olics on account of some delict he has committed.[110] It is self-evident that this crime must be public [111] before it can be the source of a loss of reputation.[112] There is no provision of reason, however, which calls for the note of notoriety in this delict. The notion of infamy of fact in itself does not postulate the note of notoriety. It is sufficient that the reputation be lost among good and prudent Catholics as the consequence of a public delict. Infamy of fact does not require notoriety of fact, much less notoriety of law with reference to the delict in question.

Canon 2294, § 2, states the general legislation of the Church that all those persons who suffer infamy of fact are forbidden to perform authorized ecclesiastical acts. Sponsorship at baptism and confirmation is one of these authorized ecclesiastical acts. There is nothing to indicate that the law calls for any different notion or added feature to the concept of infamy of fact in this particular case. Thus, it is not necessary that the delict in consequence of which one is infamous of fact be notorious.

Most of the authors are in agreement on this point. Many do not even treat the problem specifically but indicate by their translation or paraphrase of canon 766, n. 2, that they consider the element of notoriety as applying only to the excommunicated, those excluded from authorized ecclesiastical acts in themselves, and the infamous at law.[113] Others, such as Blat, (1870-1943),[114] Vidal

110 Cf. canon 2293, § 3.

111 Canon 2197, n. 1.

112 "Nimirum fundamentum huius infamiae est peccatum publicum quod, attenta qualitate et statu personae et communitatis intra quam vivit, eam reddit apud graves et honestos obiectae et vilis existimationis."—Gasparri, *op. cit.*, I, n. 306, p. 196; Reiffenstuel, *op. cit.*, VI, Lib. V, Tit. 34, n. 57, p. 558; Laymann, *Theologia Moralis,* Lib. I, Tract. V, Pars V, Cap. IV, n. 3, p. 173; Rodimer, *op. cit.*, p. 44.

113 Abbo-Hannan, *The Sacred Canons,* I, 767; Woywod, *A Practical Commentary,* I, 350; Jone, *Commentarium,* II, 38; Vermeersch-Creusen, *op. cit.*, II, n. 48, p. 28.

114 ". . . publice *criminosus;* et ex c. 2197: 'Delictum est publicum, si iam divulgatum est aut talibus contigit seu versatur in adiunctis ut prudenter iudicari possit et debeat facile divulgatum iri; quae publicitas extat quoque in sequenti: (c) *vel infamia facti . . .*'"—*Commentarium,* III, Pars I, n. 54, p. 61.

(1867-1938)[115] and Vogelpohl[116] more distinctly stated that the crime which serves as the source of the infamy of fact need only be public.

There are some authors, however, who maintain that notoriety must be present before one who labors under infamy of fact can be excluded from sponsorship at baptism and at confirmation.[117]

Thus it is clear that all the canonical references in the footnote to canon 2294, § 2, are of a confirmatory nature. They illuminate the legislation of this canon by pointing up its provisions in regard to specific authorized ecclesiastical acts in both a positive[118] and a negative manner.[119]

It is interesting to note the system of cross-reference which is employed by the legislator in this section. In canon 2294, § 2, it is stated that one who is infamous in fact is forbidden to perform authorized ecclesiastical acts. Canons 766, n. 2 and 796, n. 3, repeat this legislation in that they forbid one who suffers factual infamy to be admitted to sponsorship at baptism and at confirmation, which function evinces one particular authorized ecclesiastical act. Thus, whereas the infamous in fact are repelled from all authorized ecclesiastical acts by canon 2294, § 2, they are forbidden one particular authorized ecclesiastical act by canons 766, n. 2, and 796, n. 3.

Canon 2291, n. 8, lists the removal from the performance of authorized ecclesiastical acts as one of the principal vindictive penalties employed by the Church. Canons 766, n. 2, and 796, n. 3, point out that those who are excluded from authorized ecclesiastical acts in general are excluded from this particular authorized ecclesiastical act when they have been so punished in consequence of a notorious delict. This situation will receive further treatment in the following chapter.

115 *Ius Canonicum,* IV, Pars I, n. 264, pp. 352 and 353.

116 *The Simple Impediments to Holy Orders,* pp. 150 and 153.

117 Naz, *Traité de Droit Canonique* (4 vols., Vol. II, Paris: Letouzey and Ané, 1948), II, n. 48, p. 47; Prümmer, *op. cit.,* p. 374; Regatillo, *Ius Sacramentarium,* (2 vols., Vol. I, Sal Terrae: Santander, 1845), I, n. 62, p. 42.

118 Canons 766, n. 2 and 796, n. 3.

119 Canons 373, § 4; 1589, § 1; 1657, § 1.

Section 4. Comparison of the Effects of Infamy in Regard to Authorized Ecclesiastical Acts and a Summary of the Exclusion From the Performance of These Acts on the Part of the Infamous in Fact

In order to arrive at a better understanding of the present law on the exclusion from the performance of authorized ecclesiastical acts on the part of the infamous in fact it seems helpful to initiate a brief comparison between these effects and the effects flowing from infamy of law, as presented in canon 2294, § 1 and § 2.

The first paragraph of canon 2294 teaches that the infamous at law are unable to obtain ecclesiastical benefices, pensions, offices, and dignities. They further are unable to exercise ecclesiastical rights, functions and authorized ecclesiastical acts. As was pointed out in the previous chapter, these exclusions touch the element of validity. It is a general norm of law that these benefices, offices, pensions and dignities cannot be obtained validly. It is likewise a general norm of law that these rights, functions and authorized ecclesiastical acts cannot be exercised or performed validly.

The second paragraph of this same canon points out that those who are infamous in fact are forbidden to obtain ecclesiastical dignities, benefices and offices. They further are not permitted to perform authorized ecclesiastical acts. These exclusions touch, not the element of validity, but simply that of lawfulness. It is a general norm of law that these dignities, offices and benefices may indeed be obtained validly, albeit illicitly. Under the same norm authorized ecclesiastical acts may likewise be performed validly, but still only illicitly.

The only difference between the two lists of exclusions which affects authorized ecclesiastical acts is that, whereas the infamous at law are unable to exercise ecclesiastical right and functions (*munera*), these exclusions are left un-included among the restrictions placed upon the infamous in fact. It is clear, however, that certain rights and functions are forbidden to the infamous in fact inasmuch as they are constituted as authorized ecclesiastical acts, and thus are forbidden under this heading. Such are the right of patronage and of voting in an ecclesiastical election. The functions of the defender of the bond, the promoter of justice, the promoter of the faith, the notary, the chancellor, the messenger, the apparitor, the advocate, the procurator, the administrator of ecclesiastical property, the sponsor at baptism and the sponsor at confirmation are also denied to them. The positions of the judge, of the auditor and of the referee are offices in the strict sense of the term.[120] The law does not provide for the exclusion of the infamous in fact from other ecclesiastical functions. It seems, however, that the moral law itself would provide for such sanctions on the part of the infamous in fact in consideration of the danger of scandal arising from the performance of these functions, carried out as they are for a spiritual purpose.[121]

The principal difference between the effects of infamy of law and of infamy of fact in relation to authorized ecclesiastical acts, and the one which brings out the essential point to be remembered about infamy of fact is simply this: whereas infamy of law generally excludes a person from the valid performance of authorized ecclesiastical acts, infamy of fact never does so. Infamy of fact carries no invalidating effects. The one who is affected simply with factual infamy can validly obtain the incumbency which is forbidden to him, and validly perform any authorized ecclesiastical act. He does so illicitly, however. Woywod (1880-1941) summed up this idea quite well when he stated:

> There is a great difference between the consequences of the infamy of law and the infamy of fact. If it is an infamy of law, the person who incurred this penalty cannot validly obtain ecclesiastical benefices, pensions, offices and dignities, nor can he validly exercise the rights connected with the same nor perform a valid legal ecclesiastical act. If it is infamy of fact, the obtaining of ecclesiastical benefices, offices, etc. as well as their exercise, are illicit but valid.[122]

120 Cf. Roberti, *De Delictis et Poenis,* n. 338, p. 402.

121 Rodimer, *op. cit.,* p. 122.

122 *A Practical Commentary,* II, n. 2135, p. 458.

Section 5. The Cessation of the Exclusion From the Performance of Authorized Ecclesiastical Acts on the Part of the Infamous in Fact

The law of the Code of Canon Law orders that those who are infamous in fact are to be excluded from certain things, among which is the exercise of authorized ecclesiastical acts. The presence of this status of factual infamy is the cause for these exclusions in that the legislator has the duty to provide for the proper performance of these important actions as well as to forestall any scandal which might be given to the faithful should positions of such consequence be filled by those of unsavory reputation. [123] The exclusion from authorized ecclesiastical acts is, then, the effect of this infamy of fact. This effect, this exclusion, remains in operation for as long as the status of infamy of fact itself continues.[124] Once this status no longer continues, its effects, which are penal in character, likewise cease. It is, then, with the cessation of infamy of fact that the exclusion from the performance of authorized acts, which flow therefrom, also ceases.

Canon 2295 explains that the infamy of fact ceases when the reputation of the delinquent has been restored among good and serious Catholics. This the ordinary is in his own prudent judgment to determine after taking into consideration all the circumstances of the case, and particularly the prolonged amendment of the delinquent.[125]

Infamy of fact exists fundamentally when one has lost his reputation among good and serious Catholics because of some delict he has committed or in consequence of some immoral conduct. Thus, this infamy does not actually cease until this reputation has been recovered.[126] Since in the juridical order, some norm is absolutely

[123] Cf. Lega, *De Delictis et Poenis,* n. 289, p. 368.

[124] ". . . infamia facti, aboletur per emendationem; dum ipsa perdurat, judicio Ordinarii, *repelluntur infames* ab ordinibus recipiendis, a dignitatibus, beneficiis, officiis, ab exercendo sacro ministerio et ab actibus legitimis ecclesiasticis."—Raus, *Institutiones canonicae,* n. 460, p. 709.

[125] ". . . infamia facti cum bona existimatio apud fideles probos et graves, omnibus perpensis adiunctis et praesertim diuturna rei emendatione, fuerit, prudenti Ordinarii iudicio, recuperta."—Canon 2295.

[126] This natural state of ignominy cannot be taken away by means of any action of positive law. It must cease in the same manner in which it originated,

necessary in order that one may certify just when such a state exists, the law places upon the ordinary the burden of declaring its presence. In like manner, it is left to the prudent judgment of this same public superior to determine just when this state ceases. Within the juridical approach, then, it is the judgment of the ordinary that determines when the state of infamy of fact ceases.[127] The term "ordinary" is here to be taken in the sense of canon 198, § 1, and applies to that ordinary to whom the penitent is subject.[128]

In the formation of this judgment, which indeed is of much practical importance, the ordinary is to take into consideration all the circumstances of the individual case, and particularly the prolonged period of amendment on the side of the person in question. These are norms which the law provides for assisting the ordinary in his judgment on whether or not the reputation in question has been restored in the light of the positive signs of amendment on the part of the guilty party and his return to good favor in the eyes of the faithful.

The principal means by which the reputation of one who is infamous in fact may be restored is the practice over a continued period of time, of penance and amendment, which reflects the change that has been wrought in his way of life, and thus shows him worthy of acceptance in the good graces of the community. It is such a period that the ordinary is to hold in special regard when forming his judgment.

The duration of this period of amendment is not determined by the law beyond the very general word "*diuturna*." This follows from the very nature of infamy, in that this period must at least be so long that it allows for the recovery of the earlier good reputation. In general, the length of this period may be said to depend upon the nature of the delict or sinful actions, the degree of publicity

that is, through action on the part of the delinquent which can restore his reputation in the sight of good men. Cf. Lega, *op. cit.*, n. 290, p. 368.

[127] Vogelpohl distinguishes between *common* infamy of fact, which he defines as "that infamy which exists among the people" and *canonical* infamy of fact, which is this *common* infamy once it has been judged to be present by the ordinary.—*The Simple Impediments to Holy Orders,* p. 155.

[128] Blat, *Commentarium,* V, n. 127, p. 178.

present, the former status of the delinquent, the excellence of the virtues of the community where the repentence takes place, and the outward manifestation of the excellence of the penitent's virtues.[129] As a practical norm, however, certain specific periods have been suggested. The Sacred Congregation of the Council in many of its decisions concerning the cessation of infamy has indicated a period of three years' duration.[130] Vogelpohl holds this period as sufficient.[131] Other authors agree and base their opinion upon an analogy with canon 672, § 1, which treats of the case of dismissed religious who seek to return to the religious life. In this connection there is mention of a three-year period of amendment.[132] Others recommend a period of two years.[133] Cocchi sums up the question in this manner:

> *Per quantum temporis spatium emendatio rei durare debeat ut diuturna dici possit, ex iure praecedenti certe non constat; quidam biennium exigebant, et etiam minus quando accedebant signa extraordinaria poenitentiae; hodie res relinquitur prudenti Ordinarii iudicio.*[134]

The essential point to be noted here is that, in practice, it is the judgment of the ordinary which rules the day. Even should the infamy of fact cease in reality, that is, even if the reputation of the delinquent be regained or restored among good and serious Catholics, the legal effects of infamy of fact remain until the judgment of the ordinary is made. It is only with such a favorable judgment that these effects cease. Thus, one may be re-admitted to the performance

[129] Vogelpohl, *op. cit.*, p. 160.

[130] Cf. S.C.C., *Spoletana*, 19 ian. 1737—*Fontes*, n. 3467; S.C.C., *Elboren.*, 9 febr., 16 mart. 1737—*Fontes*, n. 3470; S.C.C., *Salernitana*, 9 febr. 1760—*Fontes*, n. 3693; S.C.C., *Terulen.*, 3 iul. 1762—*Fontes*, n. 3720; S.C.C., *Terulen.*, 27 aug., 24 sept. 1763—*Fontes*, n. 3731.

[131] Vogelpohl, *op. cit.*, p. 160.

[132] "The prolonged amendment (*diuturna emendatio*) very likely means laudable conduct for three years, as in the case spoken of in canon 672."—Woywod, *op. cit.*, II, n. 2136, p. 458; cf. Jone, *op. cit.*, III, p. 486; Conte a Coronata, IV, n. 1828, pp. 274-375; Sipos, *Enchiridion*, n. 239, p. 847, note 6.

[133] Berutti, *op. cit.*, VI, n. 88, p. 226.

[134] Cocchi, *Commentarium*, VIII, n. 112, p. 194.

of authorized ecclesiastical acts only after the prudent judgment of the ordinary that his good name has been regained or restored.

There is some question whether the judgment of the ordinary need be an explicit one. It seems preferable that such a judgment be clearly and explicitly expressed. It seems evident, however, that such a judgment is implied when the ordinary calls his subject to orders, or confers an office or a benefice upon one who had been excluded from these because of infamy of fact.[135] The same conclusion may be reached under the same circumstances in the matter of an appointment to a position that carries with it the performance of authorized ecclesiastical acts.

A comparison between infamy of law and infamy of fact in their very nature reveals the latter to be a relative thing. Infamy of law is a juridical penalty inflicted by means of the positive law as a punishment for certain serious crimes. These crimes are fixed and their effects stabilized in the law. This reflects a public advertence to and punishment of an evil deed. Once such a deed is perpetrated, infamy of law follows either immediately or upon a later judicial sentence.

Infamy of fact, on the other hand, connotes a natural status. It is the natural reaction of men to the evil conduct of others. It has its foundation in the very nature of things. The positive law recognizes this natural institution by attaching juridical effects to it. This action of the positive law reflects and voices as it were the natural law itself, which regards such persons as unworthy in relation to certain rights and capacities.[136]

It is obvious, however, that whereas the perpetration of a crime to which legal infamy is attached will always (all things being equal) result in this juridical status, no such definiteness exists in regard to infamy of fact. The natural reactions of good and serious people, even when anchored to a certain degree by a strong moral code, are subject to various influences of time, place and personality which

[135] "Dicemus proinde implicitum iudicium Ordinarii, quo clerico conferuntur ab eodem Ordinario ordines, officia aut beneficia aut exercitium sacri ministerii, sufficere ad recuperandam famam, dummodo habeatur diuturna emandatio."—Conte a Coronata, IV, n. 1828, pp. 274-275.

[136] Lega, *op. cit.*, n. 289, p. 368.

tend to color their outlook. The reactions of good and serious Catholics to certain crimes, occupations and ways of life have not always been what they are today. Further, they differ even today from one locale to another. The existence of the status of factual infamy, then, is a relative thing. It is contingent upon these various factors.

The locale influences the presence of infamy of fact in that the standards of modesty, the sensitivity to certain sins, and the repugnance to certain crimes differ from place to place.[137] Christian modesty, for example, is not judged by the same standards on a tropical Pacific island as it is in our great urban centers. A blasphemer might be subject to infamy of fact in one place while not in another.[138]

Time also affects infamy of fact in that with its passing the occupations which once were held in such ill repute that their occupants were actually liable to infamy of fact have come to be greatly respected. Such positions as those of the tavern keeper, executioner, actor, musician and policeman might be numbered among these.[139]

The personal dignity of the person involved also is a factor in the matter of determining the presence of infamy of fact. Crimes or sins committed by one of special dignity might lead to his loss of reputation among good and serious Catholics, whereas such an effect would not follow in the case of one of lesser rank. Thus, drunkenness in a priest would certainly tend to render him infamous in fact, whereas it would not necessarily have this effect in regard to a layman.[140]

These observations all tend to bring out the relative nature of infamy of fact. A person may, then, be infamous in fact in one place and not in another.[141]

137 Cf. Rodimer, *op. cit.*, p. 53; Vogelpohl, *op. cit.*, p. 151.

138 ". . . sic de blasphemis vulgaribus in quibusdam regionibus, qui quasi ex inopinato blasphemant, forte mitius iudicandum est."—Regatillo, *Ius Sacramentarium,* I, n. 62, p. 42.

139 Vogelpohl, *op. cit.*, pp. 151-152; Prümmer, *Manuale,* p. 667.

140 Gasparri, *op. cit.*, I, n. 308, p. 199; Laymann, *op. cit.*, Lib. I, Tract. V, Pars V, Cap. IV, n. 4, p. 173.

141 "*Infames infamia facti* et *criminosi* diversi in diversis regionibus censentur, de quo iudicium ad loci Ordinarium spectat";—Regatillo, *Ius Sacramentarium,* I, n. 62, p. 42.

The juridical effects of infamy of fact are operative only in that place in which the loss of reputation is suffered. When one suffers infamy of law he is incapable (with the mitigations noted in Chapter III) of performing authorized ecclesiastical acts anywhere until he is dispensed. When one is infamous in fact, however, one is excluded from the performance of these acts only in that place in which this status exists, that is, in that place in which he has lost his good name among good and serious Catholics. The judgment of the ordinary which is instrumental in certifying that the juridical effects of infamy of fact actually obtain, as also his judgment which brings about the cessation of these effects, applies only to the territory or the community over which this ordinary has jurisdiction.[142]

142 "Infamia facti delinquentem non afficit ultra terminos territorii aut iurisdictionis Ordinarii qui cuisdem declarationem emisit."—Conte a Coronata, IV, n. 1826, p. 273.

CHAPTER V

THE EXCLUSION FROM THE PERFORMANCE OF AUTHORIZED ECCLESIASTICAL ACTS IN THE NATURE OF A VINDICTIVE PENALTY

Article I. The Notion of the Vindictive Penalty

Canon 2291 presents a list of certain common vindictive penalties, to which all the faithful are subject according to the gravity of their offenses. Among these penalties is included the exclusion from the performance of authorized ecclesiastical acts. The law thus states that the faithful may be punished by being forbidden the exercise of these authorized ecclesiastical acts. This exclusion from the performance of authorized ecclesiastical acts differs from the ones previously considered in that it is direct and immediate. Whereas previously it has been noted that various groups or categories of the faithful are excluded from these actions because they are excommunicated or suffer legal or factual infamy, now it is clear that such a removal can be directly inflicted as a penalty in its own right without any relation to any other penalty or status of punishment.

An ecclesiastical penalty [1] is the deprivation of some good, which deprivation is inflicted by legitimate authority for the purpose of correcting a delinquent and of punishing his crime.[2] In the Church,

[1] "Quamvis etiam censura sit poena, tamen hoc nomen maxime proprium est *poenae vindicativae* 'quae *directe* ad delicti *expiationem* tendit ita ut eius remissio a cessatione contumaciae delinquentis non pendeat.' (Can. 2286)"—Chelodi-Ciprotti, *op. cit.*, n. 46, p. 62.

[2] Canon 2215; ". . . '*ad delinquentis correctionem et delicti punitionem*' quibus verbis denotatur *finis* poenarum; finis autem huiusmodi *triplex* est; *seu*: *delinquentis conversio,* cum Ecclesia pro suo supremo fine curare debeat salutem animarum ad quam pertinet delinquentis emendatio; hunc finem habent *censurae* seu poenae medicinales quae feruntur ad infringendam contumacium rei, et *remedia poenalia* et *poenitentiae* quae feruntur ad curanda vulnera delinquentis *vel* ad auxilium reo praebendum;—*ordinis socialis conservatio,* ideo Ecclesia deterrere debet fideles a criminum admissione, quod facit poenas statuens *tum* medicinales *tum* vindicativas;—*iustitiae socialis reparatio,* cum enim haec postulet ut delictum non maneat impunitum, poenae ab Ecclesia

delinquents are punished by means of the infliction of medicinal penalties or censures, of vindictive penalties, and of penal remedies and penances.[3] The essential and ultimate purpose of an ecclesiastical penalty is the preservation and protection of the social order in the Church. Its immediate end, which ordinarily serves as a means for the obtaining of this ultimate goal, is the correction and rehabilitation of the delinquent. It seeks to induce the delinquent to make reparation for his offense and his violation of the social order as well as to remove whatever scandal may have been caused.[4] A penalty is termed vindictive when it tends directly towards the punishment of the crime, that is, when this ultimate or essential purpose receives special emphasis.[5] Whereas the medicinal penalty or censure looks primarily towards the amendment of the individual delinquent, the vindictive penalty concerns itself chiefly with the restoration of the violated social order. Its primary concern is the good of the community and the expiation of the crime.[6] It looks

infliguntur in vindictam delicti et ad scandali reparationem quasi *reactio* ordinis contra *deordinationem;* ad hunc finem ordinantur praesertim poenae vindicativae."—Cocchi, *op. cit.*, VIII, n. 20, p. 45, cf. Sipos, *op. cit.*, n. 229, p. 815; Raus, *op. cit.*, n. 443, p. 686.

[3] Canon 2216.

[4] Ayrinhac-Lydon, *Penal Legislation*, p. 26; Beste, *Introductio in Codicem*, p. 1015; Berutti, *Institutiones*, VI, n. 83, p. 213; ". . . finis intrinsecus a quo Ecclesia abstrahere nequit est *reparatio ordinis laesi* ad quam essentialiter pertinet iustitia criminalis *seu* potestas punitiva. . . ."—Cocchi, *op. cit.*, n. 20, p. 45.

[5] Canon 2286.

[6] The reason for which a crime is punished "is the re-establishment of the confidence of the members of society that their rights are adequately guaranteed by social authority, a confidence that might be dangerously shaken if a grave transgression remained unpunished."—Abbo-Hannan, *The Sacred Canons*, II, 799; "The reformation of the delinquent is only a secondary purpose of vindictive penalties, a purpose that is at least not excluded from their aim";—Abbo-Hannan, *op. cit.*, II, 850. A vindictive penalty is therefore a "malum privationis vel passionis fideli delinquenti directe, in ultionem delicti a competente ecclesiastica potestate inflictum, ad tuendum ordinem socialem ecclesiae, et indirecte ad emandationem delinquentis."—Wernz-Vidal, *Ius Canonicum*, VII, n. 332, p. 363; Conte a Coronata, IV, n. 1819, p. 265; Vermeersch-Creusen, *Epitome*, III, n. 489, p. 299; Jone, *Commentarium*, III, 481; Lega, *De Delictis et Poenis*, n. 199, p. 270; Berutti, *op. cit.*, VIII, n. 83, p. 213.

primarily to the violation of the law rather than the violater of the law.[7]

The vindictive penalty further differs from the censure in that, whereas the latter aims primarily at the amendment of the delinquent and thus demands absolution as soon as he has receded from his contumacy,[8] the vindictive penalty in and of its nature (*per se*) continues in existence even after the repentance of the delinquent.[9] It is inflicted for a certain period of time or even perpetually, and the repentance of the delinquent gives him no right to demand its expiation.[10] This temporal element of vindictive penalties is an exclusive characteristic, and many times it serves as the principal means by which a particular penalty may be properly identified.[11]

Vindictive penalties may be determinate or indeterminate; of a *latae sententiae* or a *ferendae sententiat* character; and they may derive either *a iure* or *ab homine.*

A penalty is determinate or specific when the law or precept defines it specifically.[12] It is so clearly specified that there can be no doubt as to what is meant. In order to qualify it as a determinate penalty, the law or the precept must state the quality and quantity of the penalty, the good of which the delinquent is deprived, and the length of time involved for its observance.[13] Whenever the law or the precept neglects to specify the penalty that is to be levied, the good whose loss will be involved, or the duration of the time for the observance of the penalty, such a penalty is referred to as indeterminate, inasmuch as the law leaves these factors to the prudent discretion of the judge or the superior for their specific determination.[14] This may involve the question whether any penalty

[7] Chelodi-Ciprotti, *Ius Canonicum De Delictis et Poenis,* n. 46, p. 62.

[8] Canon 2241.

[9] Cf. canon 2286; Conte a Coronata, IV, n. 1819, p. 265; Sipos, *op. cit.,* n. 238, p. 844.

[10] Woywod, *op. cit.,* II, n. 2051, pp. 412-413; Wernz-Vidal, *op. cit.,* n. 332, p. 363; Conte a Coronata, *op. cit.,* IV, n. 1819, p. 265; Sipos, *Enchiridion,* n. 238, p. 844.

[11] Woywod, *A Practical Commentary,* II, n. 2051, p. 413.

[12] Canon 2217, n. 1.

[13] Berutti, *op. cit.,* VI, n. 19, p. 64.

[14] Canon 2217, n. 1; Berutti, *op. cit.,* n. 19, p. 64.

at all is to be inflicted, or what type of penalty, or in what degree or for what length of time it is to be imposed.[15]

With reference to the manner in which they are inflicted, vindictive penalties may be divided into *latae sententiae* penalties and *ferendae sententiae* penalties. A vindictive penalty is termed *latae sententiae* when a determinate penalty is attached to a law or a precept in such a way that it is incurred automatically upon the commission of the crime involved. It is referred to as *ferendae sententiae* when the penalty needs to be inflicted by a judge or a superior.[16] This division points out the proximate agency of the punishment, that is, either the law in its being violated or the superior in his subsequent action. The *latae sententiae* penalty may be considered as inflicted upon the potential delinquent by the lawgiver at the moment of the promulgation of the law or the precept. Thus the term *latae sententiae* is appropriate, because in some manner the condemnatory sentence has already been extrajudicially passed upon the delinquent.[17] All *latae sententiae* vindictive penalties are determinate or specific penalties. *Ferendae sententiae* vindictive penalties, on the other hand, may be determinate or indeterminate.[18] They are termed *ferendae sententiae* because at the time of the commission of the delict the sentence has not yet been passed, and thus the delinquent is not bound to observe the penalty unless and until that time at which the penalty is legitimately inflicted upon him through the action of the judge or the superior.[19]

A penalty is always understood to be *ferendae sententiae* unless it is expressly stated that it is *latae sententiae* or incurred automatically, through the use of such terms as *ipso facto, ipso iure,* and *eo ipso*.[20]

[15] Cf. Augustine, *A Commentary,* VIII, 72; Ayrinhac-Lydon, *op. cit.*, n. 35, p. 27; Ferreres, *Institutiones Canonicae* (2 vols., Vol. II, ed. altera, Barcinone: Eugenius Subirana, 1920), II, n. 968, p. 408.

[16] Canon 2217, § 1, n. 2.

[17] Berutti, *op. cit.*, VI, n. 19, p. 65.

[18] Blat, *Commentarium,* V, n. 34, p. 50; Berutti, *op. cit.*, VI, n. 19, p. 65; Christ, *Dispensation from Vindicative Penalties,* p. 57.

[19] Berutti, *op. cit.*, VI, n. 19, p. 65.

[20] Cf. canon 2217, § 2; Abbo-Hannan, *op. cit.*, II, 801.

Vindictive penalties are also divided into those which are derived *a iure* and those which are derived *ab homine.* A penalty is derived *a iure* when a determinate penalty is established in the law itself whether it be then inflicted as a *latae sententiae* or a *ferendae sententiae* penalty.[21] This division looks to the penal law's origin, or the manner in which its enactment becomes an operative and applicable penalty.[22] The penalty is referred to as deriving *ab homine* when it is inflicted, either by way of a particular precept or by way of a condemnatory judicial sentence, even though it has been established in the law or through some precept.[23] This division looks to the manner in which the penal law is put into execution or in which the punishment is set in operation.[24] It is obvious, then, that a *ferendae sententiae* penalty, when enacted in law derives simply *a iure* prior to the condemnatory sentence; after such a sentence it derives *ab homine* as well as *a iure,* but by the direction of the law it is to be considered as deriving *ab homine.*[25] In abstraction from all further discussion on this point, it seems the better opinion to hold that no *latae sententiae* penalty is ever to be regarded as deriving *ab homine.* This is true because the sentence which declares that such a penalty has been incurred does not change its character, i.e. does not make of it a penalty derived from man *ab homine* as well as from the law *a iure,* and it does not cause it to be reserved in the manner that a penalty derived from man *ab homine* is reserved.[26]

[21] Canon 2217, § 1, n. 3.

[22] Moriarity, *Extraordinary Absolution from Censures,* The Catholic University of America Canon Law Studies, n. 113 (Washington: D. C., The Catholic University of America Press, 1938), p. 96.

[23] Cf. canon 2217, § 1, n. 3.

[24] Moriarity, *op. cit.,* p. 96.

[25] Canon 2217, § 1, n. 3.

[26] Abbo-Hannan, *op. cit.,* II, p. 801; cf. Vermeersch-Creusen, *op. cit.,* III, n. 406, p. 243; Roberti, "An censurae latae sententiae per praeceptum constituta sit reservata?" *Appolinaris,* VI, (1933), 341; Conte a Coronata, IV, n. 1690, p. 82; Bouscaren-Ellis, *Canon Law,* p. 868; Jone, *op. cit.,* III, 418; Beste, *op. cit.,* p. 977; Sipos, *op. cit.,* n. 229, p. 816, footnote 5.

ARTICLE II. THE HISTORICAL DEVELOPMENT OF THE EXCLUSION FROM THE PERFORMANCE OF AUTHORIZED ECCLESIASTICAL ACTS IN THE NATURE OF VINDICTIVE PENALTY

Section 1. Introductory Notions

The Church is a perfect and supreme society which has been established by its Divine Founder to lead men to heaven.[27] As such, it possesses those means which are necessary for the carrying out of this purpose.[28] As was pointed out in the chapter concerning the exclusion from the performance of authorized ecclesiastical acts as the result of excommunication, in order that this end be attained it is necessary that the Church possess authority to legislate, judge and enforce laws which serve as means to this goal.[29] This is true because the Church is an external society composed of men, and is governed, according to the will of its Divine Founder, by men. Thus, it must be governed by means of laws which regulate the actions of its members in accordance with its end and purpose. Though the Church possesses supreme legislative and judiciary power, it would not be able to efficiently carry out its mission and fulfill its purpose did it not possess the right to coerce its contumacious members by means of the infliction of penalties.[30] This doctrine has been proposed as follows:

> The *"fundamentum et ratio"* of the penalties of the Church, as those of the civil power in regard to its end, is the fulfillment and attainment of her end and purpose.[31]

This right of the Church to punish its delinquent members has been exercised from its very beginning.[32] Even in Apostolic times there are examples of the exclusion of members from the Church as a penalty for their offenses.[33] It must be noted, however, that al-

[27] Cf. Ottaviani, *op. cit.*, I, n. 98, p. 173.

[28] Cf. Ottaviani, *op. cit.*, I, n. 109, pp. 194-196.

[29] Cf. Ottaviani, *op. cit.*, I, nn. 36-38, pp. 80-128.

[30] Cf. Ottaviani, *ibid.*, nn. 164-170, pp. 294-310.

[31] Christ, *op. cit.*, p. 1.

[32] Cf. Ottaviani, *ibid.*, nn. 171-177, pp. 311-324.

[33] Cf. Matthew, 18:18; 18:15-17; I Timothy, 1:18-20; I Cor., 5:1-5; I Cor., 5:11 and 13; Romans, 16:17; Titus, 3:10; I Cor., 16:22.

though these and similar penalties were inflicted and served as a foundation for the legislation of later times there was no well organized and definite penal system in this primitive period. Because of the infancy of the Church and the persecutions raging against it no such clearly defined system could be expected.

Terms and concepts were not employed with the same precision and meaning they were to acquire in later times. As an example of this it is noted that the term "excommunication" had such a broad connotation that it was used in designation of all ecclesiastical penalties.[34] The term "censure" was likewise used in this broad sense.[35] There was, further, no clear distinction between the internal or penitential forum and the external or judicial forum.[36] Delinquent members of the Church were customarily chastised in the penitential forum, and thus the punishments inflicted partook more of the nature of penances than penalties in the strict sense. This identification of the penitential system of the Church with its penal system remained in force until the disappearance of public penances in the West in the twelfth century.[37]

In this early period there was likewise no clear distinction between vindictive and medicinal penalties. It seems that the majority of the penalties imposed at that time would be designated today as vindictive in nature, since the public aspect of the Church and the repair of the violated social order were primarily stressed,[38] although the amendment of the delinquent was not ignored.[39] Further, the penalties were usually enjoined for a definite period of time.[40]

[34] Hyland, *op. cit.*, p. 19.

[35] Moriarity, *op. cit.*, p. 5.

[36] Morinus, *Commentarius Historicus de Disciplina in Administratione Sacramenti Poenitentiae Tredecim Primis Saeculis in Ecclesia Occidentali, et huc usque in Orientali Observata* (Parisiis, 1651), lib. I, cap. 9-10.

[37] Morinus, *op. cit.*, lib. VII, cap. 7.

[38] Rainer, *Suspension of Clerics,* The Catholic University of America Canon Law Studies, n. 111 (Washington, D. C.: The Catholic University of America, 1937), pp. 13-14.

[39] Cappello, *De Censuris,* n. 7, p. 8.

[40] Christ, *op. cit.*, p. 6; Council of Agde (506), c. 60: "Si episcopus est, tribus mensibus se a communione suspendat; presbyter duobus mensibus se abstineat."—Mansi, VIII, 559.

A definite change in the formation and development of the penal system of the Church took place with the conclusion of the period of persecution at the beginning of the fourth century. At that time the various bishops were more readily able to convene and to make laws of more general application, while at the same time the enactment of papal law became more frequent.[41] It was, however, only in the twelfth century that the penal law of the Church became distinct from its penitential system, and thus the gradual evolution and precision in the disciplinary legislation of the Church continued its development.

Section 2. Survey of Roman Law

The right of the Church to punish its delinquent members as a necessary means towards the accomplishment of its end is God-given. As such, it takes its origin neither from Roman Law nor from any other human source. Since, however, many principles and institutes of Roman Law were adopted by the Church and incorporated into its juridical system; and since many particular crimes and penalties were likewise appropriated from this source, a brief survey of Roman penal law as applied to those actions now known as authorized ecclesiastical acts is in order.

It was not uncommon in the Roman legal system that persons be forbidden to perform the duties of certain important offices as the result of a crime they had committed. These penalties, vindictive in nature, embraced many acts which are now included within the concept of authorized ecclesiastical acts by the Code of Canon Law. Such punishments were common particularly in cases relating to judicial offices. Thus the law states that it was not unusual for the governors to forbid certain persons to act as an advocate either for his lifetime or for a determined period.[42] The penalty was also frequently broadened in that the practce of law in any capacity was forbidden. As a result of this punishment the party in question was not permitted to transact any legal business whatsoever. Such penal-

[41] Christ, *op. cit.*, p. 21.

[42] D. (48.19) 9.

ties were customarily levied against delinquent advocates, notaries, students of law and other members of the legal profession.[43]

Before proceeding to the review of more specific injunctions, one may with interest note that Roman Law contained the generic prohibition of the conferring of honors upon unworthy persons. The portals to positions of honor and dignity were not open to those who lived wicked and evil lives.[44] The law declared, in general, that the prohibition to accept any honor could in the nature of a penalty be imposed upon anyone.[46] There were also a great many particular crimes which were punished with the exclusion from honors and dignities. This point is emphasized because all the present authorized ecclesiastical acts are considered as involving a position of honor and dignity. Thus, soldiers who had received a dishonorable discharge were not permitted to become candidates for any honorable office.[47] Further, those who had belonged to the lowest class of certain occupations and others who occupied base and dishonorable positions were not permitted to enjoy any position of dignity. If they occupied such a position they were to be deprived of it.[48]

One who had incurred a debt to the government was punished by being excluded from consideration for any official position of honor before he had discharged his debt.[49] Deprivation of a position of dignity was to follow as punishment for one who had perjured himself during the course of a criminal trial.[50] The law reiterated that those who stand accused of crime could not be raised to any new dignity before having established their innocence.[51] Serfs were banned from elevation to any position of dignity.[53] There were many similar cases.[54]

[43] D. (48.10) 9.
[44] C. (12.1) 2.
[46] D. (48.22) 7.
[47] C. (10.54) 1.
[48] C. (12.1) 6.
[49] C. (11.32) 1.
[50] C. (12.1) 17.
[51] C. (10.58) 1.
[53] C. (11.67) 1.
[54] Cf. C. (10.59) 2; D. (48.7) 1; D. (48.12) 2; D. (48.12) 3, 4, 5, 6; C. (12.24) 2

Roman Law also contained specific penalties which resulted in the exclusion of the delinquent from particular employments which come within the category of the present authorized ecclesiastical acts. One convicted of a crime involving private violence was, in addition to other penalties, not permitted to be a judge.[55] The same punishment was inflicted upon one convicted of extortion.[56] Those judges who were alleged to have been bribed or corrupted by money in other ways were usually punished by being taken off the court roster.[57] The conviction of a crime of dishonesty and other misdeeds also resulted in the deprivation of this office.[58] There were also other examples of this punishment.[59]

Those notaries who in consequence of preoccupation with their own affairs failed to appear in the imperial palace for a period of five continuous years were punished by being deprived of this function.[60]

Advocates, when they betrayed their trust by delivering documents to their client's opponent, were to receive several punishments, all of which implied the impossibility of continued functioning in this office.[61] Exclusion from this position for a limited period of time was the punishment meted out to those who were guilty of reading a forged document during the course of a judicial hearing in court.[62]

The office of the procurator was forbidden to those who had allowed their body to be used like that of a woman. Those convicted of capital crimes were dealt with in a like manner.[63]

Penalties were also inflicted upon those who maladministered imperial property. Those once convicted of a breach of trust were deprived of all offices of trust, and could not be reinstated.[64] Convic-

[55] D. (48.7) 1.
[56] D. (48.11) 6.
[57] D. (48.19) 38.
[58] C. (12.1) 12.
[59] D. (48.12) 2, 3, 4, 5, 6.
[60] C. (12.7) 2.
[61] D. (48.19) 38.
[62] D. (48.9) 13.
[63] D. (3.1) 1.
[64] C. (12.24) 2.

tion of the more specific crime of fraud on the part of a recording clerk resulted in the loss of this office also.[65]

Section 3. The Law in the Pseudo-Isidorian Decretals

The Pseudo-Isidorian Decretals are of little value in providing direct references to the exclusion, by way of vindictive penalty, from actions now known as authorized ecclesiastical acts. There are, of course, many examples of this type of penalty, but few if any references to exclusion from the acts in question. The texts make it obvious that those who were guilty of certain crimes were not able to perform the judicial functions that are now classified among the authorized ecclesiastical acts. This conclusion is reached by deduction, however, and not from the text of the legislation itself.

It is clear from the law of the decretals that those whose life was suspect in any way were not permitted to lodge a suit in court or to accuse another judicially.[66] This was true of criminals [67] and of those who conspired againse their bishop [68] as well as foreigners,[69] of those who disobeyed the laws of the Church,[70] of heretics, murderers, the excommunicated, thieves, persons guilty of sacrilege, adulterers, persons who patronized fortunetellers,[72] and many others.[73]

The right to give testimony, which history shows to have always been closely associated with the authorized ecclesiastical acts of the present law, was taken away from those who disobeyed the laws

65 C. (10.70) 12.

66 *Capitula Angilramni,* Cor. Par. XII—Hinschius, *op. cit.*, p. 761.

67 Pseudo-Fabianus, Ep. I, cap. 6—Hinschius, *op. cit.*, p. 159, Jaffé, n. +92.

68 Pseudo-Callistus, Ep. II, cap. 8—Hinschius, *op. cit.*, p. 138, Jaffé, n. +86.

69 Pseudo-Stephanus, Ep. II, cap. 7—Hinschius, *op. cit.*, p. 184, Jaffé, n. +131.

70 Pseudo-Eutychianus, Ep. II, cap. 8—Hinschius, *op. cit.*, p. 212, Jaffé, n. +146.

72 Pseudo-Eutychianus, Ep. II, cap. 8—Hinschius, *op. cit.*, p. 211, Jaffé, n. +146.

73 Cf. Pseudo-Fabianus, Ep. I, cap. 5—Hinschius, *op. cit.*, p. 158, Jaffé, n. +92; Pseudo-Fabianus, Ep. I, cap. 12—Hinschius, *op. cit.*, p. 162, Jaffé, n. +92; *Capitula Angilramni*, Cor. Par. XIII and XIV—Hinschius, *op. cit.*, p. 761; *Capitula Angilramni,* Cor. Par. Sal. X—Hinschius, *op. cit.*, p. 767.

of the Church.[74] In another general penalty, clerics who conspired against their bishops were to be deprived of all positions of honor.[75]

It is clear that since the perpetrators of these various crimes were punished with these minor exclusions, the more important authorized ecclesiastical acts, at least in the judicial sphere, were likewise out of bounds for such criminals.

It is also to be noted that foreigners were forbidden to become judges.[76] This was not, however, a penalty in the strict sense.

Section 4. The Law in the *Corpus Iuris Canonici*

The law prior to the Code of Canon Law in general, as also that of the *Corpus Iuris Canonici* in particular, does not supply a great many references to the exclusions from authorized ecclesiastical acts in the nature of vindictive penalties. The principal reason for this seems to lie in the general imprecision of terms, an imprecision which was only gradually corrected. Thus, it is to be noted that the term "excommunication" was used in earlier legislation in designation of all ecclesiastical punishments and penalties. "It was only in the twelfth or thirteenth century that its technical meaning became definitely fixed, and the term employed to designate exclusively one of the three penalties which were thereafter distinguished from all others by the name of censures." [77] The extremely wide comprehension of the term "infamous" also contributes to this condition. So many different classes of criminals and crimes were included under this heading [78] that it is difficult to discover many references to the

[74] Pseudo-Eutychianus, Ep. II, cap. 8—Hinschius, *op. cit.*, p. 212, Jaffé, n. +146.

[75] Pseudo-Callistus, Ep. II, cap. 9—Hinschius, *op. cit.*, p. 138, Jaffé, n. +86.

[76] Pseudo-Stephanus, Ep. II, cap. 7—Hinschius, *op. cit.*, p. 184, Jaffé, n. +131.

[77] Ayrinhac-Lydon, *Penal Legislation*, n. 110, p. 85.

[78] "Infames esse eas personas dicimus, quae pro aliqua culpa notantur infamia, idest omnes, qui Christianae legis normam abiiciunt, et itatuta ecclesiastica contemnunt: similiter fures, sacrilegos, et omnes capitalibus criminibus irretitos; sepulchrorum quoque violatores, et Apostolorum, atque successorum eorum, reliquorumque patrum statuta libenter violantes, et omnes, qui adversus patres armantur, qui in omni mundo infamia notantur: similiter et incestuosos, homicidas, periuros, raptores, maleficos, veneficos, adulteros, de bellis publicis fugientes, et qui indigna sibi petunt loca tenere, aut facultates ecclesiae abstra-

exclusion from authorized ecclesiastical acts or individual authorized ecclesiastical acts independent of these wider categories of excommunication and infamy. This lack of precision is also to be noted in comparison with the vindictive penalties levied by the Code of Canon Law itself. Whereas the Code punishes a crime with a specific penalty, e.g., the exclusion from the performance of authorized ecclesiastical acts, either one or several of them, the former law simply refers to the delinquent as being subjected to penance.[79]

In spite of these difficulties several significant examples of the exclusion from the performance of authorized ecclesiastical acts in the nature of a vindictive penalty are to be found in the *Corpus Iuris Canonici* and contemporary legislation. Canon 18 of the Council of Milan (1287) pointed out that those who were guilty of perjury were to be punished by being forbidden the performance of law-approved acts.[80] Pope Leo X (1513-1521) in his Constitution "*Exsurge Domine*" of June 15, 1520, made it clear that those who were guilty of embracing the errors of Luther in any way were to be punished by being incapable of performing any of these actions.[81]

Those who were guilty of heresy or of aiding heretics in any way were punished with excommunication. If they failed to amend within a year, they automatically incurred other penalties, some of which involved exclusion from the performance of authorized ecclesiastical acts. Thus, a judge guilty of this crime was deprived of his office to the extent that his sentences were invalid, and no causes could be brought before him. An advocate could likewise no longer

hunt iniuite, et qui fratres calumniantur, aut accusant et non probant, vel qui contra innocentes principum animos ad iracundiam provocant, et omnes anathematizatos, vel pro suis sceleribus ab ecclesia pulsos, et omnes, quos ecclesiasticae, vel saeculi leges infames pronuntiant."—c. 17, C. VI, q. 1; cf. Pseudo-Stephanus, Ep. I and II, cap. 2—Hinschius, *op. cit.*, p. 182, Jaffé, n. +131; Pseudo-Eusebius, Ep. III, cap. 18—Hinschius, *op. cit.*, p. 239, Jaffé, n. +165.

[79] E.g., c. 5, C. XXXI, q. 1; c. 6, C. XXXIV, qq. 1, 2; c. 21, X, *de sponsalibus et matrimoniis,* IV, 1; c. 5, X, *de eo qui duxit in matrimonium quam polluit per adulterium,* IV, 7.

[80] ". . . periuri . . . sunt ab omni actu legitimo repellendi . . ."—Mansi, XXIV, 878.

[81] *Fontes,* n. 76.

carry out his judicial functions. Any actions performed by a notary guilty of this crime were also declared invalid. The law went on to state that those who were engaged in similar occupations, ". . . *Et in similibus idem praecipimus obsevari,*" and were guilty of this crime were to receive like punishments. The right of active voice in elections was also forfeited in consequence of such actions.[82] Later legislation punished heretics, those who aided them in any way, and within these categories also their children to the second generation by forbidding them admittance to any public office or preferment.[83] The glossator explained that the position of the judge, of the notary and of other similar functions were included within the scope of this legislation.[84]

The law contained the example of one who bought a right of patronage so as to be able to present a son, a relative, or anyone he wished, and stated that such a person was to be deprived of this right. Anyone buying or selling the right of patronage was to be so punished.[85] This was the case because *"ius patronatus per se vendi non potest."* [86]

A patron or advocate who was guilty, whether in person (*per se*) or through another (*per alios*) of killing or injuring another cleric was to be punished with exclusion from his position.[87]

In addition to these specific exclusions from positions now involving the performance of authorized ecclesiastical acts, the law of this period abounds in more generic disqualifications of a vindictive nature. Thus, those who were guilty of schism were perpetually deprived and made juridically incapable of again receiving any ecclesiastical offices, honors, and dignities.[88] Crimes of impurity were frequently punished in this manner also. Thus, priests charged with adultery, if they did not submit to the required canonical

[82] C. 13, *de haereticis,* V, 7.

[83] C. 2, *de haereticis,* V, 2, in VI°.

[84] *Glossa ordinaria* ad c. 2, *de haereticis,* V, 2, in VI°, s.v. *publicum.*

[85] C. 6, X, *de iure patronatus,* III, 38.

[86] C. 16, X, *de iure patronatus,* III, 38.

[87] C. 12, X, *de poenis,* V, 37.

[88] C. 1, *de schismaticis,* V, 3, in VI°; c. 1, X, *de schismaticis et ordinatis ab eis,* V, 8.

purgation, were to be suspended from office.[89] Those who were guilty of conspiracy against their bishop [90] as well as those who aided or co-operated with them in any way received a like punishment.[91] Murderers,[92] apostates from religion [93] and other criminals were also excluded from or deprived of ecclesiastical honors, offices and dignities.[94]

Section 5. The Law From the Council of Trent to the Code of Canon Law

Ecclesiastical legislation from the Council of Trent to the Code of Canon Law provided additional examples of vindictive penalties which excluded the delinquent from the performance of "legitimate acts" in general, and also several individual acts, which are now considered authorized ecclesiastical acts.

Those persons who were guilty of meddling in papal elections as well as those who co-operated with them were punished by being deprived of the right of patronage and also of the active and passive voice in elections. This deprivation also extended to any jurisdiction they possessed just as it extended to any offices and honors they held. In addition, these delinquents were declared juridically incapable of acquiring ecclesiastical honors and dignities. Most important of all for this study, they were incapable of performing "legitimate acts." [95]

Pope Paul IV (1555-1559) further decreed that among other punishments those who were guilty of heresy were excluded from several authorized ecclesiastical acts. Judges guilty of this crime were unable to pass a valid sentence, or even to have causes tried before them. Advocates were forbidden to practice their profession, and

89 C. 5, X, *de adulteriis et stupro,* V, 16; cf. also c. 28, C. XXVII, q. 1.

90 C. 23, C. XI, q. 1.

91 C. 1, *de poenis,* V, 8, in Clem.

92 C. 1, *de homicidio,* V, 4, in VI°.

93 C. 69, D. L.

94 Cf. c. 7, D. L; c. 13, X, *de haereticis,* V, 7; Leo X, const. *Exsurge Domine,* 15 iun. 1520—*Fontes,* n. 76.

95 Paulus IV, const. *Cum secundum,* 16 dec. 1558, nn. 2, 3, 5.—*Bull. Rom. Taur.,* VI, 545.

the documents drawn up by notaries guilty of this crime were devoid of legal value. Heretics were also deprived of their passive voice in elections.[96]

The exercise of the office of the notary was also forbidden either perpetually or for a determined period of time to those notaries who, upon investigation by the bishop, were found to be delinquent or incompetent in the fulfillment of their duties.[97]

The legislation depriving one of the right of patronage if he attempted to transfer this right by sale was repeated in this period and extended to embrace any other means of transfer.[98] The Council of Trent also decreed that, in addition to other penalties one vested with the right of patronage who

> presumed to convert to his own use and usurp *per se* or *per alios*, by force or fear, or even by means of supposititious persons, whether clerical or lay, or by any fraud or colored pretext whatever, the perogatives, properties, rents and rights, even those held in fee or under lease, revenues, profits or any incomes whatever, belonging to any church or benefices, secular or regular, eleemosynary institutions or any other pious places, which ought to be used for the needs of the ministers and the poor. . . .[99]

was to be *eo ipso* deprived of this right. Even interference in these matters, and under any pretext, was punished with the automatic loss of this right.[100] In addition, the right of presentation was lost to the patron if he did not present his candidate within the time specified by law.[101]

The administrators of ecclesiastical hospitals who, after having been warned by the ordinary, neglected to discharge their duty of

[96] Const. "*Cum ex apostolatus,* 15 febr. 1559, § 5—*Fontes,* n. 94; cf. c. 13, X, *de haereticis,* V, 7.

[97] Conc. Trident., sess. XXII, *de ref.,* c. 10.

[98] Conc. Trident., sess. XXV, *de ref.,* c. 9.

[99] Conc. Trident., sess. XXII, *de ref.,* c. 11—translation by Schroeder, *op. cit.,* p. 158.

[100] Conc. Trident., sess. XXV, *de ref.,* c. 9; Conc. Trident., sess. XXII, *de ref.,* c. 11.

[101] Paulus IV, const. *Postquam,* 20 iul. 1558, § 2—*Fontes,* n. 93.

hospitality in the degree to which they were bound became subject to deprivation of their position as punishment.[102] Another authorized ecclesiastical act forbidden as the result of certain crimes was that of the sponsor at baptism. Public criminals and persons guilty of heresy were both excluded from this important function.[103]

In addition to the more specific penalties already mentioned, the law from the Council of Trent to the Code of Canon Law contained many prohibitions of a general nature which appear to embrace all the present authorized ecclesiastical acts. Those who were convicted of the crime of blasphemy for a second time were unable to obtain any further ecclesiastical honors or dignities. If a third conviction followed, they were punished *ipso iure* with the deprivation of any dignities, magistracies, honors and offices they already possessed. Those who were aware of such blasphemies were bound to reveal them under threat of similar penalties.[104]

Clerics who kept concubines were to be excluded from the administration of their benefices for as long a period as the ordinary deemed advisable. If they continued this sinful relationship, they were to be deprived of any ecclesiastical offices they held, and disqualified from consideration for any other ecclesiastical honors, dignities and offices until they mended their ways.[105] Those who were guilty of other crimes, such as apostacy from religion,[106] heresy,[107] and neglect of the clerical garb[108] were subject to similar penalties. Abductors and all who aided or co-operated with them were likewise disqualified for all ecclesiastical dignities.[109]

The Council of Trent added dueling to the list of crimes which *ipso facto* brought infamy of law to the delinquent.[110] The penalties

[102] Conc. Trident., sess. XXV, *de ref.*, c. 8.

[103] *Rituale Romanum, Pauli V Pontifiic Maximi jussu editum, et Benedicto XIV auctum et castigatum,* tit. II, cap. 1, *De Sacramento Baptismi*, nn. 22-26.

[104] Julius III, (1550-1555) const. *In multis deprevatis,* 1 febr. 1554—*Bull. Rom. Taur.*, VI, 479.

[105] Conc. Trident., sess. XXV, *de ref.*, c. 14.

[106] Paulus IV, const., *Postquam,* 20 iul. 1558, § 2—*Fontes,* n. 93.

[107] Paulus IV, const., *Cum ex apostolatus,* 15 febr. 1559, § 2—*Fontes,* n. 94.

[108] Conc. Trident., sess. XIV, *de ref.*, c. 6.

[109] Conc. Trident., sess. XXIV, *de ref. matrim.*, c. 6.

[110] Conc. Trident., sess. XXV, *de ref.*, c. 19.

as enacted by the Council were extended to even private duels by Pope Gregory XIII (1572-1585),[111] and to the whole world by Clement VIII (1592-1605). It was this latter Constitution which penalized any participating clerics with the privation of ecclesiastical dignities and offices possessed as well as with disqualification for others in the future.[112]

Article III. commentary on the present law

Section 1. Statement of the Law

Canon 2291 lists the principal vindictive penalties which can be imposed on all the faithful in the Church in proportion to the gravity of their crimes.[113] Among these is included the exclusion from the exercise of authorized ecclesiastical acts.[114] Thus, as has already been pointed out, the exclusion from the performance of authorized ecclesiastical acts may be enjoined as a vindictive penalty in its own right independently of other penalties or penal states.

This exclusion is a vindictive penalty. Its nature and characteristics have been outlined in Article I of this chapter. The heading in the Code itself to Chapter I, Title IX, Section II, Part II, of Book V points out that the punishments mentioned in this canon are the common vindictive penalties. They are designated as common in contradistinction to the penalties enumerated in canon 2298, which are peculiar to clerics.[115] Common vindictive penalties are, then, those which can be inflicted upon all the members of the Church, that is, upon all the faithful, whether clerics, religious or laymen.[116] As Della Rocca succinctly states:

[111] Const. *Ad tollendum,* 5 dec. 1582—*Fontes,* n. 149.

[112] Clement VIII, const. *Illius vices,* 17 aug. 1592—*Fontes,* n. 176.

[113] "Poenae vindicativae quae omnes fideles pro delictorum gravitate afficere possunt, in Ecclesiae praesertim sunt: . . ."

[114] "Remotio ab actibus legitimis ecclesiasticis exercendis."—Canon 2291, n. 8.

[115] Blat, *Commentarium,* V, n. 121, p. 174; Wernz-Vidal, *Ius Canonicum,* VII, n. 342, p. 379.

[116] ". . . omnes fideles, viros ac mulieres, sive clerici sint illi, sive laici, aut religiosi. . . ."—Blat, *op. cit.,* V, n. 123, p. 174.

> The Code divides vindictive penalties into two classes: *common,* in so far as they may be imposed on any delinquent, whether clerical or layman; and *special,* or those reserved to clerics.[117]

Those penalties which may be imposed on all the faithful are to be inflicted in proportion to the gravity of the crime in question. This declaration of canon 2291 is a re-statement of the fundamental ecclesiastical jurisprudence concerning the infliction of penalties, a jurisprudence which is found both in the former law [118] and in the present discipline:

> *In poenis decernendis servetur aequa proportio cum delicto, habita ratione imputabilitatis, scandali et damni; quare attendi debent non modo obiectum et gravitas legis, sed etiam aetas, scientia, institutio, sexus, conditio, status mentis delinquentis, dignitas personae quae delicto offenditur, aut quae delictum committit, finis intentus, locus et tempus quo delictum commissum est, num ex passionis impetu vel ob gravem metum delinquens egerit, num eum delicti poenituerit eiusdemque malos effectus evitare ipse studuerit, aliaque similia.*[119]

A penalty is to be inflicted which is in proportion to the gravity of the crime which has been committed.[120] This gravity or quantity

[117] *Manual of Canon Law* (Milwaukee: Bruce, 1959), n. 394, p. 574; cf. Ayrinhac-Lydon, *op. cit.,* n. 158, p. 120; Woywod, *op. cit.,* II, n. 2132, p. 456; Regatillo-Zalba, *op. cit.,* III, n. 1076, p. 937; Conte a Coronata, IV, n. 1824, p. 269; Chelodi-Ciprotti, *op. cit.,* n. 49, p. 65; Blat, *op. cit.,* V, n. 121, p. 174; Wernz-Vidal, *op. cit.,* n. 459, p. 708.

[118] "Sane cum vir discretus existas; plenius nosti quod in excessibus singulorum, non solum quantitas et qualitas delicti, sed aetas, scientia et sexus, atque conditio delinquentis sunt attendenda; et non solum secundum locum et tempus quo delictum committitur, unicuique poenitentia debet indici: cum idem excessus, magis sit in uno quam in alio puniendus."—c. 6, X, *de homicidio voluntario vel casuali,* V, 12.

[119] Canon 2218, § 1.

[120] This requirement has already been observed in those cases in which the law has levied a determinate penalty for a specific crime. There remain many cases, however, wherein the matter is left to the prudent discretion of the judge or the superior, and even in the case of determinate penalties a certain degree of latitude is permitted to the magistrate. Cf. canon 2223, § 3;

of the crime is to be measured not only by the gravity of the law violated but also by the greater or lesser degree of imputability or by the resulting injury.[121] Thus, canon 2218, § 1, points out that these elements of imputability, scandal, and injury are to be kept in view. In order that this necessary proportion be arrived at, however, the canon adds that not only the objective element, i.e., the object and gravity of the law offended against, be considered, but also that those subjective and circumstantial elements which might affect the imputability involved and the injury done be likewise considered. Thus the age, the instruction, the education, the sex, and the state of mind of the delinquent are to be taken into consideration. Circumstances such as the dignity of the person offended, the dignity of the delinquent, the purpose of the action, and the time and place in which it was performed, are also worthy of notice. The influence of possible grave fear or passion on the delinquent, his repentance and his efforts to prevent the evil effects of the delict, as also other similar circumstances are duly to be weighed and appraised before a proportionate penalty is selected as the requisite punishment.[122]

These penalties in due proportion to the crime may be imposed, then, on all the faithful in the Church.[123] This imposition of the penalty may derive from the law itself or through a judge or a superior.[124]

The list of the common vindictive penalties presented in canon 2291 does not offer an exhaustive or all-inclusive enumeration. It is rather presented in exemplification of the principal vindictive penalties common to the clergy, the laity and the religious alike.[125]

Vermeersch-Creusen, *op. cit.*, III, n. 409, p. 246; Conte a Coronata, IV, n. 1691, p. 84; Beste, *op. cit.*, p. 977.

121 Canon 2196.

122 Cf. canon 2218, § 1; Ayrinhac-Lydon, *op. cit.*, n. 36, pp. 28-29; Vermeersch-Creusen, *op. cit.*, III, n. 409, p. 246; Blat, *op. cit.*, V, n. 35, pp. 51-52.

123 ". . . seu hac religiosa societate perfecta."—Blat, *op. cit.*, V, n. 123, p. 174.

124 Cf. Blat, *loc. cit.*

125 Ayrinhac-Lydon, *op. cit.*, n. 158, p. 120; Augustine, *op. cit.*, VIII, p. 245; Jone, *op. cit.*, III, p. 483; Conte a Coronata, IV, n. 1824, p. 269; Chelodi-

The use of the word "*praesertim*" makes this evident. In selecting this term the legislator points out that, although these are the customary common vindictive penalties, others which seem more apt to secure the purpose of the penalty in the particular case may be employed at the prudent discretion of the judge or the superior.[126] This official should beware, however, lest he overreach the limits of his competency in these matters or inflict such penalties as are contrary to the present law and customs in the Church.[127]

The exclusion from the performance of authorized ecclesiastical acts as a vindictive penalty is expressed by the term "*remotio*." In order that a complete understanding of this legislation be attained, it is necessary to determine the force of this expression. In other words, when one is excluded from the performance of these actions, does this exclusion involve the invalid or merely the illicit performance of them?

The first thing to be noticed is that the term "*remotio*" is general in nature. Of itself it does not specify the quality of the prohibition involved. It, as in the case of canon 2263 and the excommunicated, merely testifies to the exclusion from authorized ecclesiastical acts. In order to determine the precise effect of this exclusion, one must consult the particular law or precept in question. There are, however, several general principles which must be noted in this regard. The rule of canon 11 is of capital importance:

> *Irritantes aut inhabilitantes eae tantum leges habendae sunt, quibus aut actum esse nullum aut inhabilem esse personam expresse vel aequivalenter statuitur.*

The prescription of canon 2296, § 1, is also to be recalled:

> *Si agatur de rebus ad quas assequendas capacitas iure communi statuitur, inhabilitas poenam infligere una Sedis Apostolica potest.*

Ciprotti, *op. cit.*, n. 49, p. 65; Blat, *op. cit.*, V, n. 123, p. 174; Berutti, *op. cit.*, VI, n. 86, p. 217; Della Rocca, *op. cit.*, n. 394, p. 574.

126 Vermeersch-Creusen, *op. cit.*, III, n. 492, p. 301; Beste, *op. cit.*, p. 1017; Wernz-Vidal, *op. cit.*, VII, n. 342, p. 379; Cocchi, *op. cit.*, VIII, n. 109, p. 191; Sipos, *op. cit.*, n. 239, p. 845.

127 Berutti, *op cit.*, VI, n. 87, p. 217.

This is of importance since the law of the Code does state the rules of capacity for many of the functions which involve the performance of authorized ecclesiastical acts.

In an effort to determine the precise significance of the exclusion from authorized ecclesiastical acts as provided for in canon 2291, n. 8, and keeping these basic principles in view, the writer proposes in the following section to deal with an investigation of those vindictive penalties in the law of the Code which involve this exclusion. It will be noted that such an investigation reveals a threefold division concerning this matter:

1. Those canons which directly exclude the delinquent from the performance of authorized ecclesiastical acts in general;
2. Those canons which directly exclude the delinquent from the performance of one or several particular authorized ecclesiastical acts;
3. Those canons which indirectly exclude the delinquent from the performance of authorized ecclesiastical acts by depriving him of ecclesiastical offices, dignities and functions.

Section 2. Exemplification in the Law of the Code

A. THE CANONS ENTAILING A DIRECT EXCLUSION FROM THE PERFORMANCE OF AUTHORIZED ECCLESIASTICAL ACTS

Canon 2315 points out that a person who is suspected of heresy, and who after admonition has not removed the cause for suspicion, is to be forbidden to exercise authorized ecclesiastical acts.[128]

From the psychological approach, suspicion spells out a doubt, together with a positive leaning toward one side. In law, suspicion may be occasioned in consequence of some well-founded presumption or as the result of some circumstantial evidence. It is, then, a judgment formed about someone without sufficient evidence, that is based on certain bits of evidence or on likely indications.

Three types of suspicion are generally noted by the authors: *Light* suspicion is that which is based on completely insufficient evi-

128 "Suspectus de haeresi, qui monitus causam suspicionis non removeat, actibus legitimis prohibeatur, . . ."—Canon 2315.

dence and thus admits of no conclusion. Forcible (*vehemens*) suspicion is that which rests upon evidence sufficient to reach a sound conclusion. Intense (*violenta*) suspicion rests upon an almost certain foundation, and amounts to the establishment of moral certitude. It is the forcible suspicion with which the law of canon 2315 is concerned.[129]

In general, it may be said that those persons are suspect of heresy who of their own accord and knowingly aid the propagation of heresy in any way or who communicate with heretics in sacred rites against the prescripts of the sacred canons.[130] This suspicion may arise from the law itself, which attaches it to certain actions, or from a person's mode of life, which might give rise to such a suspicion independently of any provision of law.[131]

The law declares those to be *ipso facto* suspect of heresy who knowingly and willingly assist in the propagation of heresy, or who take an active part in non-Catholic rites, or even a passive part when there is danger of scandal or perversion; [132] who contract marriage with the implicit or explicit understanding that the children are to be brought up outside of the Catholic Church; who presume to offer their children to non-Catholic ministers for baptism; who knowingly have their children or wards brought up in a non-Catholic religion; [133] who obstinately remain under the penalty of excommunication for a year; [134] who are guilty of simony in the administration or reception of the sacraments; [135] who cast away the Sacred Species, or carry off or retain them for an evil purpose; [137] or who appeal from the laws, decrees, or mandates of the reigning

[129] Cf. Augustine, *op. cit.*, VIII, p. 284; Conte a Coronata, IV, n. 1868, pp. 316-317.

[130] Cf. canons 2316 and 1258; Conte a Coronata, IV, n. 1868, p. 316.

[131] Ayrinhac-Lydon, *op. cit.*, n. 204, p. 159; Conte a Coronata, IV, n. 1868, pp. 317-318; *contra*, Cocchi, *op. cit.*, VIII, n. 139, p. 230, and Chelodi-Ciprotti, *op. cit.*, n. 59, p. 77.

[132] Cf. canon 2316.

[133] Cf. canon 2316.

[134] Canon 2340, § 1.

[135] Canon 2371.

[137] Canon 2320.

Roman Pontiff to a general council.[138] The Holy Office added to this list those who call in non-Catholic ministers to officiate at the funeral of those persons who have been denied ecclesiastical burial.[139]

Certain ways of acting and speaking may also give rise in the minds of prudent men to the suspicion that one's faith is not sound. Such practices as fortune-telling, divination, magic, and grave abuses in regard to the sacraments may well lay the foundation for such suspicion.[140] Such suspicion must be well-founded in the judgment of the canonical judge or superior before it is of any juridical value.[141]

One suspected of heresy, who after admonition has not removed the cause for this suspicion, is to be forbidden the exercise of authorized ecclesiastical acts.[142] The law is clear in demanding that the person under suspicion must be warned. This provision flows from the fundamental jurisprudence of canon 2307, which teaches that, when a person stands in the proximate occasion of committing a crime, or when an investigation has created a grave suspicion that he has committed a crime, he is to be warned by the ordinary either in person or by means of another appointed for that purpose. The warning must grant a reasonable amount of time within which the cause of suspicion is to be removed,[143] on the supposition of course that this removal is morally possible.[144]

The penalty enacted in canon 2315 is of a *ferendae sententiae* character in its mode of execution, and thus the provisions of canon 2223, § 3, are to be kept in mind. The warning or admonition is to be made in the canonical procedure outlined in canons 2143 and 2309. Any pronounced sentence which forbids the exercise of authorized ecclesiastical acts apart from this prior warning is invalid and of no juridical effect.[145]

The text of canon 2315 (*"actibus legitimis prohibeatur"*), when

[138] Canon 2332.

[139] S. C. S. off., resp., 23 febr. 1926—Bouscaren-O'Connor, *The Canon Law Digest*, IV, p. 423.

[140] Cf. Conte a Coronata, IV, n. 1868, p. 318.

[141] Ayrinhac-Lyon, *op. cit.*, n. 204, p. 159.

[142] Canon 2315.

[143] Augustine, *op. cit.*, VIII, 286.

[144] Ayrinhac-Lydon, *op. cit.*, n. 205, p. 159.

[145] Conte a Coronata, IV, n. 1869, p. 319.

taken in conjunction with the principle of canon 11, makes it clear that this exclusion from authorized ecclesiastical acts does not involve invalidity. Authorized ecclesiastical acts performed in spite of it would indeed be illicit, but nevertheless valid.

Canon 2350, § 2, states that persons who lay hands on themselves shall, if death ensues, be deprived of ecclesiastical burial in accordance with the precept of canon 1240, n. 3. If they do not die, they are to be excluded from the performance of authorized ecclesiastical acts. The attempt at suicide then is punished with the vindictive penalty of exclusion from the performance of the authorized ecclesiastical acts. An attempted delict occurs when one institutes or omits actions which of their nature lead to the commission of a crime, but does not complete the crime, either because he changes his mind, or because the completion is not possible in view of the insufficiency or inadequacy of the means employed.[146] If the law decrees a special penalty for an attempted delict, this attempt constitutes a true delict.[147] Such is the case in canon 2350, § 2.

This penalty is of the *ferendae sententiae* variety. There is nothing to indicate that when such a sentence is passed the performance of authorized ecclesiastical acts in spite of it would be invalid. The law simply states: "... *arceantur ab actibus legitimis ecclesiasticis.*" Thus in virtue of the principle of canon 11 this law prevents the licit but not the valid performance of these acts.

Men who, with a view to marriage or for the gratification of lust, carry off a woman by force or deceit against her will, or a woman of minor age who consents to elope without the knowledge or against the objection of her parents or guardian, are automatically excluded from the performance of authorized ecclesiastical acts according to canon 2353.

> Abduction may be considered as a crime or as a marriage impediment. As a crime it consists in carrying off a female against her will from a place of safety into another in which she is in the captor's power. Or, in a stricter and more usual sense, it may be defined as the carrying off or taking

146 Canon 2212, § 1.

147 Canon 2212, § 4.

> away of a virtuous woman from a free and safe place to another place morally different, where she is under the abductor's control for the purpose of marriage or gratification of lust. It is called abduction by violence when the woman is carried off against her will, by force or deceit; and abduction by seduction or elopement when a minor is taken with her own consent, but without the knowledge or against the will of her parents or guardian.[148]

This exclusion from authorized ecclesiastical acts is a *latae sententiae* vindictive penalty. The text of the law makes this clear: "*. . . ipso iure exclusus habeatur ab actibus legitimis ecclesiasticis. . . .*" It seems evident from the words and the principle of canon 11 that the imposition of such a penalty does not invalidate the performance of these acts.

A lay person who by process of law has been declared guilty of the crime of homicide, of the abduction of minors of either sex, of selling a human being as a slave or for any other evil purpose, of usury, of robbery, of theft under aggravating circumstances which change the species of the sin or of ordinary theft in a very grave matter, of incendiarism or malicious and very grave destruction of things, of serious mutilation, of a dire inflicting of wounds, or of heedless violence, shall automatically be excluded from the performance of authorized ecclesiastical acts.[149]

The crimes enumerated in this canon are of the mixed forum, i.e., they have an effect on both civil and religious society, and thus either tribunal is competent to deal with them.[150] In these days they are left almost exclusively to the jurisdiction of the civil courts. The Church; however, adds its penalty as a means of reparation for the injury done to the ecclesiastical social order.[151] The ecclesiastical penalty is a *latae sententiae* penalty which follows immediately upon the condemnation of the delinquent through due process of law. This condemnation must be carried out according to the correct judicial

[148] Ayrinhac-Lydon, *op. cit.*, n. 311, pp. 247-248.

[149] Canon 2354, § 1.

[150] Canon 1553, § 2.

[151] Ayrinhac-Lydon, *op. cit.*, n. 313, p. 250; Conte a Coronata, IV, n. 2043, p. 519.

procedure of the place in question if the civil law adjudicates the case. If the lay person were guilty of the crime but not convicted, the ecclesiastical penalty would not be incurred, since it follows only upon his conviction in due process of law.[152] If, on the other hand, an innocent person is convicted according to the rules of due legal process, Conte a Coronata holds that he is bound to observe the penalty in the external forum with a view to forestalling scandal, even though he is not bound in the internal forum.[153]

The homicide as mentioned in canon 2354, § 1, must be unjust, voluntary and consummated.[154] Abduction involves the violent or deceitful carrying off of persons of either sex who are under the age of puberty from a safe place to one which is not safe for them. The motive of the abductor plays no essential part in this action.[156] The sale of a man into slavery or for some other evil purpose was often referred to in the former law under the name of *plagium*.[157] The usury spoken of in this canon is that which is understood and condemned by modern legislation, i.e., excessive interest.[158] Since this concept of usury is much more lenient than that of the former canon law, any case of usury condemned under modern standards would likewise offend against the ecclesiastical concept.[159] Rapine, plunder or robbery implies the use of force whether physical or moral.[160]

The terminology in canon 2354, § 1, "*ipso iure exclusus habeatur ab actibus legitimis ecclesiasticis* . . ." does not seem to permit the conclusion that the performance of authorized ecclesiastical acts following the incurring of this penalty would be invalid.

[152] Conte a Coronata, n. 2043, p. 519.

[153] *Loc. cit.*

[154] Ayrinhac-Lydon, *op. cit.*, n. 313, p. 249.

[156] Conte a Coronata, IV, n. 2035, p. 514; Ayrinhac-Lydon, *op. cit.*, n. 313, p. 250.

[157] This crime is thus described: "Crimen publicum quo quis dolose subripit sui iuris existentem vel servum alienum, sive detineat illum, vel vendat, donet, permutet, vel alio contractu, quo dominium rerum transfertur, aliis tradat."—Reiffenstuel, *op. cit.*, VI, Lib. V, tit. 18, n. 58, p. 418.

[158] Ayrinhac-Lydon, *op. cit.*, n. 313, p. 250.

[159] Conte a Coronata, IV, n. 2037, p. 515.

[160] Ayrinhac-Lydon, *op. cit.*, n. 313, p. 250; Conte a Coronata, IV, n. 2038, p. 516.

Canon 2357, § 2, points out that persons who have committed a public crime of adultery, or who publicly live in concubinage, or who in due process of law have been condemned for other offenses against the sixth commandment are to be excluded from the performance of authorized ecclesiastical acts until they have given signs of true repentance.

A crime is public when it has already been divulged or was committed under or attended with such circumstances that its divulgement may and must be prudently considered as readily following.[161] The American civil law does not seem to possess a distinct notion of just what constitutes adultery.[162] This crime is not defined in the Code of Canon Law, but according to traditional canonical jurisprudence it consists in sexual intercourse of a married person with another person other than his or her spouse.[163] Concubinage involves an agreement between a man and a woman habitually to engage in marital relations in a union which remains however without any appearance of a valid marriage.[164] It is a state between mere fornication and the will to live as husband and wife[165] and in the law is contemplated as public in the sense stated above. The other delicts against the sixth commandment referred to here are distinct from those already mentioned in paragraph one of canon 2357, and special penalties are provided for them.[166]

At first glance canon 2357, § 2, seems strange in that it is a vindictive penalty which seems to partake of the nature of a censure, since it decrees that the exclusion from the performance of authorized ecclesiastical acts is to continue until the delinquent has given signs of true repentance. This sign of repentance and receding

161 Canon 2197, n. 1.

162 Augustine, *op. cit.*, VIII, 415.

163 "Adulterium est alieni thori violatio."—*Dictum* of Gratian to § 3 of c. 2, C. 36, q. 1.

164 Ayrinhac-Lydon, *Marriage Legislation in the New Code of Canon Law* (3. rev. ed., New York, Boston, Cincinnati, Chicago, San Francisco: Benziger Brothers, 1957), n. 174, p. 182.

165 Cf. Gasparri, *Tractatus de Matrimonio* (2 vols., Vol. I, ed. nova, Typis Polyglottis Vaticanis: Romae, 1932), I, n. 737, p. 450; Jone, *op. cit.*, III, 537.

166 Ayrinhac-Lydon, *Penal Legislation*, n. 317, p. 253; cf. Jone, *op. cit.*, III, 537.

from contumacy is, as has been noted, the sign whereby a censure calls for absolution.[167] Ordinarily this would not have the same effect in the case of a vindictive penalty. It is characteristic of vindictive penalties that a determined time be set for the punishment in question. In this case the period of punishment is simply determined or measured by the period required by the delinquent to indicate his repentance through external manifestation.

This penalty is a *ferendae sententiae* penalty which may be leveled after a civil as well as an ecclesiastical condemnation.[168] The judge regarding the presence of a true repentance is to be the ecclesiastical authority involved.[169]

Once again it is to be noted that the text of this law (*"excludantur ab actibus legitimis ecclesiasticis"*) does not seem to give any indication that the performance of authorized ecclesiastical acts is made invalid by the prohibition contained therein. Thus, the performance of these acts in spite of this penalty would be affected with unlawfulness, but not with invalidity.

Clerics in minor orders who are guilty of an offense against the sixth commandment are also liable to the exclusion from the performance of authorized ecclesiastical acts if their crime is one which receives specification in canon 2357, § 2. Thus, if they are guilty of public adultery, or of public concubinage, or have been condemned in due process of law.[170] For crimes against the sixth commandment other than those mentioned in canon 2357, § 1, they are liable to this exclusion.

This penalty is a *ferendae sententiae* penalty, and is not to be considered as invalidating the performance of authorized ecclesiastical acts placed in opposition to it.

[167] Cf. canon 2241, § 1.

[168] "Where the adultery or concubinage is publicly known, the ecclesiastical judge may impose these punishments before there has been a sentence of the court."—Ayrinhac-Lydon, *Penal Legislation,* n. 317, p. 253.

[169] Conte a Coronata, IV, n. 2060, p. 529; Jone, *op. cit.,* III, 537.

[170] This conviction must come about through the offices of an ecclesiastical court unless special agreements or customary law intercede. cf. "Clerici in omnibus causis sive contentiosis sive criminalibus apud iudicem ecclesiasticum conveniri debent, nisi aliter pro locis particularibus legitime provisum fuerit."—Canon 120, § 1.

Canon 2375 states that Catholics who dare to contract a mixed marriage, even though validly, without a dispensation from the Church, are automatically excluded from the performance of authorized ecclesiastical acts until they have obtained a dispensation from the ordinary.

The mixed marriage spoken of here refers to the marriage described in canon 1060, i.e., a marriage between two baptized persons, one of whom is a Catholic, the other a member of a heretical or a schismatical sect.[171] The dispensation from this law as described in canon 1061 must be obtained in these cases. The lack of this dispensation, however, does not invalidate the marriage. The use of the words *"ausus fuerit"* by the legislator refer to the fact that full knowledge and deliberation are called for in this case, so that any diminution of imputability on the part of the intellect or the will excuses from this penalty.[172] Thus, Augustine aptly remarked:

> The *"ausi fuerit"* is vérified if the Catholic party, knowing that a dispensation is necessary and possessing the necessary means of communicating with the ecclesiastical authorities, neglects to ask for the dispensation.[173]

This penalty is a *latae sententiae* penalty, which remains in effect until a dispensation is obtained from the ordinary. The dispensation referred to here is the dispensation from the penalty inflicted by this law and not the dispensation from the impediment of mixed religion.[174] This is clear from the fact that the ordinary cannot dispense from this impediment except in virtue of special faculties.[175]

This penalty does not seem to invalidate the performance of

[171] Beste, *op. cit.*, p. 1063.

[172] Cf. canon 2229, § 2.

[173] Augustine, *op. cit.*, VIII, 453.

[174] Augustine, *loc. cit.;* Woywod, *op. cit.*, II, n. 2231, p. 514; Conte a Coronata, IV, n. 2170, p. 656.

[175] Jone, *op. cit.*, III, 549; Ayrinhac-Lydon, *Marriage Legislation*, n. 101, pp. 102-103.

authorized ecclesiastical acts by one who violates the law, but rather forbids such actions under pain of unlawfulness.[176]

Canon 2385 declares that without prejudice to the precepts of canon 646, a religious who apostatizes from his religious institute is, in addition to the automatic incurring of excommunication, likewise excluded from the performance of authorized ecclesiastical acts. Upon his return he is perpetually deprived of the active and passive voice in elections.

Canon 646 relates certain cases of apostasy in consequence of which the religious in question is regarded as legitimately dismissed. An apostate from religion is one who after the profession of solemn or of simple perpetual vows unlawfully departs from his religious house with the intention not to return or who, after a lawful departure from it, determines to withdraw himself from subjection to his superiors. This determination is presumed by the law to be present if within a month of the departure the religious has neither returned nor manifested his intention of returning to his superior.[177] All those religious, men or women,[178] who have made perpetual profession, whether simple or solemn, fall within the scope of this canon.[179]

These religious are *ipso facto* excluded from the performance of authorized ecclesiastical acts. Since one of these acts concerns the administration of ecclesiastical property, they would be excluded from the position of oeconome even after returning to the institute, until a dispensation is obtained.[180] This exclusion does not involve the invalid performance of these acts, however, since the law cannot, so it appears, be interpreted as invalidating or incapacitating in light of the provisions of canon 11.

176 "Catholici qui matrimonium mixtum, etsi validum, sine Ecclesiae dispensatione inire ausi fuerint, ipso facto ab actibus legitimis ecclesiasticis et Sacramentalibus exclusi manent, donec ab Ordinario dispensationem obtinuerint."—Canon 2375.

177 Canon 644.

178 "Quae de religiosis statuuntur, etsi masculino vocabulo expressa, valent etiam pari iure de mulieribus, nisi ex contextu sermonis vel ex rei natura aliud constet."—Canon 490.

179 Ayrinhac-Lydon, *Penal Legislation*, n. 357, p. 298.

180 Jone, *op. cit.*, III, 553.

In addition to this exclusion from the performance of authorized ecclesiastical acts in general, the apostate from religion is likewise *ipso facto* perpetually deprived of his active and passive voice, i.e., his right of voting and of being voted for,[181] when and if he returns to his institute.[182] This exclusion actually adds only one note to the penalty since the right of suffrage in ecclesiastical elections is already comprehended by the exclusion from authorized ecclesiastical acts.[183] It differs, however, from the exclusion from these acts in general in that it involves validity, i.e., one is prevented under pain of invalidity from possessing either active or passive voice in elections.[184] This is true in the case of voting, for canon 167, § 1, n. 5, includes those who are deprived, be it by the law of the Code or by particular legislation, of the general right of voting in ecclesiastical elections in consequence of the legitimate sentence of a judge within the group of persons who are excluded from voting.[185] Paragraph two of the same canon states that, if such persons are admitted to vote, their vote is invalid.[186] Thus, this vindictive penalty would make the use of the active voice illicit in virtue of the exclusion from authorized ecclesiastical acts in general. In virtue of the particular prohibition in regard to active and passive voice together with the precepts of canon 167, § 1, n. 5, and § 2, however, such use must be regarded as invalid.

It seems that the passive voice or right to be voted for is also lost in such a way as a result of this penalty that the delinquent could not validly be elected to office.[187] Thus Riesner points out:

[181] Cf. canon 578, n. 3.

[182] ". . . et si redierit, perpetuo caret voce activa et passiva. . . ."—Canon 2385.

[183] Canon 2256, n. 2.

[184] *Contra*, Augustine, *op. cit.*, VIII, 470.

[185] "Nequeunt suffragium ferre: . . . 5°—Carentes voce activa sive ob legitimam iudicis sententiam sive ex iure communi aut particulari."—Canon 167, § 1, n. 5.

[186] "Si quis ex praedictis admittatur, eius suffragium est nullum. . . ."—Canon 167, § 2; cf. Roelker, Invalidating Laws (Paterson: St. Anthony Guild Press, 1955), p. 149; Mock, *Disqualification of Electors in Ecclesiastical Elections*, p. 127.

[187] *Contra*, Augustine, *op. cit.*, VIII, 470.

> After the apostate returns to the institute he cannot validly vote in the chapters of the institute, nor can he validly be elected to an office that is obtained through an election.[188]

Conte a Coronata seems to be of the same opinion, for he states:

> *Vi huius poenae apostata ad religionem reversus eligi non potest ad officia religionis. . . .*[189]

Roelker also points to this canon as an example of an invalidating penal law.[190] Jone concurs for, in pointing out that even women religious guilty of this delict are able to cast a vote in those elections which concern the reappointment of the regular confessor to a second or a third term, he states:

> *. . . cum in hoc casu ad normam can. 526 etiam illae religiosae concurrere possint, quae in aliis negotiis non habent ius ferendi suffragium.*[191]

It seems clear, then, that the penalty stated in canon 2385 with the words: *"et si redierit, perpetuo caret voce activa et passiva, . . ."* does come within the scope of canon 11, and thus is an incapacitating penal law wrich rules out the validly of acts placed contrary to it.

The procedural law of the Church provides two cases in which a delinquent is to be excluded from the performance of authorized ecclesiastical acts as the result of a vindictive penalty. According to canon 1743, § 3, if a party who is obliged to answer a question refuses to do so, or does answer but is found afterwards to have told a lie, he is to be punished with exclusion from the performance of the authorized ecclesiastical acts for a time which the judge will fix in line with the attendant circumstances.

[188] *Apostates and Fugitives from Religious Institutes,* The Catholic University of America Canon Law Studies, n. 168 (Washington, D. C.: The Catholic University of America Press, 1942), p. 92.

[189] *Institutiones Iuris Canonici,* IV, n. 2189, p. 669.

[190] Roelker, *op. cit.,* p. 153.

[191] Jone, *op. cit.,* III, 554.

The judge is obliged to interrogate the parties for the purpose of establishing the truth of a fact when the public interest demands that it be established beyond doubt. In other cases, he may question one of the parties, not only at the request of the other party, but also *ex officio,* whenever it is necessary to clarify some proof which has been advanced. The parties may be so questioned by the judge at any stage of the trial before the conclusion of the cause.[192] The parties are bound to answer the legitimate questions of the judge in a truthful manner; they are not, however, bound to answer questions concerning a delict they have committed.[193] When the parties fail in the manner described above they are subject to the *ferendae sententiae* exclusion from the performance of authorized ecclesiastical acts. This exclusion (*"remotione ab actibus legitimis ecclesiasticis"*) does not involve the invalidity of their performance, but it renders such execution illicit.

Witnesses who, in answer to a legitimate question of the judge, knowingly affirm a falsehood or conceal the truth are subject to this same exclusion. Those who presume to induce a witness or expert by a promise or in any other way to give false testimony or to conceal the truth are likewise subject to this same exclusion.[194] Witnesses who are not excused by law [195] and who are legitimately questioned by the judge are bound to answer and tell the truth.[196] The use of the terms "knowingly" (*"scienter"*) and "presume" (*praesumpserint"*) by the legislator indicates the necessity of full knowledge and deliberation in these actions, so that any diminution of imputability, whether on the part of the intellect or on the part of the will, excuses from these penalties.[197]

It is disputed among the authors whether these rules apply to *ferendae sententiae* penalties such as the present one. McCoy seems to favor the view that *ferendae sententiae* penalties are also included

[192] Canon 1742, §§ 1-3.

[193] Canon 1743, § 1.

[194] Canon 1755, § 3.

[195] Cf. canons 1757, § 3, n. 2; 1755, § 2, nn. 1 and 2.

[196] Cf. canon 1755, § 1.

[197] Canon 2229, § 2.

within the purview of these regulations.[198] Others, however, feel that these rules conform to the very nature of *latae sententiae* penalties and apply only to them.[199] At any rate, the exclusion envisioned by canon 1755, § 3, does not entail the invalidity of the performance of authorized ecclesiastical acts carried out in contravention of the standing prohibition.

The Code of Canon Law provides special regulations in relation to those who are excluded from the performance of authorized ecclesiastical acts as the result of a vindictive penalty in regard to the exercise of sponsorship at baptism and at confirmation, which actions are themselves numbered among the authorized ecclesiastical acts of canon 2256, n. 2. As has been noted, the vindictive penalties in the law of the Code which exclude the delinquent from the performance of authorized ecclesiastical acts generally refer to the licit performance of these acts. Some exception is made, however, when it is a question of sponsorship at baptism and at confirmation. Canon 765, n. 2, declares that one cannot be a valid sponsor at baptism if he has been excluded from the performance of authorized ecclesiastical acts and a declaratory or condemnatory sentence has been rendered. If the delict in consequence of which he has suffered this exclusion from the performance of these acts be notorious,[200] he cannot licitly be admitted to this position.[201]

198 ". . . Since, however, this distinction (between simple and perfect *dolus*) is made by the Code only in reference to *latae sententiae* penalties, some canonists maintain that the distinction does not hold for *ferendae sententiae* penalties. The majority of post-Code authors, however, adhere to the same distinction even for *ferendae sententiae* penalties. This seems logical for the Code itself contains twenty instances in which *ferendae sententiae* penalties are enacted for crimes which according to canon 2229, § 2, would presuppose perfect *dolus*. For the expressions which in reference to *latae sententiae* penalties postulate full knowledge and deliberation (v.g. *praesumpserit, scienter*) are also used when the law imposes *ferendae sententiae* penalties."—McCoy, *Force and Fear in Relation to Delictual Imputability and Penal Responsibility,* The Catholic University of America Canon Law Studies, n. 200, (Washington, D. C.: The Catholic University of America Press, 1944), pp. 102-103.

199 "*Agitur in hoc canone de incursione poenae latae sententiae; nam de inflictione ponae ferendae sententiae superius ad can. 2223, § 2 et 3, sermo erat.*" —Beste, *op. cit.*, p. 982; Blat, *op. cit.*, V, n. 49, p. 72.

200 Canon 2197, n. 2-3.

201 Canon 766, n. 2.

These prescriptions are ratified in the case of sponsorship at confirmation by canons 795, n. 2, and 796, n. 3. In other cases, those who have been excluded from the performance of authorized ecclesiastical acts in general may validly and licitly perform these functions. Thus, whenever no sentence has been passed and the involved delict is not notorious, one who has been excluded from the performance of authorized ecclesiastical acts in consequence of a vindictive penalty may validly and licitly be admitted to the position of sponsorship at baptism and at confirmation.

B. The Canons Entailing a Strict Exclusion from the Performance of Individual Authorized Ecclesiastical Acts

There are also examples in the law of the Code in which vindictive penalties are inflicted which exclude the delinquent from the performance of individual authorized ecclesiastical acts. Thus, if a patron of a church, either in person or by means of others, presumes to convert to his own use and usurp ecclesiastical goods of any kind, whether personal or real, or to prevent those to whom goods rightfully belong from receiving the fruits of the income from the ecclesiastical goods, he is automatically deprived of his right of patronage in addition to being *ipso iure* excommunicated.[202]

In addition to the nullity of the act and the obligation, which is to be enforced even with the use of a censure, to make restitution of the goods unlawfully acquired, and the duty to repair the damages which may have been caused, one who presumes to alienate ecclesiastical goods or gives his consent thereto in violation of canons 534 and 1532 in addition to other penalties is to be deprived of his right of patronage, and his position of administration if the goods involved have a value of over 1,000 but of less than 30,000 francs.[203] Special faculties concerning the limits of alienation are to be recalled in this regard.

Religious who have committed the crimes delineated in canon 2334 and 2335 [204] shall in addition to the penalties decreed in these

[202] Canon 2346.

[203] Canon 2347, § 1, n. 2.

[204] Those who issue laws, mandates, or decrees against the liberty and rights

canons be deprived of their active and passive voice in elections.[205]

Religious who are guilty of forging or falsifying letters, decrees or rescripts of the Holy See, or who with full knowledge of the forgery make use of the letters, decrees or rescripts, in addition to the automatic incurring of excommunication reserved in a special manner to the Holy See are to be deprived of their active and passive voice in elections.[206]

The priest who commits the crime of solicitation dealth with in canon 904, in addition to other penalties, is to be deprived of his active and passive voice in the elections and is incapable of acquiring them again.[207]

Religious who in a notable manner violate the law of community life which is prescribed by their constitutions and who do not amend upon a warning are to be punished even with the privation of the active and passive voice in elections.[208]

Those electors in ecclesiastical elections who have solicited or freely admitted the interference of lay persons or secular authorities who unlawfully and in violation of canonical liberty presume to interfere in elections conducted by a college of clerics or religious are automatically deprived of the right to vote in the particular elections involved. Those who knowingly consented to be elected under such circumstances are automatically rendered incapable of the office or benefice in question.[209]

Without prejudice to canon 729,[210] persons who commit simony

of the Church; those who either directly or indirectly impede the exercise of ecclesiastical jurisdiction in the internal or the external forum, having recourse for that purpose to any lay authority, are *ipso facto* excommunicated with an excommunication reserved to the Holy See in a special manner. Those who have themselves enrolled in the Masonic sect or in similar associations which plot against the Church or the legitimate civil authority automatically contract an excommunication reserved in a simple manner to the Holy See.

205 Canon 2346, § 1.

206 Canon 2360, § 2.

207 Canon 2368, § 1.

208 Cf. canon 2389.

209 Canon 2390, § 2.

210 This canon decrees that in addition to the penalties levied on persons guilty of simony, the simoniacal contract is itself null and void as is the simoniacal filling of a benefice, office, or dignity, even though the simony in-

in any ecclesiastical office, benefice or dignity, are automatically for all time deprived of the right of election, presentation, or nomination.[211] Automatically deprived of these same rights in the particular cause involved are also those who show disregard for the authority of the person who has the right of confirmation or institution by presuming themselves to confer the office, benefice or dignity.[212]

C. The Canons Entailing an Indirect Exclusion from the Performance of Authorized Ecclesiastical Acts

There are also other vindictive penalties in the Code which indirectly exclude the delinquents from the performance of authorized ecclesiastical acts. This is accomplished by way of an exclusion from or a deprivation of various offices, dignities, and positions in the Church. As has already been noted, almost all the authorized ecclesiastical acts that receive mention in the Code can be included within one of these categories.

Thus, e.g., those who offend against canons 827, 828, and 840, § 1, concerning Mass stipends are to be punished by the ordinary in proportion to their guilt even with the deprivation of ecclesiastical office.[213] If the cleric remains under the censure of suspension for half a year, he is to be seriously admonished; if he does not give up his contumacy within a month, he is to be deprived of any ecclesiastical offices he holds.[214]

All apostates from the Christian faith and each and every heretic or schismatic, if they have been admonished and do not repent, are to be deprived of any dignity, office, or other position they may have in the Church.[215] Clerics who conspire against the authority

volved was committed by a person not the beneficiary of the appointment, and even though it was committed without the latter's knowledge, provided that it was not committed fraudulently either with a view to prejudicing the latter or of proceeding over his protest.

211 Canon 2392, n. 2.

212 Canon 2393.

213 Canon 2324.

214 Canon 2340, § 2.

215 Canon 2314, § 1, n. 2.

of the Roman Pontiff, or of his legates, or of their own proper ordinary, or against their legitimate commands, shall be deprived of dignities, benefices and other offices.[216] The Code contains many other examples of penal canons which indirectly exclude one from the performance of authorized ecclesiastical acts in these ways.[217]

It is to be noted that the canons referred to in the sections devoted to those penal laws which exclude one from the performance of some individual authorized ecclesiastical acts and those which indirectly exclude one from the performance of these acts relate to deprivation.

Deprivation (*privatio*) is one of the common vindictive penalties spoken of in canon 2291. It is mentioned both here among the common vindictive penalties and again among those which are peculiar to clerics.[218]

As spoken of in an earlier section of the Code, deprivation is one of the means by which an ecclesiastical office is lost.[219] The loss involves the incumbent's title to the office in question together with its accompanying rights and obligations.[220] In general, then, deprivation is spoken of as a canonical act by which an ecclesiastical office is taken away from a cleric who is unwilling to lose it.[221]

Deprivation may be penal or administrative. Penal deprivation, "*quae proprio nomine privatio vocatur,*" [222] has the character of a penalty, and thus postulates the commission of a delict for which it is the punishment.[223] This penal deprivation (*privatio*) may be a *latae* or a *ferendae sententiae* penalty, which in turn derives *a iure* or *ab homine*. Non-penal or administrative deprivation does not possess a penal character; rather, it is concerned primarily with the promotion of the common good. It is called simply "removal"

[216] Canon 2331, § 2.

[217] Cf. canons 2322, n. 1; 188, n. 4; 2341; 2355; 2388, § 1; 2396; 2406, § 1; 2408; 2336, § 1; 2343, § 2; 2345; 2354, § 2; 2359, §§ 2 and 3; 2360, § 2; 2368, § 1; 2381, n. 2; 2394; 2395; 2403.

[218] Cf. canons 2291, nn. 7, 10, 11; 2298, nn. 4, 6, 9, 11.

[219] Canon 183, § 1.

[220] Abbo-Hannan, *op. cit.*, I, 242.

[221] Cf. Abbo-Hannan, *op. cit.*, I, 247; Conte a Coronata, IV, n. 266, p. 313.

[222] Conte a Coronata, IV, n. 266, p. 314; Abbo-Hannan, *op. cit.*, I, 247.

[223] Abbo-Hannan, *loc. cit.*

and is "decreed by a competent superior for a just cause and with due regard to the demands of natural equity and the formalities requisite under the law." [224]

Various forms of procedure are required in these cases of penal deprivation. Judicial procedure is required in cases of the deprivation of office for an irremovable incumbent, except in those few cases wherein a special manner of procedure is imposed by law.[225] A not strictly judicial procedure is to be followed in those cases which deal with clerics who violate the law of residence, with clerics who live in concubinage, and with pastors negligent in the fulfillment of their pastoral duties.[226] An administrative decree may be employed in cases of deprivation of office for removable incumbents. This decree must be issued according to the norms of the law.[227]

Non-penal deprivation or removal does not postulate a crime as a basis, although one may be present in an individual case. This removal is an act of ordinary administration. The special modes of procedure described are to be employed when the case concerns the removal of a pastor. In other cases the demands of natural equity must be observed, though no special procedure is required. In each case the removal becomes effective only when authentic notification of it has been sent to the incumbent by the superior. Recourse, without suspensive effect, may be interposed with the Holy See.[228]

The effect of penal privation and removal is a complete loss of the office.[229]

As has been noted, penal deprivation (*privatio*) is a vindictive penalty, which can be inflicted on all members of the Church. In the outline presented above it is treated by the Code in connection with ecclesiastical offices, and these offices are normally to be understood in the strict sense of the term, unless the contrary appears

[224] Abbo-Hannan, *op. cit.*, I, 247-248; cf. canon 192, § 3; Conte a Coronata, IV, n. 266, p. 314.

[225] Canon 192, § 2; Conte a Coronata, IV, n. 267, p. 314.

[226] Canon 2168-2185; Conte a Coronata, IV, n. 267, p. 316.

[227] Cf. canon 2225.

[228] Cf. canon 192, § 3.

[229] "Effectus privationis poenalis et amotionis administrativae est plena vacatio officii."—Conte a Coronata, IV, n. 269, p. 317.

from the context.[230] Nevertheless, this penalty is frequently inflicted in relation to the use of the active and the passive voice, dignities, benefices and *munera* within the Church. Thus, in these cases, *privatio* has a broader meaning than is pointed to by canon 183, § 1,[231] and canon 192. In these cases, "deprivation is a punishment by which an offender is deprived of an office, benefice, dignity, functions, or active or passive vote, which he has in his possession." [232] Thus once one has been penally deprived of the office, right, dignity or *munera* in question according to the norms of the law, any actions performed in spite of this deprivation would be not only illicit but invalid as well.[233]

The above presented examples of the exclusion from the performance of some individual authorized ecclesiastical acts as well as those of indirect exclusion from these actions are not, then, examples of the common vindictive penalty spoken of in canon 2291, n. 8 [234] but rather illustrations of the various penal deprivations indicated in numbers 7 and 11 of the same canon.[235] These penal deprivations are of a more serious nature than are the penalties which exclude one from the performance of authorized ecclesiastical acts in general, in that they result in the complete loss of the office, right, dignity or position in question, and thus result in the invalidity of acts placed contrary to what the law demands.

Thus, in summary, one may state that the exemplifications in the law of the Code of the vindictive penalty stated in canon 2291, n. 8,

230 Canon 145, § 2.

231 "Amittitur officium ecclesiasticum renuntiatione, privatione, amotione, translatione, lapsu temporis praefiniti."—Canon 183, § 1.

232 Christ, *op cit.*, p. 151.

233 Cf. Roelker, *op. cit.*, p. 155.

234 "Remotio ab actibus legitimis ecclesiasticis exercendis."

235 The penalty enacted in canon 2346 concerning the deprivation of the right of patronage corresponds to canon 2291, n. 7, which speaks of the deprivation of rights. The deprivations listed in canons 2347, § 1, n. 2; 2392, n. 2, and 2993, have the same correspondence. The penalties delineated in canon 2336, § 1; 2360, § 2; 2368, § 1; 2389; 2390, § 2, which relate to the deprivation of active and passive voice correspond to canon 2291, n. 11. The deprivations adverted to in 2324 and 2340, § 2, find their source in canon 2298, n. 6, which speaks of the penal deprivation of a benefice or of an office with or without a pension.

i.e., *"Remotio ab actibus legitimis ecclesiasticis exercendis,"* are of such a nature that, should this exclusion be incurred, the performance of these acts in contravention of it would indeed be illicit but still valid.[236] This seems true because the texts of these laws do not meet the requirements specified by canon 11 for an invalidating or disqualifying law.

Laws are referred to as invalidating or disqualifying with relation to their effect. A law is invalidating when it directly provides that the act referred to is null. It is disqualifying or incapacitating when it directly provides that the person in question is incapable of a particular act.[237] The effect of both of these laws is to make invalid any action placed contrary to them. Because of the severe restrictions placed by these laws it is essential that they be clearly identified. Thus canon 11 states that only those laws are invalidating or incapacitating which state expressly or equivalently either that the act is null or that the person is disqualified.

There is, however, a divergence among the commentators as to the explanation of the essential terms *"expresse"* and *"equivalenter."* According to one view, invalidation or disqualification is stated *expressly* when the legislator uses words the direct and proper signification of which declare this juridic effect. Such terms would be: *nullus, irritus, inhabilis.* These states of invalidity or incapacity are *equivalently* decreed when the legislator uses words which do not

[236] "Acts placed by those who are excluded from the exercise of the legitimate acts are valid, but they are illicit unless there is a just cause to warrant their exercise."—Riesner, *op. cit.*, pp. 89, 92; *"Remotio ab actibus legitimis ecclesiasticis,* qui in can. 2256, 2°, recensentur, *exercendis* licite, aut post sententiam condemnatoriam vel declaratariam etiam valide, iuxta can. 765, 2° quoad baptismum, can. 795, 2° quoad confirmationem, quae ad alios actus legitimos ecclesiasticos non immerito extenditur ad normam can. 20, quando nempe 'hac de re desit expressum praescriptum' in Codice."—Blat, *op. cit.*, V, n. 123, p. 175; "Competens Superior ab omnibus vel ab aliquibus tantum potest delinquentem in poenam removere; quo fit ut illicite eosdem ipse exerceret, vel etiam invalide si id expresse de quibusdam in iure caveatur: ad normam siquidem cann. 765, n. 2° et 795, n. 2° exclusus ab actibus legitimis sententia condemnatoria vel declaratoria inhabilis manet ad munus patrini exercendum pro sacramento baptismi et confirmationis."—Berutti, *op. cit.*, VI, n. 87, n. 221.

[237] Cf. Bouscaren-Ellis, *op. cit.*, p. 25; Conte a Coronata, IV, n. 21, p. 34. Cf. canons 103, § 1; 150, § 1; 169; 1017, § 2; 968; 1067; 1080; 1437.

adequately express in themselves these conditions, but which do clearly reveal his intention of producing these effects. Such terms would include: *effectum non sortitur nisi* . . . as found in canon 116, *contractus vicaret, nisi* . . . as found in canon 534, § 1, and *conferri valide nequeunt* . . . as found in canon 154.[238]

Others hold that both categories just mentioned constitute an express declaration of an invalidating or incapacitating law. Laws *equivalently* state these effects when they introduce a condition through the use of such particles as *si* or *dummodo,* and when they provide a formality which determines the nature of the act itself, even though nothing is said expressly or explicitly about the quality of the act or the capability of the person. Canon 148, which determines the various ways in which appointment to ecclesiastical offices may be made, is cited as an illustration of this equivalent expression.[239]

The canons under consideration do not seem to come within the requirements outlined by canon 11 for invalidating or incapacitating laws. An investigation of their texts does not seem to warrant their being included within the realm of *"expresse"* or *"aequivalenter"* invalidating or incapacitating legislation.

Those vindictive penalties, however, by which one is directly deprived of some individual authorized ecclesiastical acts, or indirectly excluded through privation of office, dignities, rights and *munera,* are of a more serious nature. Deprivation of these involves their complete loss, so that any acts placed after such loss of office, dignity, right, or position would be not only illicit but also invalid.

Section 3. The Influence of Canon 2232, § 1

In considering the exclusion from the performance of authorized ecclesiastical acts as a vindictive penalty, one must once again recall the provisions of canon 2232, § 1. Since this canon has been commented upon in the chapters dealing with excommunication and infamy of law, it will be treated only briefly here.

In virtue of canon 2232, § 1, one who is conscious of his delict

[238] Jone, *op. cit.,* I, 30; Beste, *op. cit.,* p. 68.

[239] Cf. Conte a Coronata, I, n. 21, pp. 34-35; Roelker, *op. cit.,* p. 99.

is bound by the *latae sententiae* vindictive penalty consequent upon it in both the external and internal forum. Before a declaratory sentence has been issued, however, he is excused from the observance of the penalty whenever he cannot observe it without loss of reputation. Further, no one can demand its observance in the external forum unless the delict involved is notorious. The precept of canon 2223, § 4, binds, however, in that it commands the respective superior to issue a declaratory sentence in those cases in which an interested party demands it or the public good requires it.

Thus, those who are excluded from the performance of authorized ecclesiastical acts in consequence of a *latae sententiae* vindictive penalty, but who cannot observe this penalty without loss of reputation in a case in which no declaratory sentence has been given, are excused from its observance. In the external forum no one can demand its observance unless the delict involved is notorious, or the conditions outlined in canon 2223, § 4, are fulfilled.

The powers of the confessor to suspend the observance of *latae sententiae* vindictive penalties as presented in canon 2290 will be noted in the following section. It is of interest here to briefly compare these powers with those which are granted the delinquent himself in canon 2232, § 1. Although the grants of canon 2232, § 1, are extensive and can be enjoyed without the necessity of approaching a confessor, the submission of the case to a confessor and the application of canon 2290 results in greater benefits for the delinquent. This is true because the suspension of the observance of the penalty by the confessor involves freedom from the penalty not only in the external forum but in the internal forum as well. Further, the performance of actions forbidden him by the penalty is permitted not only at those times when their omission would result in his loss of reputation, but also at other times when no such danger exists.[240] "In other words, canon 2232, § 1, excuses in the external forum only [241] in such acts as occasion infamy, while canon 2290, § 1, allows a complete suspension of the vindicative penalty." [242]

[240] Vermeersch-Creusen, *Epitome,* III, n. 491, pp. 300-301.

[241] It is disputed by the authors whether the suspension of the penalty is of avail for both forums. Cf. Conte a Coronata, IV, n. 1723, p. 128.

[242] Christ, *op. cit.*, p. 179.

The second paragraph of canon 2290 goes even further in that it involves not merely a suspension of the penalty but a dispensation itself.

Throughout the course of this study the possible effect of canon 2232, § 1, upon the exclusion from the performance of authorized ecclesiastical acts by various groups of delinquents has been considered. In order that the precise value of this legislation be ascertained, however, it is essential to possess a clear conception of the second paragraph of this canon as well.

Canon 2232, § 2, states:

> *Sententia declaratoria poenam ad momentum commissi delicti retrotrahit.*

A *latae sententiae* penalty is one which is attached to a law or a precept in such a way that the mere fact of the violation of the law or the precept suffices for incurring it.[243] The penalty, then, is incurred at the moment the delict is committed. The declaratory sentence does not inflict the penalty. It is merely an official declaration that the crime has been committed and the penalty incurred. This sentence brings the entire matter clearly into the external forum, and thus eliminates the excusing causes listed in paragraph one.

It has been noted throughout the course of this study that many delinquents are excluded from the performance of authorized ecclesiastical acts in such a way that any attempt at their performance is marked with invalidity. The far reaching effect of such exclusions has been pointed out in many cases. The very important positions which come within the judicial, administrative and sacramental framework of the Church, and which are comprehended within the concept of authorized ecclesiastical acts have been noted. The extreme importance and value of canon 2232, § 1, has therefore been carefully considered. An incorrect interpretation of canon 2232, § 2, could therefore lead to a great deal of confusion, especially regarding the validity of actions placed by those who take advantage of the norm incorporated in canon 2232, § 1.

243 Canon 2217, n. 2.

The second paragraph of canon 2232 does not imply that, once a declaratory sentence has been issued, the penalty has a retroactive effect which in an absolute sense reaches back to the moment when the delict was committed. This retroactive effect flows from the very nature of a *latae sententiae* penalty and a declaratory sentence.[244] The law, however, has provided for certain exceptions in this regard, and certainly does not intend to interfere with them in any way by the statement of this paragraph. To state it briefly: the law in canon 2232, § 1, makes it clear that in certain specific cases one is excused from the observance of *latae sententiae* vindictive penalties. The acts placed in these circumstances and under these conditions are valid and licit. A subsequent declaratory sentence does not invalidate them.[245]

Canon 2232, § 2, simply points out that the *latae sententiae* penalty in question is incurred the moment the delict is committed. This is restricted, however, to those cases in which the delinquent is not excused from the observance of the penalty by the law itself. Once the delinquent is excused from the observance of the penalty, even though the penalty is incurred at the time of the commission of the delict, it does not produce its complete effect precisely because of this suspension.[246] The application of these principles to the performance of authorized ecclesiastical acts is of vital importance.

Section 4. The Cessation of the Exclusion From the Performance of Authorized Ecclesiastical Acts in the Nature of a Vindictive Penalty

The exclusion from the performance of authorized ecclesiastical acts as a vindictive penalty has been discussed. It now remains to determine if and when such an exclusion comes to an end. The exclusion from the performance of authorized ecclesiastical acts is,

[244] Cf. Chelodi-Ciprotti, *op. cit.*, n. 28, p. 34.

[245] "Cum in casu infamiae excusatio a poena observanda ab ipsa lege detur, actus positi inter sententiam declaratoriam et delictum commissum valide positi sunt et licite, nec sententia declaratoria subsequenti rescinduntur."—Conte a Coronata, IV, n. 1723, p. 129; "Actus autem positi ante sententiam declaratoriam retinent suum valorem."—Jone, *op. cit.*, III, 434; cf. also Tatarczuk, *op. cit.*, n. 7, pp. 108-109.

[246] Cf. Conte a Coronata, *loc. cit.*

in the situation contemplated, the vindictive penalty itself. It is not the result of another penalty or penal status. It constitutes the penalty that has been inflicted in consequence of a delict. The object of this section, then, is to determine when and how this vindictive penalty ceases, when and how the delinquent may be relieved of his exclusion from the exercise of the authorized ecclesiastical acts. Much of the matter calling for treatment here has already been dealt with in section 4 of the chapter dealing with the incapacity for the performance of authorized ecclesiastical acts as the result of infamy of law, and hence will not be dealt with at length here.

Canon 2289 contains the general principle relating to the cessation of vindictive penalties. It teaches that the vindictive penalty ceases on its expiation or its dispensation granted by him who has, in accordance with canon 2236, legitimate authority for dispensing. The means of cessation are spelled out more clearly in Canon 2289 than in canon 2236, § 1, which states in general that censures are remitted by way of absolution, while vindictive penalties cease by way of a dispensation.[247]

It is evident that vindictive penalties cease in other ways besides by way of dispensation.[248] If they are inflicted for a definite time or under a certain condition, they cease automatically when the time has elapsed or the condition is fulfilled.[249] The death of the delinquent and the agency of legal prescription [250] likewise cause vindictive penalties to cease. In general, however, vindictive penalties, if imposed with a temporal indefiniteness, cease through the granting of a dispensation, and all may be remitted in this manner.

The discussion regarding the exact meaning of the term "dispensa-

[247] "Remissio poenae sive per absolutionem, si agatur de censuris, sive per dispensationem, si de poenis vindicativis. . . ."—Canon 2236, § 1.

[248] This dispensation differs fundamentally from the absolution given in the case of censures in that, whereas the latter is an act demanded by justice, since the law demands absolution from censure once the delinquent has receded from his contumacy, a dispensation is in the nature of a favor, because it is *contra legem,* need not necessarily be granted, and the delinquent has no strict right to it.—Cf. Conte a Coronata, IV, n. 1736, p. 141; Bouscaren-Ellis, *op. cit.,* p. 876.

[249] Cf. canon 2289.

[250] Wernz-Vidal, *op. cit.,* VII, nn. 205-206, pp. 230-232.

tion" in this regard has been referred to in the chapter that deals with infamy of law. The dispute centers around the question whether the dispensation spoken of in canons 2289 and 2236, § 1, is to be identified with that of canon 80. Canon 80 defines a dispensation as a relaxation of the law in a particular case. For centuries the relaxation of vindictive penalties was considered in the sense of this definition, and it is only in more recent times that some commentators have come to regard it in a wider and more arbitrary sense. The traditional opinion seems to be the correct one.[251]

Canon 2236 singles out those who possess the proper power for dispensing from vindictive penalties. It states in the first place that the remission of a penalty, by way of absolution in the case of censures or by way of dispensation in the case of vindictive penalties, may be granted only by him who has established the penalty, or by his competent superior or successor, or by him to whom this faculty has been committed. Those who can exempt others from the observance of a law can also remit the penalty attached to that law.[252] These two paragraphs recount the persons who possess such dispensatory power in their own right.

It is a clear principle of jurisprudence that he who establishes a vindictive penalty has the power to dispense from it. The successor of the legislator possesses this power because he is officially identified with his predecessor. He occupies the same office and enjoys all jurisdiction of that office.[253] It is clear that the superior of the legislator possesses this power of dispensation as well, since the jurisdiction of the legislator depends upon that of the superior.

On the basis of these principles it is clear that the Roman Pontiff as the supreme head of the Church possesses the power to dispense from any vindictive penalty of whatever kind of classification. In the case of *latae sententiae* vindictive penalties established in the law of the Code this power resides in the sovereign pontiff alone.

251 Christ, *op. cit.*, pp. 67-70.

252 Canon 2236, §§ 1 and 2.

253 Christ, *op. cit.*, p. 85; "Is qui in ius succedit alterius, eo iure, quo ille, uti debebit."—Reg. 46, R.J., in VI°.

Ordinaries apart from him enjoy only a derived power in this regard.[254]

The residential bishop has the power to dispense from all vindictive penalties of particular or diocesan law established by himself or his predecessors. As regards the general law of the Code, he is competent for dispensing from *ferendae sententiae* vindictive penalties, for once such a penalty is inflicted by a court or by a particular penal precept it becomes a penalty *ab homine,* and as such comes within the jurisdiction of the ordinary who issued the particular penal precept, or whose court rendered the decision.[255]

Canon 2236, § 1, also speaks of one to whom the dispensatory power has been committed. This is based on the fundamental principle that one who possesses the right to accomplish something, also possesses the right to commission another to accomplish it in his place.[256] Thus a superior with the proper jurisdiction, together with his successor or superior, can grant the power to another for dispensing from vindictive penalties established or inflicted by himself.

Paragraph two of canon 2236 states an exception to the general norm of law enacted in the first paragraph when it teaches that one who can exempt others from the observance of a law can also remit the penalty attached to that law. Thus even one who possesses delegated jurisdiction, whether from the law or *ab homine,* is able to remit the penalty involved.[257] Thus, as Chelodi-[258] Ciprotti points out, an ordinary who is able to dispense from the law of residence can also remit the penalty of canon 2381 concerning this matter. There are further exceptions to the general norm of the law which are to be treated presently. It is to be noted here, however, that canon 81 grants very broad powers to the ordinary regarding dispensation from the law of the Code. In general, ordinaries subordinate to the Roman Pontiff cannot dispense from the universal law of the Church, even in a particular case, except when the power

[254] Canon 2236, § 1; Christ, *op. cit.,* p. 87; Conte a Coronata, IV, n. 1736, p. 142.

[255] Cf. canon 2217, § 3; Ayrinhac-Lydon, *op. cit.,* n. 70, p. 53.

[256] Wernz-Vidal, *op. cit.,* VII, n. 210, p. 234.

[257] Conte a Coronata, IV, n. 1736, p. 143.

[258] *Op. cit.,* n. 29, p. 36, footnote 1.

has been granted to them explicitly or implicitly, or also in those cases in which recourse to the Holy See to obtain the faculty is difficult, the delay occasioned by such recourse will probably result in great harm, and the dispensation is one which the Holy See is accustomed to grant.[259] Thus in the cases embraced by this canon the ordinary may, in virtue of canon 2236, § 2, dispense from the penalties involved.[260]

The powers of ordinaries in regard to the dispensation from vindictive penalties enacted in the law of the Code is extended in canon 2237. In public cases the ordinary may remit all *latae sententiae* penalties enacted in the law of the Code with the exception of:

> (1) cases brought to court;
>
> (2) censures reserved to the Apostolic See;
>
> (3) penalties which incapacitate the delinquent from obtaining benefices, offices, dignities, functions in the Church, or an active and passive vote, as well as those which entail the privation of these, or which involve perpetual suspension, infamy of law, or deprivation of the right of patronage or of a privilege or favor granted by the Apostolic See.[261]

This first paragraph determines the dispensatory power of ordinaries in public cases in regard to all *latae sententiae* vindictive penalties of the law of the Code. A public case involves more than a public delict, since the vindictive penalty incurred as a result of the delict must also be considered. A public case, therefore, in the sense of this paragraph is one which involves a formally public delict,[262] or a public vindictive penalty, or both.[263] The power granted to ordinaries in this paragraph of canon 2237 is ordinary

[259] Canon 81.

[260] Conte a Coronata, IV, n. 1736, p. 143; Augustine, *op. cit.*, VIII, 108.

[261] Canon 2237, § 1.

[262] Cf. canon 2197, n. 1.

[263] Christ, *op. cit.*, p. 136.

power which derives from their office,[264] and thus may be delegated to others.[265]

Despite this extension of the dispensing power of ordinaries in regard to the *latae sententiae* vindictive penalties as enacted in the law of the Code, a great many vindictive penalties in general and many relating to authorized ecclesiastical acts in particular are included among the exceptions to this jurisdiction.

The first exception contemplates the cases brought to the contentious forum. Thus, whenever a case is brought to the judicial court, it is considered to have been brought to the contentious forum, so that the dispensatory power of the ordinary ceases in respect to the *latae sententiae* vindictive penalties which in line with the law of the Code are involved.[266]

If any of the *latae sententiae* vindictive penalties mentioned in canon 2237, § 1, n. 3, are involved in a case which is public, the ordinary may not dispense from them. It is to be noted here that the *latae sententiae* exclusion from authorized ecclesiastical acts in general is not included among these exceptions, and thus is subject to the power granted to the ordinary in virtue of this canon.[267]

Vindictive *latae sententiae* penalties which involve a disability, while they are not to be identified with the penalty stated in canon 2291, n. 8, do have a definite bearing on the exclusion from various authorized ecclesiastical acts. Thus, e.g., the disability for the obtaining of an office, dignity, function, or active and passive vote in the Church effectively excludes a delinquent from almost every authorized ecclesiastical act. The deprivation of these things has the same effect regarding authorized ecclesiastical acts, except that this penalty looks to past acquisitions, while disability refers only to the future.

The second paragraph of canon 2237 deals with the dispensatory

[264] Canon 197, § 1; Conte a Coronata, IV, n. 1737, p. 144; Christ, *op. cit.*, p. 139.

[265] Canon 199, § 1; Conte a Coronata, *loc. cit.*; Christ, *loc. cit.*

[266] Wernz-Vidal, *op. cit.*, VII, n. 214, p. 237; Woywod, *op. cit.*, II, n. 2077, p. 425; Christ, *op. cit.*, p. 141; Conte a Coronata, IV, n. 17136, p. 146.

[267] Cf. canons 2353; 2354, § 1; 2375, which explicitly mentions a dispensation to be granted by the ordinary; 2385.

powers of ordinaries regarding *latae sententiae* penalties, as enacted in the law of the Code, when they are connected with occult cases. In occult cases, without prejudice to canons 2254 and 2290, the ordinary is able to dispense from the *latae sententiae* vindictive penalties enacted in the law of the Code, either personally or through another, with the exception of the censures reserved to the Apostolic See in a special or most special manner.[268]

An occult case, like a public one, involves not only the delict but the resulting vindictive penalty as well. Thus, if the delict is at least formally occult, the *latae sententiae* vindictive penalty incurred as a result of it is also occult, so that an occult case obtains. It is also possible to have a case in which the delict is public but the *latae sententiae* vindictive penalty is occult. This delict is considered formally occult. Thus, an occult case involves a delict which is at least formally occult, or an occult vindictive penalty, or both.[269]

The power here granted to ordinaries is ordinary power which derives from the jurisdiction inherent in their office,[270] and, as is clear from the canon itself, may be delegated to others.[271] This power seems, however, to be limited to the internal forum for its use. This seems to be true, since the use is restricted to occult cases. Canon 202, § 3, states that if the forum for which a power was granted is not mentioned, the power is understood to have been granted for both forums, unless from the nature of the particular case it is clear that the power is meant for a particular forum. This latter clause seems verified here, inasmuch as the use of the power is limited to occult cases, which inherently pertain to the internal forum.[272]

Canon 2290, § 1, treats of the suspension of the observance of *latae sententiae* vindictive penalties in the more urgent occult cases. In these cases, if through the observance of a *latae sententiae* vindictive penalty the guilty party would betray himself with resulting infamy and scandal, any confessor may in the sacramental forum

268 Canon 2237, § 2.

269 Cf. Conte a Coronata, IV, n. 1738, p. 148; Christ, *op. cit.*, p. 164.

270 Cf. canon 197, § 1; Wernz-Vidal, *op. cit.*, VII, n. 215, p. 238.

271 "Ordinarius . . . per se vel per alium remittere. . . ."—Canon 2237, § 2.

272 Blat, *op. cit.*, V, n. 59, pp. 84-85; Berutti, *op. cit.*, VI, n. 38, p. 106; Christ, *op. cit.*, pp. 165-166.

suspend the obligation of observing the penalty under these conditions: the confessor shall enjoin on the delinquent the burden of having recourse to the Sacred Penitentiary, or to the bishop if he has the faculties for dispensing, if the recourse can be had without grave inconvenience. This petition is to be made by letter or through the confessor within at least one month. The name of the delinquent is to be concealed, and the instructions of the authority to whom recourse is made are to be carried out.[273] If in some extraordinary case this recourse is impossible, the confessor himself can grant the dispensation in line with the norm enacted in canon 2254, § 3.[274]

The prescriptions which are incorporated in canon 2290 received an adequate commentary in the chapter dealing with infamy of law, and the reader is referred to that section.[275]

Thus, one who has been excluded from the performance of authorized ecclesiastical acts in virtue of a *latae sententiae* vindictive penalty and who finds himself in the above-described circumstances may take advantage of the provisions of this canon and receive a suspension of the observance of this penalty.

[273] Canon 2290, § 1.

[274] Canon 2290, § 2.

[275] For a more detailed commentary, which is beyond the scope of this work, cf. Christ, *op. cit.*, pp. 168-238.

CONCLUDING NOTE

The exclusion from the performance of authorized ecclesiastical acts has been considered under the various headings contained in the Code of Canon Law. The quality of the particular exclusion involved has been investigated. The legislation dealing with the excusing causes, suspension, and cessation of this exclusion has been treated. It remains to be noted that frequently the law of the Church punishes a particular delict with a combination of penalties. These penalties and the effects flowing from them may very well have varying influences upon the exclusion from authorized ecclesiastical acts, and thus upon the valid and licit performance of these acts.[276]

When such a penalty is incurred, the various elements must be carefully weighed in order that the correct status of the delinquent regarding the performance of authorized ecclesiastical acts may be determined. Not only must one refer to the general principles as outlined above in the various chapters, but also to the many exceptions and mitigations arising from the diversity of the nature of these acts, and incorporated as elements in the law under consideration.

The Church has shown itself by this legislation to be most solicitous that its authorized ecclesiastical acts be performed by those who are worthy of such important matters while at the same time maintaining that spirit of merciful charity which it cherishes as an inheritance from its Divine Founder.

[276] Thus in canon 2385 an apostate from religion, in addition to other penalties, automatically incurs an excommunication reserved to his proper major superior, or, if the religious institute is laical or non-exempt, to the ordinary of the place where he resides; he is automatically excluded from the performance of authorized ecclesiastical acts; if he returns to his institute he is perpetually deprived of the active and passive voice in elections. Thus the censure of excommunication and two vindictive penalties are involved, all of which have an effect upon the exclusion from the performance of authorized ecclesiastical acts.

CONCLUSIONS

1. The institute of authorized ecclesiastical acts as it is known today, that is, as it is described in canon 2256, n. 2, begins with the Code of Canon Law. It has no exact counterpart in the former law.

2. The terms *actus legitimi ecclesiastici* and *actus legitimi* have exactly the same meaning and content in the present law of the Code.

3. An excommunicated person generally cannot licitly perform any authorized ecclesiastcial act. The various canons which have a relation to the placing of these acts determine whether such actions are invalid as well as illicit.

4. The censure of excommunication is removed by way of absolution. Once this absolution has been obtained by him, the erstwhile delinquent is restored to the communion of the faithful with the result that no longer is he to be excluded from the performance of the authorized ecclesiastical acts with relation to which his earlier status of excommunication has erected a barrier or hindrance.

5. Although one is unable to determine the precise content of the *actus legitimi* of the former law, it is clear that the infamous at law were excluded from all those actions which are now described by the Code of Canon Law as authorized ecclesiastical acts.

6. The incapacity for the performance of authorized ecclesiastical acts when sustained as a result of infamy of law refers to the valid performance of these acts.

7. The law of the Code provides exceptions to the general law of canon 2294, § 1, which renders the infamous at law incapable of the performance of authorized ecclesiastical acts.

8. Infamy of law is dispensed from in other ways than by the Holy See in spite of the wording of canon 2295.

9. The incapacity for the performance of authorized ecclesiastical acts ceases when the infamy of law of which it is a result ceases. It is suspended when and for the length of time the infamy of law is suspended.

10. Infamy of fact is not a penalty in the strict sense of the term. It partakes of the nature of a penal state or status.

11. In practice, a declaration of the ordinary is necessary in order that the presence of infamy of fact be established and the subsequent effects of this juridical status be enforced.

12. It is not required that the delict in consequence of which one is infamous in fact be notorious in order that the delinquent be forbidden to act as sponsor at baptism or confirmation. It need only be public.

13. The principal difference between the effects of infamy of law and infamy of fact in relation to authorized ecclesiastical acts is this: whereas infamy of law generally excludes one from the valid performance of these acts, infamy of fact never does so.

14. The exclusion from the performance of authorized ecclesiastical acts suffered by the infamous in fact is the effect of their status. This effect remains in operation for as long as the state of infamy of fact is present. It is with the cessation of infamy of fact that the exclusion from the performance of authorized ecclesiastical acts resulting from this infamy ceases.

15. Juridically it is the judgment of the ordinary that determines when the state of infamy of fact ceases. Thus a person may be re-admitted to the performance of authorized ecclesiastical acts only after the prudent judgment of the ordinary that his good name has been restored.

16. The examples in the law of the Code of the exclusion from the performance of authorized ecclesiastical acts in the nature of a vindictive penalty refer to the licit and not the valid performance of these acts. There are some exceptions regarding sponsorship at baptism and at confirmation.

17. The *privatio* spoken of in those vindictive penalties which directly exclude the delinquent from the performance of some individual authorized ecclesiastical acts as well as those which indirectly exclude the delinquent from the performance of these acts has a broader meaning than the one pointed to in canon 183, § 1.

18. The performance of authorized ecclesiastical acts placed in virtue of canon 2232, § 1, is both valid and licit. A subsequent declaratory sentence does not invalidate them.

19. The exclusion from the performance of authorized ecclesiastical acts in the nature of a vindictive penalty ceases and is suspended according to the norms governing the cessation and suspension of vindictive penalties in general.

BIBLIOGRAPHY

Sources

Acta Apostolicae Sedis, Commentarium Officiale, Romae, 1909-1929; Civitate Vaticana, 1929-

Acta Sanctae Sedis, 41 vols., Romae, 1865-1908.

Bullarum Diplomatum et Privilegiorum Sanctorum Romanorum Pontificum Taurinensis Editio, 24 toms. in 25 vols., Augustus Taurinorum: Neapoli, 1857-1872.

Canones et Decreta Concilii Tridentini, editio Neopolitana Joseph Pallella, Neapoli, 1895.

Canon Law Digest, The, edited by T. Lincoln Bouscaren, 4 vols., Milwaukee: Bruce Publishing Company, Vol. I, 1934, Vol. II, 1943, Vol. III, 1954, Vol. IV, 1958, ed. with the aid of James I. O'Connor.

Codex Iuris Canonici, Pii X Pontificis Maximi Iussu Digestus, Benedicti Papae XV Auctoritate Promulgatus, Romae, Typis Polyglottis Vaticanis, 1917.

Codicis Iuris Canonici Fontes, cura Emi Petri Card. Gasparri editi, 9 vols., Romae (postea Civitate Vaticana): Typis Polyglottis Vaticanis, 1923-1939. (Vols. VII-IX ed. cura et studio Emi Iustiniani Card. Serédi.)

Corpus Iuris Canonici, ed. Lipsien. 2. post Aemilii Ludovici Richteri curas . . . intruxit Aemilius Friedberg, 2 vols., Lipsiae: Tauchnitz, 1879-1881. Aditio anastatice repitita, Lipsiae: Tauchnitz, 1928.

Corpus Iuris Civilis, 3 vols., Berolini, 1928-1929. *Institutiones,* quas recognovit P. Krueger, ed. stereotypa 15., 1928; *Digesta,* quae recognovit T. Mommsen et retractavit P. Kreuger, ed. stereotypa 15., 1926; *Codex Iustinianus,* quem recognovit et retractavit Paulus Krueger, ed. stereotypa 10., 1929; *Novellae,* quas recognovit R. Schoell, et absolvit G. Kroll, ed. stereotypa 5., 1928.

Decretales D. Gregorii Papae IX, suae integritati, una cum glossis restitutae, cum privilegeo Gregorii XIII, Pontif. max., et aliorum Principum, Romae, 1582.

Decretum Gratiani, emendatum et notationibus illustratum, una cum glossis, 2 vols., Romae, 1582.

Denzinger, Heinricus-Bannwart, Clemens-Umberg, Joannes, *Enchiridion Symbolorum, Definitionum et Declarationum de Rebus Fidei et Morum,* 29. ed. Carolus Rahner, Friburgi Brisgoviae, Barcinone: Herder, 1953.

Gaius, *Institutionum Iuris Civilis Commentarii Quattuor,* 5. ed., 4 vols., Lipsiae, 1886.

Hinschius, Paulus, *Decretales Pseudo-Isidorianae et Capitula Angilramni,* Lipsiae, 1863.

Jaffé, Philippus, *Regesta Pontificium Romanorum ab condita Ecclesia ad annum post Christum natum MCXCVIII,* 2. ed., correctam et auctam auspiciis Gulielmi Wattenbach, curaverunt E. Löwenfeld, F. Kaltenbrunner, P. Ewald, 2 vols., Lipsiae, 1885-1888.

Kirsch, Conradus, *Enchiridion Fontium Historiae Ecclesiasticae Antiquae,* 6. ed., aucta et emendata, quam curavit Leo Ueding, Barcelona: Herder, 1947.

Liber Sextus Decretalium D. Bonifatii Papae VIII, Clementis Papae V. Constitutiones, Extravagantes tum vigenti D. Joannis Papae XII tum Communes, haec omnia cum suis glossis suae integritati restituta, 2 vols., Augustae Taurinorum, 1588.

Mansi, J., *Sacrorum Consilorum Nova et Amplissima Collectio,* 53 vols. in 60, Parisiis, 1901-1927.

Monumenta Germaniae Historica, Legum Sectio II, *Capitularia, Tomus I, Capitularia Regnum Francorum,* Pars I, denuo edidit Alfredus Boretius, Hannoverae, 1883.

Potthast, Augustus, *Regesta Pontificum Romanorum inde ab anno post Christum natum MCXCVIII ad annum MCCCIV,* 2 vols., Berolini, 1874-1875.

Rituale Romanum, Pauli V Pontifici Maximi jussu editum, et Benedicto XIV auctum et catigatum, Ratisbonae, 1901.

Schroeder, H. J., *Canons and Decrees of the Council of Trent,* Original text with English translation, St. Louis: B. Herder Book Co., 1941.

Authors

Abbo, John A.-Hannan, Jerome D., *The Sacred Canons,* 2 vols., rev. ed., St. Louis: B. Herder Book Co., 1957.

Andreae, Joannes, *In Titulum de Regulis Iuris Novella Commentaria,* Venetiis, 1581.

Augustine, Charles, *A Commentary on the New Code of Canon Law,* 8 vols., Vol. VIII, 3. ed., St. Louis: B. Herder Book Co., 1931.

Ayrinhac, H. A.-Lydon, P. J., *Marriage Legislation in the New Code of Canon Law,* 3. rev. ed., New York, Boston, Cincinnati, Chicago, San Francisco: Benziger Brothers, 1957.

——— *Penal Legislation in the New Code of Canon Law,* new rev. ed., New York, Boston, Cincinnati, Chicago, San Francisco: Benziger Brothers, 1936.

Baisio, Guido a, *Commentaria in Decretorum Volumen,* Venetiis, 1577.

Bennington, James, *The Recipient of Confirmation,* The Catholic University of America Canon Law Studies, n. 267, Washington, D. C.: The Catholic University of America Press, 1952.

Berutti, Cristophorus, *Institutiones Iuris Canonici,* 6 vols., Vol. VI, *De Delictis et Poenis,* Taurini-Romae: Marietti, 1938.

Beste, Udalricus, *Introductio in Codicem,* 4. ed., Neapoli: M. D'Auria, 1956.

Blat, Albertus, *Commentarium Textus Codicis Iuris Canonici,* 6 vols., Vol. III, *De Rebus,* Pars I, 2. ed., 1924, Vol. V, *De Delictis et Poenis,* 1924, Romae: Collegio Angelico.

Bottoms, Archibald M., *The Discretionary Authority of the Ecclesiastical*

Judge in Matrimonial Trials of the First Instance, The Catholic University of America Canon Law Studies, n. 349, Washington, D. C.: The Catholic University of America Press, 1955.

Bouscaren, T. Lincoln-Ellis, Adam C., *Canon Law, A Text and Commentary,* 2. ed., Milwaukee: Bruce Publishing Co., 1953.

Buckland, W. W., *Manual of Roman Private Law,* London: Cambridge University Press, 1925.

——— *Textbook of Roman Law from Augustus to Justinian,* 2. ed., London: Cambridge University Press, 1932.

Cappello, Felix M., *De Censuris,* 4. ed., Taurini-Romae: Marietti, 1950.

——— *Summa Iuris Canonici,* 3 vols., Vol. III, *De Processibus, Delictis et Poenis,* 4. ed., Romae: Apud Aedes Universitas Gregorianae, 1955.

Catholic Encyclopedia, The, 15 vols. and 2 supplements, Vol. V, New York: Robert Appleton Company, 1909.

Cerato, P., *Censurae Vigentes,* 2. ed., Patavii, 1921.

Chelodi, Ioannes, *Ius Canonicum de Delictis et Poenis,* 5. ed., recognita et aucta a Pio Ciprotti, Trento: Liberia Moderna Editrice, Vicenza: Società Anonima Tipografica, 1943.

Christ, Joseph J., *Dispensation from Vindicative Penalties,* The Catholic University of America Canon Law Studies, n. 174, Washington, D. C.: The Catholic University of America Press, 1943.

Cipollini, Albertus, *De Censuris Latae Sententiae,* Taurini: Marietta, 1925.

Claeys-Bouuaert, F.-Simenon, G., *Manuale Iuris Canonici,* 3 vols., Vols. I et III, 5. ed., 1939-1943; Vol. II, 3. ed., 1947; Gandae et Leodii: H. Dessain.

Cloran, Owen M., *Previews and Practical Cases,* Milwaukee: The Bruce Publishing Company, 1951.

Cocchi, Guidus, *Commentarium in Codicem Iuris Canonici et usum scholarum,* 8 vols., Vol. VIII, *De Delictis et Poenis,* 4. ed., Taurinorum Augustae: Marietti, 1938.

Connolly, Thomas J., *The Effects of Infamy of Law,* The Catholic University of America Canon Law Studies, Licentiate Thesis, Washington, D. C., 1951.

Conte a Coronata, Matthaeus, *Institutiones Iuris Canonici,* 5 vols., Vol. I, 4. ed., 1950, Vol. II, 4. ed., 1951, Vol. IV, 4. ed., 1955, Vol. V, 3. ed., 1951, Taurini-Romae: Marietti.

Creusen, Joseph-Ellis, Adam C., *Religious Men and Women in Church Law,* 6th English edition revised and edited to conform with the 7th French edition by Adam C. Ellis, Milwaukee: Bruce Publishing Co., 1958.

Davis, Henry, *Moral and Pastoral Theology,* 4 vols., Vol. III, *Sacraments,* 7. ed., London and New York: Sheed & Ward, 1958.

——— *Moral and Pastoral Theology: A Summary,* London and New York: Sheed & Ward, 1952.

Della Rocca, Fernando, *Manual of Canon Law,* Milwaukee: Bruce Publishing Company, 1959.

Dolan, John L., *The Defensor Vinculi,* The Catholic University of America Canon Law Studies, n. 85, Washington, D. C.: The Catholic University of America, 1934.

Duerr, Charles J., *The Judicial Notary,* The Catholic University of America Canon Law Studies, n. 312, Washington, D. C.: The Catholic University of America Press, 1951.

Dugan, Henry F., *The Judiciary Department of the Diocesan Curia,* The Catholic University of America Canon Law Studies, n. 26, Washington, D. C.: The Catholic University of America, 1925.

Eltz, Louis A., *Cooperation in Crime,* The Catholic University of America Canon Law Studies, n. 156, Washington, D. C.: The Catholic University of America Press, 1942.

Ferreres, Joannes, *Institutiones Canonicae,* 2 vols., ed. altera, Barcinone: Subirana, 1920.

Gasparri, Petrus Cardinalis, *Tractatus Canonicus de Matrimonio,* 2 vols., ed. nova, Typis Polyglottis Vaticanis: Romae: 1932.

——— *Tractatus Canonicus de Sacra Ordinatione,* 2 vols., Parisiis, Lugduni, 1893.

Glynn, John C., *The Promoter of Justice,* The Catholic University of America Canon Law Studies, n. 101, Washington, D. C.: The Catholic University of America, 1936.

Godfrey, John A., *The Right of Patronage According to the Code of Canon Law,* The Catholic University of America Canon Law Studies, n. 21, Washington, D. C.: The Catholic University of America, 1924.

Greenidge, A. H. J., *Infamia: Its Place in Roman Public and Private Law,* Oxford: Clarendon Press, 1894.

Heylen, V., *De Censuris,* 4. ed., Mechliniae: H. Dessain, 1945.

Hogan, James J., *Judicial Advocates and Procurators,* The Catholic University of America Canon Law Studies, n. 133, Washington, D. C.: The Catholic University of America Press, 1941.

Hostiensis, Henricus Cardinalis, *Summa Aurea,* Lugduni, 1568.

Hughes, Philip, *A Popular History of the Catholic Church,* 7th printing, Image Books Edition by special arrangement with The Macmillan Company, Garden City, New York: Image Books, Doubleday & Co., 1957.

Hyland, Francis E., *Excommunication: Its Nature, Historical Development and Effects,* The Catholic University of America Canon Law Studies, n. 49, Washington, D. C.: The Catholic University of America, 1928.

Jone, Heribert, *Commentarium in Codicem Iuris Canonici,* 3 vols., Paderborn: Ferdinandus Schöningh, 1950-1955.

Jone, Heribert-Adelman, Urban, *Moral Theology,* rev. English trans. of 13th German edition, Westminster: The Newman Press, 1953.

Jorio, Thomas, *Theologia Moralis,* 3 vols., Vol. III, *De Sacramentis in genere et de sacramentalibus,* 4. ed., Neapoli: M. D'Auria, 1954.

Kearney, Richard J., *Sponsors at Baptism According to the Code of Canon*

Law, The Catholic University of America Canon Law Studies, n. 30, Washington, D. C.: The Catholic University of America, 1925.

Laymann, Paulus, *Theologia Moralis,* 2 vols. in 1, Venetiis, 1630.

Leage, R. W., *Roman Private Law,* 2. ed., by C. H. Ziegler, London: Macmillan & Co., 1930; Reprint, 1948.

Lega, Michael, *Praelectiones in Textum Iuris Canonici, De Delictis et Poenis,* ed. altera, Romae, 1910.

Mahoney, E. J., *Priests' Problems,* New York, Chicago, Cincinnati, Boston, San Francisco: Benziger Brothers, 1958.

McCoy, Alan E., *Force and Fear in Relation to Delictual Imputability and Penal Responsibility,* The Catholic University of America Canon Law Studies, n. 200, Washington, D. C.: The Catholic University of America Press, 1944.

Merkelbach, B., *Summa Theologiae Moralis,* 3 vols., Vol. III, *De Sacramentis,* 10. ed., Brugis, Belgica: Desclée De Brouwer, 1956.

Metz, John E., *The Recording Judge in the Ecclesiastical Collegiate Tribunal,* The Catholic University of America Canon Law Studies, n. 287, Washington, D. C.: The Catholic University of America Press, 1949.

Migne, P. J., *Patrologiae Cursus Completus, Series Latina,* 221 vols., Parisiis, 1844-1855.

Mock, Timothy, *Disqualification of Electors in Ecclesiastical Elections,* The Catholic University of America Canon Law Studies, n. 365, Washington, D. C.: The Catholic University of America Press, 1958.

Moriarity, Francis E., *Extraordinary Absolution from Censures,* The Catholic University of America Canon Law Studies, n. 113, Washington, D. C.: The Catholic University of America Press, 1938.

Morinus, Joannes, *Commentarius Historicus de Disciplina in Administratione Sacramenti Poenitentiae Tredecim Primis Saeculis in Ecclesia Occidentali, et huc usque in Orientali Observata,* Parisiis, 1651.

Naz, Raoul, *Traité de Droit Canonique,* 4 vols., Vol. II, Letouzey and Ané: Paris, 1948.

Noldin, H.-Schmidt, A.-Heinzel, G., *Summa Theologiae Moralis,* 3 vols., Vol. III, 30. ed. quam paravit Godefridus Heinzel, Westminster, Maryland: The Newman Press, 1954.

Noone, John J., *Nullity in Judicial Acts,* The Catholic University of America Canon Law Studies, n. 297, Washington, D. C.: The Catholic University of America Press, 1943.

Noval, *Commentarium Codicis Iuris Canonici, Liber IV De Processibus,* Pars I, *De Iudiciis,* Romae, 1920.

Ottaviani, Alaphridus, *Institutiones Iuris Publici Ecclesiastici,* 2 vols. in 1, Vol. I, *Ius Publicum Internum,* 3. ed., Typis Polyglottis Vaticanis, 1947.

Parsons, Anscar J., *Canonical Elections,* The Catholic University of America Canon Law Studies, n. 118, Washington, D. C.: The Catholic University of America Press, 1939.

Poulet, Dom Charles-Raemers, Sidney, *A History of the Catholic Church*, 2 vols., Authorized translation and adaptation from the 4th French edition, St. Louis and London: B. Herder Book Co., 1952.

Prince, John E., *The Diocesan Chancellor*, The Catholic University of America Canon Law Studies, n. 167, Washington, D. C.: The Catholic University of America Press, 1942.

Prümmer, Dominicus M., *Manuale Iuris Canonici*, 5. ed., Friburgi Brisgoviae: Herder, 1927.

Rainer, Eligius G., *Suspension of Clerics*, The Catholic University of America Canon Law Studies, n. 111, Washington, D. C.: The Catholic University of America, 1937.

Raus, P. J. B., *Institutiones Canonicae*, altera ed., Lugduni-Parisiis: Vitte, 1931.

Regatillo, E. F., *Ius Sacramentarium*, 2 vols., Sal Terrae: Santander, 1945.

Regatillo, E. F.-Zalba, M., *Theologiae Moralis Summa*, 3 vols., Vol. III, *De Sacramentis, De Delictis et Poenis*, Madrid: Biblioteca De Autores Cristianos, 1954.

Reiffenstuel, Anacletus, *Ius Canonicum Universum*, 5 vols. in 7, Parisiis, 1864-1870.

Riesner, Albert J., *Apostates and Fugitives from Religious Institutes*, The Catholic University of America Canon Law Studies, n. 168, Washington, D. C.: The Catholic University of America Press, 1942.

Roberti, Franciscus, *De Delictis et Poenis*, 2 vols., Vol. I, Romae: Apud Aedes Facultatis Iuridicae ad S. Apollinaris, 1938.

——— *De Processibus*, 2 vols., Vol. I, 4. ed., Civitate Vaticana: Apud Custodian Librariam Pontificii Instituti Utriusque Iuris, 1956.

Roby, Henry J., *Roman Private Law in the Times of Cicero and the Antonines*, 2 vols., London: Cambridge University Press, 1902.

Rodimer, Frank J., *The Canonical Effects of Infamy of Fact*, The Catholic University of America Canon Law Studies, n. 353, Washington, D. C.: The Catholic University of America Press, 1954.

Roelker, Edward, *Invalidating Laws*, Paterson: St. Anthony Guild Press, 1955.

Sandeus, Felinus, *Commentaria in Quinque Libros Decretalium*, 3 vols. cum indice, Venetiis, 1570.

Schmalzgrueber, Franciscus, *Ius Ecclesiasticum Universum*, 5 vols. in 12, Romae, 1843-1845.

Schmidt, John R., *The Principles of Authentic Interpretation in Canon 17 of the Code of Canon Law*, The Catholic University of America Canon Law Studies, n. 141, Washington, D. C.: The Catholic University of America Press, 1941.

Schultz, Fritz, *Classical Roman Law*, Oxford: Clarendon Press, 1954.

Sipos, Stephanus, *Enchiridion Iuris Canonici*, Editionem sextam recognovit Ladislaus Galos, Romae: Herder, 1954.

Sylvester, Prierias, *Summa Silvestrina,* 2 vols., Venetiis, 1601.

Smith, Canon George D. (ed.), *The Teachings of the Catholic Church,* 2 vols., Vol. II, New York: Macmillan Co., 1953.

Smith, S. B., *Elements of Ecclesiastical Law,* 3 vols., Vol. III, *Ecclesiastical Punishments,* 3. ed., New York: Benziger Brothers, 1888.

Sohm, Rudolph, *The Institutes of Roman Law,* 3. ed., Oxford: Clarendon Press, 1907.

Stadler, Joseph N., *Frequent Holy Communion,* The Catholic University of America Canon Law Studies, n. 263, Washington, D. C.: The Catholic University of America Press, 1947.

Suarez, Franciscus, *De Censuris, Disputationum de censuris in communi, excommunicatione, suspensione, et interdicto, itemque de irregularitate, tomus quintus, additus ad tertiam partem D. Thomae.,* Lugduni: Horatius Cardon, 1608.

Tatarczuk, Vincent A., *Infamy of Law,* The Catholic University of America Canon Law Studies, n. 357, Washington, D. C.: The Catholic University of America Press, 1954.

——— *Infamy of Law,* The Catholic University of America Canon Law Studies, Licentiate Thesis, Washington, D. C., 1953.

Trombelli, Ioannes, *Tractatus de Sacramentis,* 5 vols., Vol. II, Bononiae, 1770.

Vermeersch, A.-Creusen, I., *Epitome Iuris Canonici,* 3 vols., 7. ed., Mechliniae, Romae: H. Dessain, 1949-1956.

Vermeersch, A., *Theologiae Moralis,* 3 vols., 4. ed. by Creusen, Romae: Pontificia Università Gregoriana, 1948.

Vogelpohl, Henry J., *The Simple Impediments to Holy Orders,* The Catholic University of America Canon Law Studies, n. 224, Washington, D. C.: The Catholic University of America Press, 1945.

Wernz, Franciscus-Vidal, Petrus, *Ius Canonicum ad Codicis Normam Exactum,* 7 vols. in 8, Vol. IV, *De Rebus,* Tom. II, 1935, Vol. VII, *Ius Poenale Ecclesiasticum,* ed. altera, 1951, Romae: Apud Aedes Universitatis Gregorianae.

Woywod, Stanislaus, *A Practical Commentary on the Code of Canon Law,* 2 vols., 3. ed., New York: Wagner, 1929.

Woywod, Stanislaus-Smith, Callistus, *A Practical Commentary on the Code of Canon Law,* 2 vols. in 1, rev. and enlarged ed., New York: Wagner, 1957.

Articles

Roberti, Franciscus, "An censura latae sententiae per praeceptum constituta sit reservata?", *Apollinaris,* VI (1933), 341-348

Schwegler, Edward S., "Sponsors and Testimonials," *The Ecclesiastical Review,* CIV (1941), 254-269.

PERIODICALS

Apollinaris, Romae, 1928-

Ecclesiastical Review, The, Vols. I-XXXII, Philadelphia, 1889-1905, known as *American Ecclesiastical Review;* from 1905: *The Ecclesiastical Review,* Vols. XXXIII-CIX, Philadelphia, 1905-1943; from 1944: *The American Ecclesiastical Review,* Washington, D. C., Vol. CX, 1944-

ALPHABETICAL INDEX

BIOGRAPHICAL NOTE

William Joseph Tierney was born on July 23, 1931, in Brooklyn, New York. After receiving his elementary school education in the Hempstead, New York, public school system, he was graduated from Chaminade High School at Mineola, New York, in June, 1949. After two years of study at Mount Saint Mary's College at Emmitsburg, Maryland, he entered the Seminary of the Immaculate Conception at Huntington, New York, in September, 1951. He received the degree of Bachelor of Arts in June, 1953. He was ordained to the priesthood June 1, 1957, for the newly erected Diocese of Rockville Centre. In September, 1957, he entered the School of Canon Law at The Catholic University of America. He received the degree of Bachelor in Canon Law in June, 1958, and the degree of Licentiate in Canon Law in June, 1959.

CANON LAW STUDIES *

410. Dee, Rev. Dacian, O.F.M.Cap., A.B., J.C.L., The manifestation of conscience.
411. De La Cruz, Rev. Eufemio, J.C.L., The Leasing of church properties in the Philippines.
412. Nessel, Rev. William, O.S.F.S., M.A., J.C.L., First amendment freedoms, papal pronouncements and concordat practice.
413. Roos, Rev. John R., M.A., S.T.L., J.C.L., The seal of confession.
414. Tierney, Rev. William J., A.B., J.C.L., Authorized ecclesiastical acts.
415. Van Ommeren, Rev. William M., J.C.L., Mental illness affecting matrimonial consent.

* For a complete list of the available numbers of this series apply to the Catholic University of America Press, 620 Michigan Avenue, N.E., Washington (17), D. C., for a general catalogue.

www.ingramcontent.com/pod-product-compliance
Lightning Source LLC
LaVergne TN
LVHW050247080826
844660LV00012B/605
* 9 7 8 0 8 1 3 2 2 5 7 2 2 *